The Family in the English Revolution

For My Family

The Family in
the English Revolution

CHRISTOPHER DURSTON

306.85
D939 f

WITHDRAWN

Basil Blackwell

Copyright © Christopher Durston 1989
First published 1989
Basil Blackwell Ltd
108 Cowley Road, Oxford, OX4 1JF, UK

Basil Blackwell Inc.
432 Park Avenue South, Suite 1503
New York, NY 10016, USA

All rights reserved. Except for the quotation of short passages for the purpose of criticism and review, no part of this publication may be reproduced, stored in a retrieval system, or transmitted, in any form or by any means, electronic, mechanical, photocopying, recording or otherwise, without the prior permission of the publisher.

Except in the United States of America, this book is sold subject to the condition that it shall not, by way of trade or otherwise, be lent, re-sold, hired out, or otherwise circulated without the publisher's prior consent in any form of binding or cover other than that in which it is published and without a similar condition including this condition being imposed on the subsequent purchaser.

British Library Cataloguing in Publication Data

Durston, Christopher
    The family in the English Revolution.
    1. England. Families, 1625–1660
    I. Title
    306.8'5'0942
ISBN 0–631–15496–5

Library of Congress Cataloging in Publication Data

Durston, Christopher, 1951–
The family in the English Revolution / Christopher Durston.
    p. cm.—(The Family, sexuality, and social relations in past times)
Bibliography: p.
1. Family—Great Britain—History—17th century.
2. Great Britain—Social conditions—17th century.
3. Great Britain—History—Puritan Revolution, 1642–1660.
I.Title.   II. Series.
HQ613.D874 1989   306.8'5'0941—dc19   88-21683
ISBN 0–631–15496–5

Typeset in 10 on 12pt Sabon
by Hope Services, Abingdon
Printed in Great Britain by
T.J. Press (Padstow) Ltd., Padstow, Cornwall

Contents

	Acknowledgements	vi
	Abbreviations	viii
1	Introduction	1
2	The Debate on the Family	10
3	By the Sword Divided?	33
4	Marriage	57
5	Wives and Husbands	87
6	Parents and Children	110
7	The Family and Illicit Sexual Relations	142
8	Conclusion	160
	Bibliography	175
	Index	187

Acknowledgements

I owe thanks to a large number of institutions and individuals. I am grateful to the staffs of the British Museum Manuscripts Dept, the British Library, the Public Records Office and the Berkshire and Warwickshire Records Offices for their help and attention. I am particularly indebted to the staff of the Bodleian Library, Oxford, for their seemingly inexhaustible patience and kindness. I should also like to acknowledge the financial assistance which I received from the St Mary's College Research Fund.

A number of friends and colleagues gave me invaluable advice and support. I should like to express my thanks to my colleagues in the History Department at Strawberry Hill, and especially to Susan Doran and Christopher Harper-Bill, both of whom were a constant source of encouragement. They also read draft sections of the book and offered many helpful suggestions. In addition, I am especially grateful to Gerald Aylmer, Barry Coward, Ralph Houlbrooke and John Morrill, all of whom read a draft of the completed typescript, for their valuable suggestions for amendments and additions, and for pointing out a number of misjudgements and errors. All the mistakes that remain are, of course, entirely my own responsibility. Thanks are also due to Ruth Harvey, Sheila Marwood, Irmela Jay and Fakir Hussain.

An earlier version of the discussion in chapter 4 on the civil marriage act of 1653 appeared in the *Historical Journal* for March 1988, under the title '"Unhallowed Wedlocks": The Regulation of Marriage During the English Revolution'. I should like to thank the editors of that journal for permission to include it here.

Writing a book about family life makes one particularly aware of the importance of relationships with one's closest relatives. This book is dedicated to my family, and in particular to my mother, my father who died and my son Joel who was born during the period of its writing, and

Acknowledgements

my wife Ros, who, to borrow the Earl of Derby's phrase, is 'truly the best part of myself'. But for her constant support and encouragement, this book could not have been written.

In all quotations, spelling has been modernized. The year has been taken as starting on 1st January.

C. D.

Abbreviations

BL	British Library, London.
Bod. Lib	Bodleian Library, Oxford.
Cal. Com Advance Money	M. A. E. Green (ed.), *Calendar of the Committee for the Advance of Money* (3 vols, London, 1888).
Cal. Com. Comp.	M. A. E. Green (ed.), *Calendar of the Committee for Compounding* (5 vols, London, 1889–93).
CSPD	*Calendar of State Papers, Domestic Series.*
DNB	*Dictionary of National Biography.*
HMC	Historic Manuscripts Commission.
PRO	Public Records Office, London.
TT*	Thomason Tracts Collection (in the British Library).
WRO	Warwickshire Records Office.

* The BL reference for Thomason Tracts is given with the relevant work where it appears in the Bibliography.

1
Introduction

An important and welcome feature of the historiography of the late-twentieth century has been the shift of attention away from an earlier preoccupation with high politics and international diplomacy towards a greater interest in the beliefs and institutions which helped to shape the social and cultural experiences of our less exalted ancestors. As a result of this change of emphasis, historians have recently come to recognize the great importance of the family, one of the most ubiquitous and long-established of these institutions, which has formed the basis of the social structure of western Europe throughout the last millennium. During the last ten years in particular, the evolution of the modern family has become an area for considerable study and debate, in the course of which particular attention has been focused upon England, where the distinct, two-generational nuclear family of parents and children living apart from other relatives has been shown to be the norm since at least the fourteenth century. In his major study *The Family, Sex and Marriage in England 1500–1800*, published in 1977, Lawrence Stone argued that most of the dynamic changes which shaped the modern English family occurred during a 300-year period between 1500 and 1800.[1] These changes included the rise of close and affectionate relationships between both husbands and wives and parents and children, common features of the modern family which Stone claimed were absent from its medieval counterpart. Although subsequent detailed investigations by other historians of the family have since revealed that Stone's central thesis is unreliable,[2] his study continues to demand respect as the instigator of

---

[1] Lawrence Stone, *The Family, Sex and Marriage in England 1500–1800* (London, 1977), *passim*.
[2] The best recent survey is Ralph A. Houlbrooke, *The English Family 1450–1700* (London, 1984).

enquiries which have greatly enhanced our knowledge of the social environment of early-modern England. In many ways *The Family, Sex and Marriage* is the intellectual father of this work too, but in several important respects the present study differs both from Stone's book and from the family studies which have appeared in its wake. Whereas most of the contributions to the debate on the family have covered a period of one or more centuries and have considered the long-term evolution of the institution during periods of relative stability, this book deals with a period of only twenty years and its aim is to discover how this most traditional of social organisms fared during a brief period of intense political and religious crisis.

One of the many important axioms which social historians need to bear in mind when studying the experiences of men and women in the past is that for most of their lives the majority of them were largely uninterested in politics and theology. As Alan Everitt has pointed out in a study of provincial society in seventeenth-century England, for much of the time the local community was not 'chiefly occupied with politics at all, but with its own affairs of buying, selling, making love, marrying, bringing up a family, and with all those thousand little concerns that tied together the bonds of family life.'[3] Such domestic concerns will, of course, be central topics of this study; but so too will national political and religious developments, because, during certain periods of major upheaval, political and religious issues force themselves upon the attention of those who would prefer to ignore them, demanding that they become more involved in public affairs and affecting their lives to a much larger degree than in more tranquil times. This was particularly true of the period from 1640 to 1660, when England experienced some of the most unusual, dramatic and momentous events of its entire history and witnessed changes which were so rapid and far-reaching that, according to some historians, they constituted an English Revolution.

This revolutionary sequence of events began in November 1640 when the representatives of the English political nation arrived at Westminster to take their seats in the Long Parliament. Alarmed at the fiscal and religious policies which had been pursued by Charles I's government during the personal rule of the 1630s, the great majority of them were determined to secure major constitutional and religious reforms. Two years later, however, after prolonged efforts to resolve the differences between the king and his parliamentary opponents had foundered upon their mutual suspicion and distrust, the two sides resorted to arms. While large numbers of the nobility and gentry joined Charles I's Royalist army,

---

[3] Alan Everitt, *Change in the Provinces* (Leicester, 1969), p. 10.

a sizeable proportion of English landed society embarked upon a full-scale armed revolt against their legitimate and, as was widely believed, divinely appointed sovereign. The resultant Civil War lasted four years and brought serious social and economic dislocation to many areas of the country. The normal processes of local justice and administration were interrupted, and communities suffered material deprivation and were subjected to frequent unwelcome visitations by the often ill-disciplined soldiers of both armies. With the rival governments at Oxford and London preoccupied by the more immediate priorities of the war, the customary constraints upon political and religious debate broke down, and political and religious radicals began to find it relatively easy to spread their unorthodox and subversive opinions in print.

The period which followed the parliamentary victory in 1646 saw a series of renewed attempts by both Parliament and the leaders of the New Model Army to agree upon a compromise constitutional settlement with the defeated king. However, Charles I's reluctance to take these negotiations seriously and his decision to renew the war with Scottish assistance in 1648 finally prompted the leaders of the army to cut through the constitutional Gordian knot. During December 1648 and January 1649, England suffered a military coup, in the course of which, having purged the Parliament of all unsympathetic MPs, the army brought the king to trial for waging war against his own people, sentenced him to death and publicly executed him. In the aftermath of this act of tyrannicide, the monarchy and the House of Lords were abolished and England was declared a republic. By this stage too, the established Anglican church had been proscribed and attempts had been made to replace it with a rigid and alien Presbyterian state church. As these extraordinary events were taking place at the centre of the political stage, the ideological debate continued to widen in scope. While conservatives looked on in disbelieving horror at the attack upon the king, the radical Leveller party campaigned in London for sweeping constitutional reforms, including a substantial extension of the franchise, and other radicals advocated as solutions to the country's problems the abolition of all private property and the introduction of more equitable legal and educational systems.

By the mid 1650s, a conservative reaction had set in. In 1653, the republic gave way to a quasi-monarchical constitution headed by the dominant personality of the army, Oliver Cromwell. Cromwell's government set its face firmly against any further radical political change, but its religious and social policies continued to alienate conservative opinion. In the climate of relative religious freedom presided over by the army leaders, radical sects, like the socially subversive Quakers and Fifth

Monarchists, continued to threaten public order. In addition, in an attempt to establish their Calvinist Zion in England, the Puritan generals struggled throughout the 1650s to reform the morality of the English people, closing down brothels and unlicensed ale houses, banning stage plays and other leisure activities and outlawing the traditional customs associated with the celebration of feasts such as Christmas, Whitsun and May Day. The revolution came to an abrupt end with the return of the Stuart monarchy in 1660, but, in the course of the preceding twenty years, England had been transformed from a relatively stable political organism into an arena of intense ideological debate and wide-ranging political and religious experimentation.

This sustained attack upon the traditional authority of state and church had direct theoretical implications for the institution of the family. Like most sixteenth- and seventeenth-century European kings, Charles I was widely viewed as the father of his people, and it was generally believed that his authority rested on the same biblical sanction as that of fathers of families. Contemporary political theorists, like Sir Robert Filmer, whose *Patriarcha* was written on the eve of the Civil War, stressed that both kings and heads of families exercised their power as the descendants of the first father, Adam.[4] It was also widely accepted that the fifth commandment, 'Honour thy father and thy mother', demanded submission to the head of the state as well as to the ruler of the family, and that the well-ordered family was the foundation of a well-ordered state. Confronted, therefore, with the near collapse of the English state in the 1640s, some contemporaries argued that the political upheavals had originated in disputes within families. In 1641, the Presbyterian Thomas Edwards had argued that:

> . . . both churches and commonwealths are made of families, all issuing out from thence, they being the seminaries and nurseries of both, and if there be a ground work laid for disturbances, divisions and disorder there, what can be firm, peaceable or sure.[5]

Similarly in 1653, Robert Abbot, who had by then witnessed more than ten years of civil strife in England, declared at the beginning of his *A Christian Family Builded by God*:

> 'the first government that ever was in this world was in a

---

[4] Sir Robert Filmer, *Patriarcha* (London, 1680), *passim*, in P. Laslett (ed.) *Patriarcha and Other Political Works* (Oxford, 1949).
[5] Thomas Edwards, *Reasons Against the Independent Government of Particular Congregations* (London, 1641), p. 27 (TT).

Family; and the first disorder that ever was in the world was in a Family; and all the disorders that ever fell out since, sprung from Families. If families had been better, Churches and commonwealths all along had prospered. As we read, it was in Athens of old, the boy ruled the mother, the mother ruled the Father, and he ruled the whole City, and thence sprung many disorders which made those present times sick of them even to complaining; so hath it been in all ages, and I am sure it hath been in ours, all we that live here groan under it still, even to more than a complaint.[6]

As well as identifying the family as the source of political disorder, some observers believed that as a result of the continuing political and religious upheaval, the family was itself breaking up and would eventually disintegrate altogether. On the eve of the fighting in June 1642, Charles I warned his disaffected MPs in his answer to their Nineteen Propositions for Peace that civil war would destroy 'all distinctions of families' and four years later, Thomas Edwards complained that unless religious uniformity were reimposed, fathers 'should never have peace in their families more, or ever after have command of wives, children, servants.'[7] Similarly in 1648, William Herbert declared 'This is a time of division and insolence. . . . Now are parents against their children, now the son seeks to supplant his Father, the Mother and Daughter differ, the Brothers fight, Sisters quarrel, Infants curse . . .'[8] In the mid-1650s, John Gauden claimed that 'this is an age when men and women too, under pretence of Christian liberty, are pleading for divorces, for plurality of wives and husbands, for a ranting and fornicating devil under the notion of spiritual freedom.'[9] Perhaps the most direct parallel between political and familial breakdown, however, was drawn by the author of the Royalist pamphlet *The Maid's Prophecies*, who announced in 1648 that those who had rebelled against Charles I and had thus caused him to be separated from his wife and children, would as a result suffer problems within their own families, declaring:

> Cursed be they that parted man and wife,
> Unite them speedily, compose the strife.

---

[6] Robert Abbot, *A Christian Family Builded By God, Directing All Governors of Families How to Act* (London, 1653), dedicatory epistle (TT).
[7] J. P. Kenyon (ed.), *The Stuart Constitution* (Cambridge, 1966 edn), p. 23; Thomas Edwards, *Gangraena* (London, 1646), part 1, p. 156.
[8] William Herbert, *Quadrapartit Devotions* (London, 1648), part 4, p. 10 (TT).
[9] John Gauden, *Christ at the Wedding* (London, 1655), p. 23 (TT).

> For till the King, Queen, Princes all appear
> Like constellations fixed in their sphere,
> Shall never Father, Son, Wife, Daughter, Mother
> In England find true joy in one another.[10]

Such gloomy prognostications were not, of course, confined to the period 1640–60, but were also frequently voiced by conservative observers both earlier and later in the century; nor should they be accepted at face value as entirely reliable guides to developments in family life during the Civil War and the Interregnum. None the less, the events of the 1640s and 1650s did affect the family in a number of important ways, and some of these will be investigated in detail in the following chapters. As a traditional institution, the family was clearly threatened by the ideological ferment of the revolutionary years. Some wives and children who had imbibed the heady, anti-authoritarian theories of the political and religious radicals, began to question the absolute, patriarchal authority of their husbands and fathers. The traditional structure of the family also came under attack from writers who advocated a range of imaginative reforms, such as the introduction of divorce and polygamy, and permission to marry close relatives. A number of extreme radicals, like the Ranters, further challenged the traditional family by denouncing the Christian code of sexual ethics upon which it was founded.

While individuals were able to reduce the impact of such new ideas by simply ignoring them, it was not as easy for them to insulate themselves or their families from the realities of war and revolution. The Civil War produced deep political divisions within some families, and, as a result, many individuals found that they were forced to regard their closest kin as enemies, and were sometimes even compelled to go into battle against them. Again, the war and its aftermath caused serious financial problems within some families, and further interrupted normal family relationships by separating wives and husbands and parents and children, and producing the inevitable wartime crop of widows, orphans and bastards; such difficulties were felt particularly acutely by some of the families of the defeated Royalists after 1646. The fighting and its concomitant economic and social dislocation also caused problems for some of those who wished to marry during this period. In addition, as was mentioned above, the 1640s and 1650s witnessed concerted efforts by successive Puritan governments to reform long-established aspects of English popular culture, including some of the ceremonies associated with the most important milestones of family life; the 1640s saw the curtailment

---

[10] *The Maid's Prophecies* (London, 1648), unpag. (TT).

of the churching of women after childbirth and the rejection of godparents, and, for three years during the mid-1650s, church weddings ceased to be considered legally binding and couples were forced to marry before a justice of the peace.

As we have already noted, the widespread impression of contemporaries was that the abnormal pressures of the revolutionary years were tearing the family apart, and that they might even lead to its eventual destruction. The few modern historians who have turned their attention to the topic have tended to agree with them that the general effect was detrimental. At the end of his seminal article on the impact of the Civil War upon women, published in the 1950s, Keith Thomas speculated whether the institution of the family had 'emerged unscathed' from the maelstrom of civil war and revolution in England, concluding that it was 'hard to believe' that it had not been damaged.[11] However, from his investigations into the impact of crises within the political and social systems of medieval Europe, the French historian Georges Duby concluded that 'the family is the first refuge in which the threatened individual takes shelter when the authority of the state weakens.'[12] It would be unwise, therefore, to conclude that the impact of the English Revolution upon the family was deleterious simply because it appeared to be so to contemporaries. In the following chapters, I shall examine in detail whether the family was indeed a casualty of the war and revolution, or whether, conversely, it proved strong enough to withstand any increased external pressures, and may even have emerged from the maelstrom of the mid-seventeenth-century crisis in England with its strength and status enhanced.

Before embarking on such an investigation, however, it is necessary to add several notes of caution. At first glance, it might appear that, as an inevitable result of some of the developments outlined above, the lives of the great majority of English men and women underwent a complete transformation during the period from 1640 to 1660. Without doubt, the lives of a great many individuals were significantly affected by these largely unprecedented events, and those of a smaller number were altered almost beyond recognition. One must be careful, however, not to exaggerate the impact of political and religious change; for, although the breakdown of the English state in the early 1640s clearly did produce a number of new pressures and threats, because it involved the temporary breakdown of censorship, it may also have assured that a number of pre-existing domestic problems came into sharper historical focus. The

---

[11] Keith Thomas, 'Women and the Civil War Sects', *Past and Present*, 13 (1958), 57.
[12] Quoted by Philippe Aries in *Centuries of Childhood* (London, 1973 edn), p. 343, and by Stone in *Family, Sex and Marriage*, p. 133.

relatively abundant evidence from the 1640s and 1650s about the attitudes and activities of the lower orders may have made more apparent to historians familial tensions which have a no less real, if somewhat more shadowy, existence in earlier periods also. To take just one example, Martin Ingram's study of ecclesiastical justice in Wiltshire during the forty years which preceded the revolution has revealed that illicit sexual activity occurred with sufficient regularity to lead one to doubt whether the Ranters were solely a product of the events of the 1640s and were entirely without pre-Civil War antecedents.[13] One should be cautious, therefore, about drawing too clear a contrast between a tumultuous twenty year period in the middle of the seventeenth century and halcyon periods of calm and tranquillity before and after.

The other caveat that should be made concerns the sources. The extent to which any of the developments of the 1640s and 1650s can be investigated is, as always, determined by the amount and quality of the extant evidence. As this study is concerned primarily with close personal relationships, the most useful and revealing sources are private ones, such as letters, diaries and memoirs; these exist in some quantity for the mid-seventeenth century, but were written almost exclusively by men and women from the landed classes. In addition to such private sources, information can also be obtained from a range of more official documents, such as quarter sessions records, government papers, and some of the many thousands of books, pamphlets and newsbooks collected between 1641 and 1660 by the London bookseller George Thomason. These allow one to discover how some of those from the lower social orders were affected by the crisis, but the picture presented remains a fragmentary one. As a consequence, the dramatis personae of the following chapters includes only a few hundred of the roughly 5 million individuals alive in mid-seventeenth-century England, and contains a heavy over-representation of members of the nobility and gentry classes.

In defence of the present study, one could argue that, in reluctantly concentrating its attention upon men and women from the middle and upper social ranks, it is at least dealing with those social groupings which were most actively involved in, and directly affected by the public events of these years. None the less, it must be acknowledged that this book is deliberately less ambitious in scope than some previous studies of the family, and that it eschews the use of the quantitive techniques by which modern demographers and anthropologists investigate the long-term

---

[13] M. J. Ingram, 'Ecclesiastical Justice in Wiltshire 1600–1640, with special reference to cases concerning sex and marriage', Unpub. D.Phil. thesis, Oxford Univ. (1976), *passim*.

evolution of the social institutions of past societies. It is important, therefore, to guard against the temptation to make sweeping generalizations about early-modern English society on the basis of the small sample of families considered in the following chapters. The aim of the book is not to arrive at conclusions of general applicability to the study of the long-term institutional development of the early modern family, but rather to describe the reactions and experiences within the domestic sphere of some of those caught up in the mid-seventeenth-century crisis in England. It will perhaps also in the process throw some additional light on the nature and impact of the English Revolution, and help to explain why it proved so short-lived and abortive.

2
The Debate on the Family

Nowhere is the revolutionary nature of mid-seventeenth-century England more clearly seen than in the intense and wide-ranging ideological debates which took place during these years. Many of these intellectual discussions were concerned with proposals for fundamental political and religious change, but there were also a number of imaginative speculations and suggestions for the reform of various aspects of contemporary social organization, including the traditional patriarchal family. Arguing in 1644 in favour of freer divorce laws, the poet John Milton commented:

> What are our public immunities and privileges worth, and how shall it be judged that we fight for them with minds worthy to enjoy them, if we suffer ourselves in the meanwhile not to understand the important freedom that God and nature hath given us in the family?[1]

In calling for the introduction of a measure which, if adopted, would have had a profound impact upon family life, Milton was allying himself with a group of theorists and writers who during the 1640s and 1650s argued vigorously for the abolition or fundamental remodelling of the traditional patriarchal nuclear family.

Attacks upon the family can be found in some of the most widely read books of the 1640s and 1650s, but they were not always meant to be taken entirely seriously; for a number of authors during these years continued to uphold a well-established, pre-war literary tradition of male chauvinism, within which women and marriage were ridiculed and

---

[1] John Milton, *The Judgement of Martin Bucer* (London, 1644), in D. M. Wolfe et al. (eds), *The Complete Prose Works of John Milton* (8 vols, Yale and London, 1935–82), vol. 2, pp. 438–9.

The Debate on the Family

suspected in equal measure. One especially popular writer who expressed a fierce, if somewhat frivolous, opposition to monogamy and the family was Francis Osborne, whose *Advice to a Son* appeared in 1656. The book was published in Oxford, where Osborne had settled to supervise his son's education; it proved an immediate success with the students, selling in even greater numbers after it had been banned for suspected atheistic tendencies. It was reprinted four times within two years and, according to Sir William Petty, became one of the three most popular books of its day.[2] Osborne described marriage as 'a Clog fastened to the neck of Liberty', and 'a thraldom no wise man would sell himself to for the fairest inheritance, much less for trouble, vexation and want during life'. He warned his predominantly male readership that

> ... like a trap set for flies, it [marriage] may possibly be ointed at the entrance with a little voluptuousness, under which is contained a draught of deadly wine, more pricking and tedious than the passions it pretends to cure.[3]

Men who married women of beauty, Osborne argued, would subsequently suffer the indignity of being made cuckolds, and husbands who quarrelled with their wives would find that the law took the woman's part. He also declared that a man who married 'changeth the shape of natural freedom, and enrols himself among such as are rendered beasts of burden', and suggested that only the single life offered 'pleasure and safety'.[4]

Similar views were expressed the same year by the author of *Pray Be Not Angry, or the Woman's New Law*, who also pointed out the dangers involved in marriage and claimed that 'men may live without women, but women cannot live without men.'[5] In 1658, Osborne's friend, Thomas Pecke, recorded his hostility to marriage in his *Advice to Balaam's Ass*, asserting:

> Man of himself, Sir, is a microcosm; but this matrimonial incorporation proves often a contraction of the great world; when thousands of Acres are contracted by Pride and Prodigality into the narrow limits of a Burying-Place.[6]

---

[2] *DNB*, Francis Osborne (1593–1659).
[3] Francis Osborne, *Advice to a Son, or Directions for your Better Conduct* (Oxford, 1656), pp. 44, 50, 52 (TT).
[4] Ibid., pp. 35–63, esp. pp. 46–9, 55.
[5] G. Thorowgood, *Pray Be Not Angry or the Woman's New Law* (London, 1656), unpag. (TT).
[6] Thomas Pecke, *Advice to Balaam's Ass* (London, 1658), pp. 32–3.

Aside from this satirical tradition, a far more serious and aggressive call for the complete abolition of the familial structure of society was made by some of the most prominent theorists of the Ranter movement. The Ranters emerged in England in the late 1640s and for several years their subversive ideas and practices caused considerable alarm in more conservative circles. They believed that, as they had been redeemed or justified not through their own efforts but as a result of a predetermined decision by God, they had been freed from any obligation to conform to the moral code of their day. From this extreme antinomian standpoint, some Ranter theorists advocated the complete abolition of the family and its replacement by looser, less-structured social units, within which men and women would indulge in casual sexual relations with a variety of partners. In 1649, the Ranter writer Abiezer Coppe called upon God to punish individuals who married, and exhorted his readers to

> ... give over thy stinking family duties, and thy Gospel Ordinances as thou callest them: for under them all there lies, snapping, snarling, biting, besides covetousness, horrid hypocrisy, envy, malice, evil surmising.[7]

In 1650, the author of *A Justification of a Mad Crew* wrote of the Ranters:

> These creatures are married all, to every woman is their wife, not one woman apart from another, but all in one, and one in all: There is not a voice heard at this feast, whose wife is this woman, and whose that? and whose husband is such a one? For there is but one Husband and one Wife: and this man and wife, though made up of many thousands, lie with one another every night, and the bed is large enough to hold them all.[8]

Another Ranter was accused of arguing that 'for one man to be tied to one woman, or one woman to be tied to one man' was 'a fruit of the curse'.[9] John Pordage, the radical minister of Bradfield in Berkshire who came under the influence of Ranter ideas, was accused of telling some of his parishioners that marriage was illegal. In the early 1650s, Pordage gathered around him at Bradfield a small group of followers who attempted to put the ideas of the Ranters into practice. When the

---

[7] Abiezer Coppe, *A Second Fiery Flying Roll* (London, 1649), p. 12 (TT).
[8] *A Justification of a Mad Crew* (London, 1650) (TT), printed in J. C. Davis, *Fear, Myth and History: The Ranters and the Historians* (Cambridge, 1986), pp. 147–8.
[9] John Holland, *The Smoke of the Bottomless Pit* (London, 1651), p. 4 (TT).

Presbyterian minister Richard Baxter visited this community in an attempt to persuade one of its members to return home to his mother, he found the young man to be 'much against propriety [property], and against Relations of Magistrates, subjects, Husbands, wives, Masters, servants etc.'[10] The Ranters' critics often exaggerated when reporting the group's beliefs and activities, but there is little doubt that some Ranters were fundamentally opposed to the nuclear family.

In advocating the total abolition of the family, the Ranters and their fellow travellers were in a very small minority. Far more writers, however, were interested in discussing how the traditional structure of the family might be adapted and improved. These authors contributed to an inventive and wide-ranging debate on familial reform, which encompassed topics such as the status of women and the limits of patriarchal power, the procedures for the arranging of marriages and the choosing of spouses, and the merits of divorce, polygamy and marriages between close kin.

Within the vast majority of seventeenth-century families, the father was an absolute ruler who exercised a largely unrestrained power over his wife and children. However, during the 1640s and 1650s, some individuals began to suggest that the power of fathers should be limited in several important respects. In 1641, the prominent religious radical Katherine Chidley argued in her *Justification of the Independant Churches of Christ* that, although the husband had authority over his wife in 'bodily and civil respects', he was not entitled to be 'lord over her conscience'.[11] According to the Presbyterian author, Thomas Edwards, some of the radical religious sectaries had also claimed that wives were not obliged to obey their husbands and could dispose of family property without their permission, that parents had no right to interfere with their children's religious upbringing, and that children were not bound to obey ungodly parents.[12] A decade later, the New England minister, Thomas Cobbet, claimed that in recent years 'petty, Antichristian spirits' in both England and America had been encouraging children to disregard their parents' wishes.[13]

One important intellectual development of these years which could hardly fail to threaten the absolute power of the father within the family,

---

[10] John Pordage, *Innocence Appearing Through the Dark Mists of Pretended Guilt* (London, 1654), *passim*, esp. p. 16 (TT), Richard Baxter, *Reliquiae Baxterianae*, ed. M. Sylvester (London, 1696), p. 78.

[11] Katherine Chidley, *The Justification of the Independant Churches of Christ* (London, 1641), p. 26 (TT).

[12] Edwards, *Gangraena*, part 1, pp. 34–7.

[13] Thomas Cobbet, *A Fruitful Discourse Touching the Honour Due from Children to Parents and the Duty of Parents to Children* (London, 1656), p. 45.

was the reassessment by some writers of the traditional male view of the status and capabilities of women. The standard male attitude towards women throughout the early-modern period was one that emphasized their subservience and involved a distrust and suspicion which could easily spill over into misogyny. During the 1640s and 1650s, however, this orthodox position came under challenge from certain quarters. A number of the male writers who extolled the virtues of women during these years did so while retaining an essentially patronizing attitude towards them. In 1651, Charles Gerbier published a defence of women entitled *Elogium Heroinum*; the work was dedicated to Charles I's sister, Elizabeth of Bohemia, and argued that women were potentially the equal of men, quoting numerous examples from history of their learning and courage. Gerbier labelled those who criticized women as 'the crazy and vain wits of these times', and declared:

God made woman not of man's head, lest she should presume to over top him, nor of his foot, lest she should be villified by him, but from a rib near unto his heart, that she might ever be dear and entire to him.[14]

Another apparent champion of women was the Cambridge academic John Hall, who published in the early 1650s a series of 'paradoxes', or light-hearted literary diversions. Hall's work frequently stressed the noble nature of women, but his general approach was humorous and condescending, and his discussion of questions such as whether women should go naked or should be allowed to govern states was primarily intended to amuse and titillate his male readership.[15] In 1658, the former Royalist John Heydon, whose varied intellectual interests included astrology and Rosicrucianism, published *Advice to a Daughter*, in which he defended women from some of the attacks made by Francis Osborne. Heydon claimed that man was the 'consummation of creation', but that woman was the 'consummation of man', and he argued that the greater physical beauty of women was a sign that their souls were also superior to men's.[16] Heydon's support for women, however, was probably something of a mixed blessing, for he possessed a generally poor reputation with his contemporaries and was described by Elias Ashmole as 'an ignoramus and a cheat'.[17]

[14] Charles Gerbier, *Elogium Heroinum* (London, 1651), p. 4 (TT).
[15] John Hall, *Paradoxes* (London, 1650), ed. D. C. Allen (Gainsville, Fl., 1956), pp. 60–77. See also 2nd edn (London, 1653), pp. 120–5.
[16] John Heydon, *Advice to a Daughter. In Opposition to the Advice to a Son* (2nd edn, London, 1659), *passim*, esp. pp. 59–74 (TT).
[17] *DNB*, John Heydon (fl. 1667).

A more genuine and potentially more influential re-evaluation of the status of women emanated from the ranks of the radical political and religious writers. John Lilburne, the leader of the Leveller party which campaigned in the 1640s for a radical political programme based upon a theory of fundamental natural rights, claimed in *The Free Man's Freedom Vindicated* that 'all and every particular and individual man and woman that ever breathed in the world, are by nature all equal and alike in their power, dignity, authority and majesty...',[18] and the Ranter Abiezer Coppe insisted that 'Male and Female are all one in Christ, and they are all one to me.'[19] The Quakers, who began to emerge in the north of England in the early 1650s, accorded the women who joined their movement full equality with men in church affairs. Arguing in 1653 in favour of women preachers, one Quaker, Richard Farneworth, wrote that 'the manifestation of the spirit is given to profit withall in a daughter as well as a son.'[20] In 1655, the Quaker leader, George Fox, declared: '... may not the Spirit of Christ speak in the female as well as the male ... for the light is the same in the male and the female that cometh from Christ'; in the 1670s he reminded his followers that 'all the family of God, women as well as men, might know, possess, perform and discharge their offices and services in the house of God.'[21] Another religious radical, Richard Coppin, declared that 'in any assembly of people, a woman creature may have freedom to speak and answer as a man.'[22] By emphasizing the natural equality of men and women and advocating the greater involvement of women in public affairs, such writers were also by implication undermining patriarchy and questioning the subservient position of women within the family.

Another topic which was imaginatively debated during these years was the procedure for the arranging and solemnizing of marriage. Throughout the seventeenth century, the great majority of English men and women were responsible for choosing their own marriage partners, but their freedom of choice was constrained by a number of important factors. Most couples wished to marry with their parents' approval and were reluctant to proceed with any match they disapproved of. Within the landed classes in particular, where marriage settlements often involved

---

[18] Quoted by Howard Shaw in *The Levellers* (London, 1968), p. 100.
[19] Abiezer Coppe, *Some Sweet Sips of Spiritual Wine* (London, 1649), printed in Nigel Smith (ed.), *A Collection of Ranter Writings from the Seventeenth Century* (London, 1983), p. 66.
[20] Richard Farneworth, *A Woman Forbidden to Speak in Church* (London, 1653), p. 4 (TT).
[21] George Fox, *The Woman Learning in Silence* (London, 1655), pp. 5–6 (TT); *The Journal of George Fox*, ed. J. L. Nickalls (Cambridge, 1952), p. 668.
[22] Richard Coppin, *Michael Opposing the Dragon* (London, 1659), quoted by Davis in *Fear, Myth and History*, p. 39.

the transfer of considerable amounts of money and property, financial considerations figured prominently in pre-marital negotiations. Young, wealthy heiresses were frequently besieged by a succession of suitors and were unlikely to be allowed to marry solely for love; conversely, rich widows, who also often had a wide choice of aspiring husbands, had far more control over their own destinies.

A number of writers argued during the 1640s and 1650s that the state should intervene to discourage marriages of convenience. The restriction or abolition of the bridal portion – the often substantial cash sum that the bride brought to her new husband – was advocated by Gerrard Winstanley, the leader of the proto-communist Digger community which was formed at St George's Hill in Surrey in the late 1640s, and by the republican theorist, James Harrington. Both argued that such a measure would prevent men marrying solely for money.[23] Other reformers turned their attention to the marriage ceremony itself. The regulations governing the solemnization of marriage in early-seventeenth-century England were not always fully understood or adhered to, and some couples were married in irregular ceremonies of dubious legality. To complicate matters further, a number of sectarian writers and preachers argued during the 1640s that the members of the radical gathered churches could marry by a simple declaration before their congregations. In 1651, the radical Independent minister Hugh Peter suggested that marriage should become a civil ceremony conducted by a justice of the peace.[24] Two years later, the MPs of Barebone's Parliament adopted this proposal and, for the following three years, church weddings ceased to be legally binding.[25]

Among other radical suggestions for familial reform which surfaced during the 1640s and 1650s were the legalization of marriages between near relations, and the introduction of polygamy and divorce. The canon law of the Anglican church prohibited marriage and sexual intercourse between members of the nuclear family and other close family relatives, the precise regulations being laid down in a table of affinity based upon the Mosaic law outlined in the Old Testament book of Leviticus. In 1646, the anonymous author of the tract *Little Non-Such* argued for the removal of this canonical ban, citing numerous biblical examples of legal and successful marriages between brothers and sisters, and claiming that the natural affection between siblings would increase the likelihood of a

---

[23] Gerrard Winstanley, *The Law of Freedom in a Platform* (London, 1651), in Christopher Hill (ed.), *The Law of Freedom and Other Writings* (Cambridge, 1983), p. 388; James Harrington, *The Commonwealth of Oceana* (London, 1656), printed in H. Morley (ed.), *Ideal Commonwealths* (New York, 1901), pp. 261–72.

[24] Hugh Peter, *Good Work for a Good Magistrate* (London, 1651), postscript (TT).

[25] See below, ch. 4.

successful marital relationship. He suggested that, if such marriages were allowed, they might help to repair the familial disruption which had resulted from the 'late and common calamities' of the Civil War, and lead to a reduction in fornication and incest.[26] The following year, these arguments were reinforced in the pamphlet *A Counter-Buffe*, which stated:

> ... to such as inveigle their kindred and make them concubines, or even commit fornication with them, we wish the punishments allotted in 20 of Leviticus, to them and the like capital offenders. But such as do really (and with their good liking) make them their wives according to the holy Ordinance, we pray for, and wish them the blessings of Abraham and Sarah, Isaac and Rebecca, with the rest of the fathers and Patriarchs which married in this manner.[27]

At the end of 1647, the group of conservative Presbyterian ministers who drew up the pamphlet *A Testimony to the Truth of Jesus Christ* accused the radical sectaries of arguing that the marriage of two close relatives who shared 'a liking and mutual correspondency' was 'most lawful and according to the Primitive purity and practice'.[28]

Polygamy found a number of influential supporters. John Milton made it clear on several occasions in his writings that he saw no objection to a man having two or more wives. In *De Doctrina Christiana* he argued that a practice which had been so common among the Old Testament prophets and patriarchs could hardly be unacceptable to God, and, following a conversation with a Dutch diplomat in 1652, he seems to have acquired a reputation on the Continent as an advocate of the practice.[29] Francis Osborne, who was so opposed to the monogamous family, also commented favourably on polygamy in his *Political Reflections Upon the Government of the Turks* which appeared in 1656, claiming that, as a result of the practice, the Turks were less addicted to the 'European vanities' of horse racing, hunting and hawking, and amorous entertainments.[30] In 1657, an English translation of *The Dialogue of Polygamy* appeared; originally the work of the sixteenth-century Protestant reformer Bernardino Ochino, it was dedicated to

---

[26] *Little Non-Such or Certain New Questions Moved out of Ancient Truths* (London, 1646), *passim* (TT).

[27] *A Counter-Buffe* (London, 1647), p. 20 (TT).

[28] *A Testimony to the Truth of Jesus Christ* (London, 1647), p. 19 (TT).

[29] Wolfe (ed.), *Complete Prose Works of Milton*, vol. 6, pp. 355–68; Christopher Hill, *Milton and the English Revolution* (London, 1977), pp. 137–9.

[30] Francis Osborne, *Political Reflections Upon the Government of the Turks* (Oxford, 1656), p. 48.

Osborne and probably translated by Thomas Pecke. Justifying its appearance in the preface, the stationer informed readers that the book was not meant to be an encouragement to those who wished to desert their wives, leaving them 'with poverty, shame and, it may be, a great belly to boot', and stressed that Ochino's main argument was that the introduction of polygamy would reduce the incidence of desertion of wives by dissatisfied husbands.[31]

The following year saw the appearance of *A Remedy for Uncleanness*, another tract which advocated polygamy and which was dedicated to the head of state, Oliver Cromwell. The anonymous author urged the Protector to introduce polygamous marriages on the grounds that they would help to reduce the incidence of promiscuity and violence within families and, in particular, the killing of unwanted illegitimate babies by their mothers. Such 'impure and unnatural abominations' were, he claimed, frequently committed throughout the country. The author asserted that polygamy would 'in every way suit and comport with the nature and essence of purity and holiness in the present saints and people of God as well as those that walked with God before and after the flood.'[32] He seems to have expected a fair hearing from Cromwell, declaring in the dedicatory epistle, 'I know custom is not the mistress of your actions: you have learned to stand for Religion, equity and reason, against mouldy laws and rotten records.'[33] Cromwell's personal response is not known, but whether he was intrigued or appalled, the pamphlet was subsequently brought to the attention of the Council of State.[34]

Perhaps the most notorious of these controversies, however, was that which arose over the question of divorce. English divorce laws in the seventeenth century were very restrictive. Absolute divorce, *a vinculo matrimonii*, was only available where it could be proved that an impediment to marriage, such as impotence, had existed prior to contract. Divorce *a mensa et thoro*, the equivalent of a legal separation, could be obtained only for serious misconduct after marriage, in particular the wife's adultery. A call for the liberalization of these laws was initiated in 1643 by John Milton, whose own recent marriage to Mary Powell had proved so disastrous and who thus considered the prohibition upon divorce 'the most urgent and excessive grievance happening in domestic life.'[35] In a series of divorce tracts, *The Doctrine*

---

[31] Bernardino Ochino, *A Dialogue of Polygamy* (London, 1657), stationer's preface.
[32] *A Remedy for Uncleanness or Certain Queries Propounded to His Highness the Lord Protector* (London, 1658), p. 6 (TT).
[33] Ibid., dedicatory epistle.
[34] CSPD 1658–9, p. 71.
[35] John Milton, *Tetrachordon* (London, 1645), in Wolfe (ed.), *Complete Prose Works of Milton*, vol. 2, p. 585.

and Discipline of Divorce, The Judgement of Martin Bucer, Tetrachordon and *Colasterium*, published between 1643 and 1645, and again later in *De Doctrina Christiana*,[36] Milton argued that companionship, rather than procreation, was the chief purpose of marriage, and that husbands should therefore be permitted to divorce wives not only for adultery, but also in cases of fundamental incompatibility.

In the first of these tracts, *The Doctrine and Discipline of Divorce*, which was published in August 1643 and reissued only seven months later, Milton argued that

> indisposition, unfitness or contrareity of mind, arising from a cause in nature unchangeable, hindering and ever likely to hinder the main benefits of conjugal society, which are solace and peace, is a greater reason of divorce than natural frigidity, especially if there be no children and that there be mutual consent.[37]

In support of this view, he marshalled an impressive array of scriptural evidence, calling upon all his intellectual virtuosity to explain away Christ's apparent blanket condemnation of the practice in the New Testament. In *The Judgement of Martin Bucer*, published in July 1644, he pointed out to those who were hostile to his proposals that divorce had been supported by a number of prominent sixteenth-century Protestant reformers, and that Martin Bucer had suggested to Edward VI that it should be introduced into England in the early 1550s.[38] Over the next few months, he continued to campaign with great vigour and, in March 1645, two further divorce tracts, *Colasterium* and *Tetrachordon*, were published on the same day. These works contained his response to the criticisms which the earlier tracts had aroused; the preface to *Tetrachordon* was addressed to the MPs of the Long Parliament, to whom the poet declared 'these things both in the right constitution and in the right reformation of a commonwealth call for speediest redress.'[39] Milton's advocacy of freer divorce scandalized many of his contemporaries and was largely responsible for his acquiring the contemporary reputation of a libertine. Some, however, did come to his support. The radical sectary Mrs Attaway defended Milton and, forgetting that he had argued only in favour of divorces initiated by men, she later deserted her own 'unsanctified' husband.[40] In 1646, the eminent lawyer John Selden

---

[36] Wolfe (ed.), *Complete Prose Works of Milton*, vol. 6, pp. 371–81.
[37] Ibid., vol. 2, p. 242.
[38] Ibid., pp. 421–79.
[39] Ibid., pp. 571–758.
[40] Edwards, *Gangraena*, part 2, pp. 10–11.

published a detailed study of ancient Jewish divorce law entitled *Uxor Ebraica*, in which he argued that there might be grounds for some liberalization, and in 1651 Hugh Peter suggested that divorce cases should be heard before justices of the peace.[41]

One further controversy which surfaced during the 1640s and 1650s and which had important implications for family life was over the question of sexuality. A number of writers during these years began to dissent from the traditional view that sexual attraction was a dangerous and intrinsically sinful force. Foremost among such writers were the Ranters, who challenged the traditional sexual ethics underpinning the family by advocating indulgence in casual, multi-partner sexual intercourse. The Ranters claimed that, when performed in a spirit of 'light and love', promiscuous sexual activity was not sinful, but rather a glorification of God in his creation. In *A Second Fiery Flying Roll*, published in 1649, Abiezer Coppe argued in favour of complete sexual freedom, declaring, 'if I can, I will kiss and hug ladies, and love my neighbour's wife without sin';[42] and the following year, the author of *A Justification of a Mad Crew* asked:

> ... if I the lord in a man gain the love, affections and desires of all women, and make them sweetly to serve me, and have done so lie with them all, and use them oft as I please, and set not up an idol in my heart, by having one woman only, damning and cursing and estranging myself from all other women, is this not the truest marriage?[43]

Another Ranter, Thomas Webbe, was accused of stating that he could justifiably lie with any woman except his mother and that there was 'no heaven like women, nor no hell like marriage',[44] and Lawrence Clarkson claimed in *A Single Eye*:

> If Reason were admitted and thereby Scripture interpreted, then should they observe that Act they call Honesty to be Adultery, and that Act so called Adultery to have as much honesty as the other, for with God they are but one, and that one Act, holy, just, and good as God.[45]

---

[41] John Selden, *Uxor Ebraica* (London, 1646), *passim*; Peter, *Good Work for a Good Magistrate*, postscript.
[42] Coppe, *Second Fiery Flying Roll*, p. 9.
[43] Davis, *Fear, Myth and History*, p. 154.
[44] Edward Stokes, *The Wiltshire Rant* (London, 1652), p. 12 (TT).
[45] Smith, *Ranter Writings*, pp. 163–4.

While his outlook was in no way as extreme as that of the Ranters, there is some evidence that John Milton may also have been more liberal in his view of sexuality than most of his contemporaries. Throughout the divorce tracts, he argued that 'mere physical adultery' was a far less serious fault in a marriage partner than incompatibility, which he viewed as a form of spiritual adultery. Later, in the epic poem *Paradise Lost*, he emphasized not Adam's deception by an evil woman, but his decision to follow Eve into the wilderness out of love; and of the first couple's sexual relations in Eden, he commented:

> Whatever hypocrites austerely talk
> Of purity place and innocence
> Defaming as impure what God declares
> Pure, and commands to some, leaves free to all.[46]

Even prostitution found support from some quarters. In 1660, the author of *The Ladies' Champion* defended the practice on the grounds that prostitutes provided a relatively harmless sexual outlet for husbands whose wives were temporarily unavailable to them, either through illness or advanced pregnancy.[47]

Another diametrically opposed attitude towards sexuality which posed an additional threat to normal sexual relationships within the family was the view of some writers that, as sexual relations were so fraught with danger, they were best shunned altogether and that chastity was a higher calling. John Pordage, the radical Berkshire minister, advocated chastity, pointing to Christ as the model for what he called 'Christian Eunuchism'.[48] Nor was it only male writers who recommended abstinence; Sarah Jinnor concluded a discussion of sex and marriage in her *Woman's Almanack*, published in 1659, with the advice

> For this is my judgement, do not take distaste,
> But as I am, I wish you all be chaste,
> This is the only way, if you desire
> To be preserved from the Frenchman's fire.[49]

During the 1640s and 1650s, then, the traditional family was roundly censured by a number of intellectuals who advocated fundamental reform of its structures, traditions and relationships. But if the family had its critics during these years, it also found a number of equally influential

---

[46] John Milton, *Paradise Lost*, book 4, lines 744–7. See also Hill, *Milton*, pp. 128–30.
[47] *The Ladies' Champion* (London, 1660), pp. 5–6 (TT).
[48] Pordage, *Innocence Appearing*, p. 57.
[49] Sarah Jinnor, *The Woman's Almanack* (London, 1659), unpag. (TT).

defenders, who believed that there was considerable merit in the existing institution, and who published a number of spirited and widely read defences of the traditional family and its patriarchal structure. The task of defending the family fell to an influential group of conservative theorists which included William Herbert, Thomas Cobbet, Robert Abbot and Jeremy Taylor. William Herbert of Pointington in Somerset, a tutor for some years to the children of the Royalist Montague Bertie, Earl of Lindsey, was the author of a number of devotional works which appeared in the 1640s. In *The Child-Bearing Woman*, published in 1648, he warned his readers against those who wished to reform the family, claiming that the 'novelty of their presumptuous opinions' would 'bring again such old darkness as was at first on the face of the deep'.[50] In *The Careful Father and Pious Child*, which appeared the same year, he discussed family relationships in some detail. He pointed out that patriarchal power had been supported by St Paul, and counselled wives to honour, serve and obey their husbands, and to view them as 'God's image, his lieutenant to her on earth, the cause of her being and the fountain of her authority'. He advised the husband to 'love, comfort, Honour, maintain, Govern, instruct his wife, and be faithful to her'. Parents, he argued, ruled over their children as prophets, priests and kings, and were obliged to bring them up religiously, to pray for them and to supervise their careers and marriages.[51]

Thomas Cobbet was a New England minister whose *A Fruitful Discourse Touching the Honour due from Children to Parents and the Duty of Parents to Children* was written in 1654 and published in England in 1656. The work consisted of a detailed exposition upon the fifth commandment, in the course of which the author claimed that respect for parental authority was essential for the stability of the state. Cobbet discussed in great detail the obligation upon children to respect, honour and obey their parents, asserting:

> ... who better servants, in that relation to masters, than those that were good children to Parents? Who more obedient subjects to lawful Authority, and Fathers of the Commonwealth, than such as learned and practised filial obedience to Parents at home? Who more respective to Ministers, than those that were and are conscientiously respective to good Parents? Who more tender of their own and others chastity, of their own and others estates and names ... than such as have been conscientious honourers of their Parents.

[50] William Herbert, *The Child-Bearing Woman* (London, 1648), p. 10 (TT).
[51] Idem, *The Careful Father and Pious Child* (London, 1648), questions 659–704 (TT).

Children, he believed, should render all outward marks of respect to their parents, such as bowing to them and standing bare-headed before them; they should enjoy their company, listen to their advice and never criticize them. He warned that the dishonouring of parents was the 'very spring and root of manifold wickedness', and claimed that those who broke the fifth commandment would go on to break the others too.[52]

Another clergyman who came to the support of the traditional family was Robert Abbot, the Presbyterian minister of St Austin's, London, whose *A Christian Family Builded by God* appeared in 1653. The book contained a wealth of advice upon family matters, such as the choice of marriage partner, the arrangement of the marriage ceremony and the duties and responsibilities of spouses and children. Abbot's stance was uncompromisingly conservative; he was a firm supporter of patriarchy and urged his readers to involve God in their families at every opportunity, arguing that a family founded upon God would be a well-ordered family. Men should choose as brides, he counselled, women who had a good reputation, were modest of dress and refrained from speaking too much. Once the marriage had taken place, the woman should submit to her husband because 'the Order of Creation requires it', and should avoid the four common faults of wives – 'want of wit to know their place', 'want of love', 'Pride in Aspiring to Mastership' and 'love of the vanities of the world against the minds of their husbands'.[53] Abbot advised that, while ruling over their wives, husbands should also honour and love them; like many of his contemporaries, he saw women as 'weaker vessels' and declared:

> Weakest members are most spared, and brittle vessels are most tenderly used. It is true they are vessels, therefore they are for use; they are helps to piety, helps to society, helps to house government and helps to propagation; yet are they weaker vessels, therefore to be honoured as being for the Closet not for the Kitchen.[54]

Abbot also outlined the responsibilities of parents towards children and advised children to show their parents reverence, obedience and thankfulness.[55]

Probably the most influential of these conservative commentators on family life, however, was Jeremy Taylor. An Anglican divine who had

---
[52] Cobbet, *Fruitful Discourse, passim*, esp. pp. 9–10.
[53] Abbot, *Christian Family, passim*.
[54] Ibid., pp. 44–5.
[55] Ibid., pp. 46–59.

been associated with William Laud in the 1630s and chaplain to Charles I from 1636 to 1649, Taylor discussed family life in several tracts and sermons which appeared in print during the 1650s, including *The Marriage Ring or The Mysteriousness and Duties of Marriage*, and his extremely popular *Rules and Exercises for Holy Living*. This latter work, which was published in 1650, ran to five editions before 1656 and a further nine during Charles II's reign. Taylor was another staunch defender of patriarchy, though he saw the father's power as 'paternal and friendly, not magisterial and despotic'. He advised husbands to rule over their wives as the soul rules the body, and to show them 'love, maintenance, duty and sweetness of conversation'. He pointed out that wives had their own authority in certain spheres of family life, such as the daily supervision of children and the household budget, but emphasized that this authority was subordinate to the husband's, arguing that the husband was the sun and the wife the moon who 'shines only by his light, and rules by his authority'. Amongst the duties of parents he included educating their children, instructing them in religion and providing them with suitable candidates for marriage partners, though he counselled against undue parental interference in their choices. Children, he argued, should regard their parents as 'friends and patrons, their defence and sanctuary, their treasure and their Guide'.[56]

Because of the close relationship between the power of the father in the family and that of the ruler in the state, the patriarchal family was also defended by some of the most important political theorists of the mid-seventeenth century. In *Patriarcha*, a justification of the theory of the divine right of kings written on the eve of the civil war, Sir Robert Filmer argued that both kings and fathers of families exercised their absolute authorities as descendants of the first ruler and father, Adam. Filmer claimed that 'distinct families which had Fathers for rulers' had existed since earliest times, and declared that 'the subordination of children is the foundation of all regal authority.'[57] Thomas Hobbes, who also supported the absolute rule of monarchs, though on an entirely different basis from that of Filmer, claimed in *Leviathan*, published in the early 1650s, that fathers had possessed sovereign power over their families before the formation of civil society and had retained a considerable degree of

---

[56] Jeremy Taylor, *The Marriage Ring or the Mysteriousness and Duties of Marriage* (London, 1653), in C. P. Eden (ed.), *The Whole Works of the Right Reverend Jeremy Taylor* (10 vols, London, 1848), vol. 4, pp. 219, 221; and idem, *The Rules and Exercises for Holy Living*, (London, 1857 edn), pp. 204–10.
[57] Filmer, *Patriarcha* in Laslett (ed.), *Patriarcha and Other Political Works*, pp. 57–9.

authority after contracting into a commonwealth. This authority, he asserted, was 'not only lawful, but necessary and laudable'.[58]

Nor was it only conservative writers who saw merit in the family. The Digger leader, Gerrard Winstanley, found fault with many of the traditional institutions of his day, but, outlining his conception of an ideal communistic republic in *The Law of Freedom in a Platform* published in 1651, he was careful to refute any suggestion that individual family units would disappear, declaring:

> though the earth and storehouses be common to every family, yet every family shall live apart, as they do; and every man's house, wife, children and furniture for ornament of his house, or anything which he hath fetched in from the store-houses or provided for the necessary use of his family, is all a property to that family for the peace thereof.[59]

While Winstanley advocated the complete abolition of private property, he wished to retain the family as an uncompromisingly authoritarian and patriarchal institution. He referred to fathers as 'the first link in the chain of magistracy' and proposed that they be given wide-ranging powers and responsibilities, including the supervision of their children's education and the direction of their employment. They would also have been empowered to administer corporal punishment if their children defied them.[60] This strong support for the traditional family unit probably resulted partly from Winstanley's experiences at St George's Hill, where a group of Ranters had proved a particularly disruptive influence. It is also possible that he had heard reports of how, earlier in the century, the Puritan colonists of Massachusetts in North America had been forced to abandon their unsuccessful attempts to organize themselves into communities within which the individual lacked any meaningful familial identity.[61]

One major reason why patriarchy continued to be widely regarded as the most suitable form of family government was that very few men believed that women were capable of exercising real authority in their own right. Discussing the emergence of women preachers during the 1640s, E. M. Williams has stated that, following the outbreak of the Civil

---

[58] Thomas Hobbes, *Leviathan* (London, 1651), ed. C. B. Macpherson (Harmondsworth, 1966), pp. 284, 305, 382.
[59] Winstanley, *Law of Freedom*, p. 288.
[60] Ibid., pp. 317, 325.
[61] W. T. Davis (ed.), *Bradford's History of the Plymouth Plantation* (New York, 1908), pp. 146–7.

War, 'the Pauline injunction of female inferiority was one of the first traditions to be swept aside.'[62] In reality, however, despite the arguments of the Quakers and the other writers mentioned above, traditional attitudes proved far more persistent. Conservative writers found the views of the Quakers particularly offensive, and even amongst the radical groups the equality of women was not universally conceded. Although the Leveller leaders had based their campaign for political reform upon the idea of a fundamental natural equality and large numbers of women had actively supported them in the 1640s, there is no indication that they ever seriously considered including women in the extended franchise for which they were campaigning. Again, not all the sects followed the Quaker example; in 1658, the Baptist church at Abingdon in Berkshire forbade women to speak during church services on the grounds that this would amount to a denial of 'the inferiority of their sex'.[63] Elsewhere, the old misogynist view of women remained firmly entrenched in revolutionary England; it was typified by the author who declared in 1642:

> Then for wives, there's scarce one good of twenty. If I should say Forty I think I should not lie; for one scolds, another pouts; one is lazy, another sluttish; a third Proud, a fourth a downright Drunkard, a fifth a tittle-tattle Gossip; and so from one to a hundred, to a thousand, to many thousands: You shall scarce find one that is not Guilty of one abominable crime or another.[64]

Many male writers believed that the whole of womankind shared the blame for the Fall with the first woman, Eve. Francis Osborne, whose opposition to monogamy was based upon his low opinion of women, claimed in *Advice to a Son* that 'Eve, by her stumbling at the Serpent's solicitations, cast her Husband out of Paradise; nor are her Daughters surer of foot.'[65] Similarly, Thomas Pecke argued in his *Advice to Balaam's Ass*, published in 1658, that Eve 'was made when Adam was asleep: and plucked so much knowledge from the Tree of Knowledge as to bequeath most of her daughters that Serpentine desire of making their Husbands know some Good and much Evil.'[66] The following year, William Hill reminded the readers of his *A New Year's Gift for Women* that women were all 'Daughters of Eve, who was the author of much

---

[62] E. M. Williams, 'Women Preachers in the Civil War', *Journal of Modern History*, 1 (1929), 561.
[63] Quoted by Hill in *Milton*, p. 118.
[64] *A Strange Wonder or a Wonder in a Woman* (London, 1642), p. 2 (TT).
[65] Osborne, *Advice to a Son*, p. 45.
[66] Pecke, *Balaam's Ass*, p. 31.

more evil to Mankind in seducing her Husband to eat of the forbidden fruit, than Judas was in betraying our Saviour.'[67] Another writer claimed that women had inherited from Eve discontentedness, curiosity and unreliability,[68] and a number of works which appeared during the 1640s and 1650s included the traditional distinction between the 'good' and 'bad' woman. *A Brief Anatomy of Women*, which appeared in 1653, contrasted the destructive powers of evil women, who ensnared men with their physical attractions and whose beauty was like 'Indian apples, seemingly fair without but poison within', with the minority of subservient good women who were 'helpful, comfortable and generally useful to man, as that without them the world would be at a period'.[69] William Hill added a third element to this categorization, roundly criticizing a group he labelled 'Marthas' for their preoccupation with material concerns.[70]

Evident throughout this literature is a considerable male disquiet and anxiety over what was seen as the failure of contemporary women to conduct themselves in ways which matched their subordinate status. William Hill lamented the absence of 'poverty of spirit' and humility amongst women,[71] and Thomas Pecke complained:

> Nothing is more indecent and distasteful than that a woman should act the part of an Eagle . . . yet sometimes we see that the Husband hath only the name of master, whilst the wife exercises a Tyrannical Monarchy over the family.[72]

This same fear is expressed in many of the popular songs and ballads of the period, such as *An Invective Against the Pride of Women*, and Edward Foord's *Wine and Women*. The former condemned women who attempted to educate themselves, declaring:

> Their soaring thoughts to Books advance
> 'Tis odds that may undo 'um
> For ever since Dame Eve's mischance
> That villanous itch sticks to 'um.[73]

---

[67] William Hill, *A New Year's Gift for Women* (London, 1659), dedicatory epistle (TT).
[68] John Brinsley, *A Looking Glass for Good Women* (London, 1645), p. 6 (TT).
[69] J. S., *A Brief Anatomy of Women* (London, 1653), p. 3 (TT).
[70] William Hill, *New Year's Gift*, pp. 32–8.
[71] Ibid., dedicatory epistle.
[72] Pecke, *Balaam's Ass*, p. 44.
[73] *An Invective Against The Pride Of Women* (London, 1657), unpag. (TT).

Foord emphasized the manipulative nature of women in verses such as:

> Women they say the Weaker Vessels are
> If so, it is a Paradox to me
> That those that never were trained up in war
> So often should obtain the victory
> For your fair women still in every place
> Do conquer valiant men with their bare Face . . .

He even intimated that women should bear some of the responsibility for the civil conflicts that England was experiencing, declaring:

> 'Tis envious Women in a troubled State
> That do incense their Husbands to rebel.[74]

In addition to defending the power structure within the traditional family and reinforcing the idea of female subservience, conservative writers also vigorously opposed any proposals for major familial reform. Suggestions that the marriage service should become a secular ceremony were opposed by both Jeremy Taylor and John Gauden. Taylor's sermon, *The Marriage Ring or The Mysteriousness and Duties of Marriage*, was published in May 1653, just a few weeks before the members of Barebone's Parliament voted to make church weddings invalid. The author explained to his readers that, if marriage was not 'in Christ and the church', it would lose its 'mysteriousness' and declared '. . . it concerns all that enter into those golden fetters to see that Christ and His church be in at every of its periods, and that it be entirely conducted and overruled by religion.'[75] Another tract attacking civil marriage, *Christ at the Wedding*, was written by the conservative divine, John Gauden. Gauden was almost certainly also the author of much of the highly popular *Eikon Basilike*, which had appeared in the wake of Charles I's execution and contained details of what purported to be the king's last prayers and devotions. In *Christ at the Wedding*, he addressed the MPs of Cromwell's first Protectorate Parliament, calling upon them to reverse the decision of Barebone's Parliament to introduce a secular marriage service, and stressing the importance of the prayers and religious instruction included in the religious ceremony.[76]

Shortly after the appearance in 1646 of the tract *Little Non-Such*, which had proposed that marriages should be permitted within the forbidden degrees of consanguinity, the proposal was attacked by the

---

[74] Edward Foord, *Wine and Women* (London, 1646), pp. 16, 28 (TT).
[75] Taylor, *Marriage Ring* in Eden (ed.), *Whole Works of Jeremy Taylor*, vol. 4, p. 212.
[76] Gauden, *Christ at the Wedding*, passim.

Presbyterian Thomas Edwards in the pamphlet *Animadversions Touching a Pamphlet Entitled Little Non-Such*.[77] In 1652, the Anglican clergyman Henry Hammond again criticized marriages between close kin in his *Letter of Resolution to Six Queries of Present Use in The Church of England*, in which he discussed some of the major religious controversies dividing his contemporaries. After giving a detailed exposition of the provisions of the Mosaic law, Hammond concluded that such marriages were forbidden unless allowed by special divine dispensation. Another of Hammond's six queries concerned polygamy; his judgement on this practice was that it had only been permitted amongst the Old Testament Jews because the increase in their numbers was of paramount concern, and that it had subsequently been specifically forbidden by Christ.[78] Robert Abbot also firmly rejected both polygamy and incestuous marriages in *A Christian Family Builded by God*.[79]

Conservative moralists considered John Milton's call for the introduction of divorce particularly outrageous and devoted much of their attention to refuting the poet's arguments. The first major attack upon Milton's proposals was that outlined in the tract *An Answer to a Book entitled The Doctrine and Discipline of Divorce*, which appeared in 1644. The anonymous author questioned Milton's motives, suggesting that his call for general reform had been precipitated by his own unfortunate marital experiences, and had considerable fun at the poet's expense by arguing that it was surely possible to consider the suitability of a prospective spouse as a companion before any marriage took place, and declaring that, if companionship was indeed the main end of marriage, God would have created a second man to befriend Adam. He also accused Milton of having unrealistically high expectations of a partner, declaring '. . . we believe you count no woman to due conversation accessible as to you, except she can speak Hebrew, Greek, Latin and French, and dispute the canon law as well as you.' In a more serious vein, he went on to question Milton's biblical exegesis and to point out that his arguments could equally easily be used to justify the divorce of husbands by wives. 'Contrareity of mind', he suggested, could be remedied by means of medicine, diet and 'the soft words and carriage of a patient man or woman', whereas the result of liberalization would be the break-up of the family. If divorce became easily available, he argued:

> many thousands of lustful and libidinous men would be parting from their wives every week and marrying others; and upon this,

[77] The pamphlet, which has not survived, is referred to in *A Counter-Buffe*.
[78] Henry Hammond, *A Letter of Resolution to Six Queries of Present Use in the Church of England* (London, 1652), pp. 35–82 (TT).
[79] Abbot, *Christian Family*, pp. 27–9.

who would keep the children of these divorces which sometimes they would leave in their wives' bellies? how shall they come by their portions, of whom or where? and how shall the wife be endowed of her husband's estate? Nay commonly to what reproach would the woman be left who was not fit for anyone's company? and so who would venture upon her again? And so by this means, through her just cause of discouragement, she would probably hazard herself upon some dishonest or disgraceful course, with a hundred more the like inconveniences, even as the overturning and overthrowing of all humane society.[80]

Milton's proposals were also attacked by Henry Hammond. In his *Practical Catechism*, written specifically for a popular readership and published in 1645, Hammond argued that the only justifiable ground for divorce was adultery by the wife, which could cause families 'great inconveniences and mischiefs', such as disputes over inheritance. Seven years later, he returned to the question in *A Letter of Resolution*, where he reviewed the literary controversy on the subject and attempted to vindicate the conservative position 'from the prejudices under which it hath fallen, and to which the pride and lusts of men have subjected it in these licentious days'.[82] Another firm opponent of divorce was John Heydon, who declared in *Advice to a Daughter*:

Some have complained of the Christian religion, in that it ties men so strictly in this point, and when matches happen ill, there is no remedy. But, surely, if liberty or change were granted, all would grow to confusion: and it would open a sluice to many mischiefs arising out of heat only, which now by necessity are cooled and made tame again.[83]

Finally, a great deal of conservative advice on sexual matters appeared in print during the revolutionary years and the traditional approach to sexual matters was firmly restated by a number of the most influential commentators upon family life. Extramarital sexual relations were widely condemned. Fornication – sexual relations between unmarried men and women – was frequently deplored. Gerrard Winstanley, the

---

[80] *An Answer to a Book Entitled the Doctrine and Discipline of Divorce* (London, 1644), pp. 8–9 (TT).
[81] Henry Hammond, *A Practical Catechism* (London, 1645), p. 81 (TT).
[82] Hammond, *Letter of Resolution*, pp. 83–173.
[83] Heydon, *Advice to a Daughter*, pp. 66–7.

Digger leader, went out of his way to denounce the Ranter advocacy of free love, which he described as 'the destroying power of creation'. In *A New Year's Gift for Parliament and Army*, he declared:

> ... they report that we diggers hold women to be common, and live in that bestialness. For my part, I declare against it. I own this to be the truth, that the earth ought to be a common treasury to all, but as for women, let every man have his own wife, and every woman her own husband; and I know none of the diggers that act in such an unrational excess of female community. If any should, I profess to have nothing to do with such people, but leave them to their own master who will pay them with torment of mind and diseases in their bodies.[84]

Still greater criticism was levelled against adultery, particularly on the part of the married woman, as this involved the violation of a man's property and was thus a sin with a social dimension. Rape, prostitution and homosexuality were also roundly denounced. Winstanley described rape as 'robbery of a woman's bodily freedom', and advocated the death penalty for men convicted of the crime. He would also have executed men found guilty of repeated adultery.[85] Prostitution was condemned by William Herbert, who advised husbands not to waste their bodies on whores.[86] Francis Osborne described homosexuality as an 'unnatural heat' and 'an impiety not to be credited by an honest heart', and he warned any 'handsome, young and beardless' readers who might decide to travel to Italy to beware 'the lusts of men as well as the affections of women.'[87]

Married men and women, for whom sexual relations were somewhat grudgingly acknowledged to be permissible, were counselled by the conservative theorists of family life to exercise a restrained and moderate indulgence in marital intercourse. In *Holy Living*, Jeremy Taylor instructed married couples that their sexual relations should be 'moderate so as to consist with health', not 'too expensive of time', and 'without violent, transporting desires or too sensual applications'. The primary purpose of sexual intercourse within marriage, he argued, was to prevent fornication and to lighten the cares and sadness of household affairs, and

---

[84] Winstanley, *Law of Freedom*, p. 177. See also Christopher Hill, *The World Turned Upside Down: Radical Ideas During the English Revolution* (London, 1972), p. 257.
[85] Winstanley, *Law of Freedom*, p. 388.
[86] Herbert, *Careful Father*, question 685.
[87] Osborne, *Advice to a Son*, p. 84.

he urged his readers not to 'separate the sensuality from those ends that hallow it', warning them:

> ... it is a sad truth that many married persons, thinking that the flood-gates of liberty are set wide open, without measure or constraints ... have felt the final rewards of intemperance and lust, by their unlawful using of lawful permissions.

Holy Living also included an exhaustive list of techniques aimed at subduing passion and lust. Nevertheless, despite all these injunctions, Taylor also stated that spouses should never refuse each other normal sexual relations, and both he and William Herbert argued against those who had claimed that individuals should aspire to celibacy as a higher state than marriage.[88]

The years of revolutionary crisis in mid-seventeenth-century England witnessed, then, an extensive and lively intellectual discussion of many aspects of contemporary family life and sexual relations. In the course of this discussion, writers produced both imaginative programmes for reform and vigorous apologies for the familial status quo. Just how much influence these writers exerted is, however, difficult to assess. As intellectual ideas often have little or no effect, or results which are totally unintended and undesired, it is never easy for historians to evaluate the scale and nature of their impact upon the societies which produce them. Many of the titles mentioned above were certainly readily available and some are known to have reached a wide audience. But seventeeth-century England was only a semi-literate society and then, as now, the relationship between intellectuals and their less enquiring contemporaries was one of detachment and mutual suspicion. In the following chapters we shall consider the extent to which the lives of those who lived through the English Revolution were influenced by the literary works mentioned above, and also whether family life was more affected by intellectual theories or by the extraordinary events of these disturbed years.

---

[88] Taylor, *Holy Living*, pp. 97–102, and *Marriage Ring* in Eden (ed.), *Whole Works of Jeremy Taylor*, vol. 4, p. 211; Herbert, *Careful Father*, questions 560–6.

3
By the Sword Divided?

During the summer of 1642, after numerous attempts to reach a peaceful accommodation between the king and his parliamentary opponents had all proved unsuccessful, both sides made their preparations for war and, in the autumn, full-scale armed conflict ensued. Few English men or women had had any first-hand experience of warfare, but most viewed the prospect of civil war as extremely alarming. Their concern was well justified, for during the following four years, the fighting caused widespread social disruption and personal inconvenience, and some of their worst fears became reality. For many, one of the most distressing features of the conflict was the fact that it was a 'war without an enemy', which created deep enmities and divisions between those who in more normal times would have been natural friends and allies. Contemporaries were particularly shocked by divisions within families; for some indeed this seemed to be the quintessential feature of the war. At the beginning of 1643, a petition claiming to represent the views of a number of widows was published in London; calling for an end to the fighting, it declared:

> We have a tender sense of all those miseries which have drowned the face of this kingdom in a sea of blood, of those dreadful domestic wars which have engaged brother against brother, our sons one against the other, the sons of our bowels, with hostile and unbrotherly hatred, destroying one another, so that England seems to be turned mad with a Theban fury and those civil and fraternal differences were re-enacted on this our English stage.[1]

[1] *The Widows' Lamentation* (London, 1643), p. 4 (TT).

Several years later, the author of *The Scourge of Civil Warre, The Blessing of Peace* declared that 'War makes the Father's throat a sheath for the Son's sword',[2] and, reflecting upon the events of the Civil War period in his commonplace book, Sir John Oglander of Nunwell on the Isle of Wight commented, 'Thou would think it strange if I should tell thee there was a time in England when brothers killed brothers, cousins cousins, and friends their friends'.[3] Similarly, in his autobiography the Derbyshire yeoman Leonard Wheatcroft wrote of the 1640s 'then there was civil wars in England betwixt King and Parliament: then was father against son, and son against father, and brother against brother.'[4] In order to assess the accuracy of such contemporary observations, in this chapter we shall consider the relationship between family loyalty and political affiliation during the Civil War years, and investigate both the extent and the repercussions of divided civil-war allegiance within families.

During the summer of 1642, as war became increasingly unavoidable, many individuals were forced to make an often agonizing choice between supporting their lawful sovereign, Charles I, who many believed ruled with divine sanction, or his opponents in Parliament. In their efforts to discover the cause or causes of the Civil War and the reasons why individuals chose to fight either for or against the king, historians have suggested a variety of factors which may have influenced allegiance, including financial circumstance, religious affiliation and the rivalries within provincial communities. While such considerations were undoubtedly important, another factor which also influenced those who became actively involved in the war was the pressure brought to bear by their relatives. Many examples could be cited of individuals who claimed that their civil war allegiance had been decided by family pressures. Numbers of Royalists, such as Charles, Viscount Standish, Sir Christopher Wray, Robert Villiers, George Bisse and Giles Lockett claimed after the end of the war that they had been forced to fight for the king by their parents.[5] In May 1647, Francis Baildon of Yorkshire stated that he had been taken to the Royalist garrison at Skipton by his guardian, Francis Malham.[6] In 1650, it was reported that Thomas Cresheld of Church Honiborn in Worcestershire had persuaded his kinsman, William Harrison, to fight for the king and had supplied him with money and

---

[2] *The Scourge of Civil Warre, The Blessing of Peace* (London, 1645), unpag. (TT).
[3] F. Bamford (ed.), *A Royalist's Notebook* (London, 1936), pp. 103–4.
[4] C. Kerry (ed.), 'The Autobiography of Leonard Wheatcroft', *Journal of the Derbyshire Archaeological and Natural History Society*, 21 (1899), 27.
[5] *Cal. Com. Comp.*, vol. 2, pp. 1075, 1361; vol. 3, pp. 1688, 1799, 1928.
[6] Ibid., vol. 3, p. 1748.

arms.⁷ On other occasions, familial pressure was aimed not at persuading individuals to adopt a partisan position, but at keeping them neutral. Edward Dennis of Sharwell on the Isle of Wight was persuaded to return home from the Royalist wartime headquarters at Oxford through the influence of his mother and a friend and, at the start of the war, Anne, Lady Beauchamp of Eddington in Wiltshire, sent her two sons Edward and William Lewis to France and refused to allow them to return 'lest their uncles, the marquis of Hertford and the earl of Dorset, should engage them in the war.'⁸

Whatever considerations influenced individuals most when they were making up their minds whether to fight for Parliament or the king, in many cases members of the same nuclear family arrived at very different decisions and, as a result, found themselves numbering their closest relatives among their enemies. It is possible that a few particularly shrewd individuals, whose primary motivation was the protection of their families against all eventualities, may have deliberately divided their close relatives between the two sides. According to Lucy Hutchinson, one man who did this was Robert Pierrepont, Earl of Kingston. While Pierrepont's eldest son Henry fought for the King, a younger son, Francis, served as a colonel for Parliament, and Hutchinson later claimed that at the start of the war the earl had 'divided his sons between both parties and concealed himself'.⁹ Cary Gardiner also suggested that this was happening; writing to her sister-in-law during the early months of the war, she declared 'the world now accounts it policy for the father to be one one side and the son on th'other'.¹⁰ However, even if these women were correct and some families had decided to hedge their bets in this way, such machination was probably comparatively rare. Serious political and religious differences between close kin were much more commonly the result of accidental divergence of personal conviction and, as such, frequently caused considerable pain and regret within families. They were, none the less, a common occurrence and often spectacular in scale.

There are many examples of deep wartime divisions between fathers and sons. At the battle of Edgehill, the first major engagement of the war which took place in the autumn of 1642, two of the Royalist peers in the king's lifeguard, William Feilding, Earl of Denbigh, and Henry Carey, Earl of Dover, charged against their own sons, Basil Feilding and John

---

⁷ *Cal. Com. Advance Money*, vol. 3, p. 1287.
⁸ Ibid., vol. 1, p. 569; vol. 2, p. 1003.
⁹ *DNB*, Robert Pierrepont (1584–1643); and Lucy Hutchinson, *Memoirs of the Life of Colonel Hutchinson*, ed. C. H. Firth (London, 1906 edn), p. 92.
¹⁰ F. P. Verney and M. M. Verney, *Memorials of the Verney Family during the Seventeenth Century* (2 vols, London, 1904), vol. 1, p. 242.

Carey, Viscount Rochford, who were both members of the Earl of Essex's parliamentary army.[11] Sir Edmund Verney of Claydon in Buckinghamshire, another prominent Royalist who was killed at Edgehill while defending the king's standard, had a son, Sir Ralph Verney, who adhered to Parliament; Henry Belasyse of Durham was a Royalist, but his son Thomas Belasyse, Viscount Fauconberg, supported Parliament and later married one of Oliver Cromwell's daughters: Robert Rich, Earl of Warwick, supported Parliament, but his son Robert, Baron Rich of Leighs, was at Oxford during the war: Edward Bulstrode, an Inner Temple lawyer, acted as a judge for Parliament throughout the 1640s and 1650s, while his son, Sir Richard, was in arms as a Royalist; Sir John Corbet sat in the Long Parliament as MP for Shropshire during the war, while his eldest son John fought for Charles I.[12]

Brothers were also frequently at odds: Sir John Coke of Derbyshire was a Parliamentarian, but his younger brother Thomas a Royalist; Richard Neville of Billingbear in Berkshire was a Royalist colonel, but his brother Henry a Parliamentarian and republican theorist; Sir Edward Hungerford of Wiltshire fought for Parliament, while his half-brother Anthony was in arms for the king; the Royalist Sir William Fleetwood of Aldwinckle in Northamptonshire, was the elder brother of the parliamentary colonel Charles Fleetwood, and the Royalist Mountjoy Blount, Earl of Newport, was the illegitimate half-brother of the Parliamentarian Robert Rich, Earl of Warwick; Sir Walter Vane, younger brother of the republican Sir Henry Vane the younger, was a Royalist; and the poet John Milton, who was a staunch supporter of Parliament throughout the 1640s, had a Royalist brother, Sir Christopher Milton; Henry Lilburne, brother of the committed Parliamentarian John Lilburne, was killed in 1648 fighting for the king. Some brothers also exhibited a marked divergence in religious outlook. Arthur Penington, brother of the Quaker Isaac Penington the younger, was a Roman Catholic; the Puritan parliamentary general Edward Montagu, Earl of Manchester, had a Catholic brother Walter, who was abbot of a religious house at Pontoise in France; and Timothy Rogers, a Presbyterian divine in Essex, had an elder brother Nehemiah, who was an former associate of William Laud and a Royalist in the 1640s.[13]

[11] Edward Hyde, Earl of Clarendon, *The History of Rebellion and Civil Wars in England*, ed. W. Dunn Macray (6 vols, Oxford, 1888), vol. 2, pp. 352–6; *DNB*, William Feilding (d. 1643), Basil Feilding (d. 1674).
[12] *DNB*, Sir Edmund Verney (1590–1642), Sir Ralph Verney (1613–96), John Belasyse (1614–89), Thomas Belasyse (1627–1700), Robert Rich (1587–1658), Edward Bulstrode (1588–1659), Sir Richard Bulstrode (1610–1711), Sir John Corbet (1594–1662).
[13] *DNB*, Sir John Coke (1563–1644), Henry Neville (1620–94), Anthony Hungerford (d. 1657), Sir Edward Hungerford (1596–1648), Charles Fleetwood (d. 1692), Mountjoy

Divided allegiance was also a marked feature of the families of the regicides, the group of committed revolutionaries who signed Charles I's death warrant in 1649. Two of the regicides, John Lisle of Wootton on the Isle of Wight and Sir Thomas Mauleverer of Allerton Mauleverer in Yorkshire, had Royalist sons, William Lisle and Richard Mauleverer. A number of other regicides had Royalist brothers: William Goffe of Stanmer in Sussex, a staunch Puritan and regicide and one of Cromwell's major-generals in the 1650s, had an elder brother Stephen, who was a Royalist and who converted to Roman Catholicism in the early 1650s; and the regicides William Heveningham, Sir William Monson and Sir John Danvers, were the brothers of the Royalists Arthur Heveningham, Sir John Monson and Henry Danvers, Earl of Danby.[14]

Many additional examples could be cited of political division between more distant relatives, and between affinal kin who were connected through marriage. The cousin of the Royalist Sir Richard Bulstrode was the Parliamentarian Bulstrode Whitelocke; the second cousin of the Parliamentarian Isaac Penington the elder was the Royalist admiral, Sir John Penington; the mother of the regicide Simon Mayne of Dinton in Buckinghamshire was a member of the Royalist Lovelace family of Hurley in Berkshire; the Royalist Robert Dormer, Earl of Carnarvon, was the son-in-law of the Parliamentarian Philip Herbert, Earl of Pembroke; the parliamentary general Robert Devereux, Earl of Essex, was the brother-in-law of the Royalist William Seymour, Earl of Hertford: the Royalist Sir Edward Ford of Uppark in Sussex was the brother-in-law of the New Model Army officer Henry Ireton; and the regicide Anthony Stapley of Patcham in Sussex was the brother-in-law,

---

Blount (1597?–1665), Sir Henry Vane the younger (1613–62), John Milton (1608–70), Sir Christopher Milton (1615–93), Sir Isaac Penington the elder (1587–1660), Isaac Penington the younger (1616–79), Edward Montagu (1602–71), Nehemiah Rogers (1593–1660), Timothy Rogeers (1589–1650); Pauline Gregg, *Free-Born John* (london, 1961), pp. 97, 247, 305; A. Collins (ed.), *Letters and Memorials of State . . . Writen and Collected by Sir Henry Sydney* (2 vols, London, 1746), vol. 2, pp. 674–7; Violet A. Rowe, *Sir Henry Vane the Younger* (London, 1970), p. 241; C. G. Durston, 'Berkshire and its County Gentry 1625–49', Unpub. PhD. thesis, Reading Univ. (1977), vol. 2, pp. 116–23.

[14] *DNB*, John Lisle (1610?–1664), Sir Thomas Mauleverer (d. 1655), William Heveningham (1604–78), Sir John Monson (1600–83), Sir William Monson (d.1672), Henry Danvers (1573–1644), Sir John Danvers (1588–1655), Stephen Goffe (1605–81), William Goffe (d. 1679?); W. H. Blaauw, 'Passages of the Civil War in Sussex from 1642 to 1660', *Sussex Archaeological Collections*, 5 (1852), 83–4; Mark Noble *Lives of the English Regicides* (2 vols, London, 1798), vol. 1, pp. 163–70. William Heveningham sat as a commissioner at the king's trial on three occasions and was present when the sentence was passed, though he did not actually sign the death warrant.

by a previous wife, of the prominent Royalist Lord Goring, and in 1658 his children joined with Goring in a plot against Cromwell.[15]

One particularly good example of a family deeply divided by the conflicts of the 1640s, is the Sidney (or Sydney) family of Penshurst in Kent. At the beginning of the Civil War, Robert Sidney, Earl of Leicester, joined the king at Oxford, but in 1644 he retired to Penshurst and apart from taking charge of Charles I's children for some months after the king's execution in 1649, he took no further part in the political events of the 1640s. His relatives, however, adopted a range of divergent political stances; his brother-in-law, the Earl of Northumberland, supported Parliament, as did his two sons Philip and Algernon; his son-in-law Henry Spencer, Earl of Sunderland, was killed at the first battle of Newbury while fighting for the king, and his sister-in-law, the Countess of Carlisle, fell foul of the authorities in 1648 for abetting the Royalist rising of the Earl of Holland. The family's disagreements persisted on into the 1650s, when Philip, Lord Lisle, was closely associated with the Cromwellian Protectorate, to which his republican brother Algernon was so fervently opposed.[16]

Even the two families which could be considered as the leaders of the opposing factions during the Civil War – the Cromwells and the royal family – were not totally consistent in their allegiance. At the end of the war, Oliver Cromwell's uncle, Sir Oliver Cromwell, was obliged to pay a composition fine for his Royalist activities, and his son, Oliver's cousin Henry Cromwell, was in arms for the king.[17] Two of Charles I's nephews, Prince Rupert and Prince Maurice, the children of his sister, Elizabeth of Bohemia, were in arms for their uncle during the Civil War; their elder brother Charles Louis, however, who was also in England, deserted the king on the outbreak of war and settled in London, where he placed himself under the protection of Parliament and took the Presbyterian covenant, perhaps hoping that in the event of a parliamentary victory and the subsequent deposition of Charles, he would be considered as a possible replacement for his uncle.[18]

---

[15] *DNB*, Edward Bulstrode (1588–1659), Sir Isaac Penington the elder (1587–1660), Sir John Penington (1568–1646), Simon Mayne (1612–61), Robert Dormer (d. 1643), Philip Herbert (1584–1650), Robert Devereux (1591–1646), William Seymour (1588–1660), Sir Edward Ford (1605–70); Blaauw, 'Civil War in Sussex', pp. 66–7.

[16] *DNB*, Algernon Sidney (1622–83), Philip Sidney (1619–98), Robert Sidney (1595–1677); and R. W. Blencowe (ed.), *The Sydney Papers* (London, 1825), p. xxxii. For the Sidney family correspondence see also HMC *De L'Isle and Dudley MSS*, vol. 6, 1626–98, *passim*.

[17] *Cal. Com. Comp..* vol. 2, pp. 978–9.

[18] W. Bray (ed.), *The Diary and Correspondence of John Evelyn* (London, 1906), p. 895, n. a; Clarendon, *History of Rebellion*, vol. 3, pp. 324–5.

Serious ideological disagreement between kin was clearly, then, far from uncommon, but what was its effect upon relationships within the family? According to the Earl of Clarendon, Charles I's muted response to Charles Louis's defection was to take 'no other notice, than sometimes to express that he was sorry on his nephew's behalf that he thought fit to declare such a compliance'.[19] But Charles may have been much more hurt than he was prepared to admit, for elswhere such divisions caused deep regrets. Like his father Sir Edmund, Edmund Verney supported the king at the start of the Civil War. Writing to his Parliamentarian brother, Sir Ralph, in September 1642, he told him that Ralph's parliamentary sympathies 'much troubled' him, and were 'a great grief' to their father.[20] Edward, Lord Montagu of Boughton, was also very distressed to discover that members of his family were in opposition to the king. In the spring of 1642, as the armed struggle approached, he wrote to his nephew, Viscount Mandeville, the future Earl of Manchester, advising him to disassociate himself from the parliamentary cause, and he urged Mandeville's brother to remind him of 'Solomon's rule, Fear God, Honour the King'.[21] Some months later, when Parliament took Montagu into custody, it was suggested that he should be held at the house of his daughter, who was married to John Manners, the Parliamentarian Earl of Rutland. Montagu made it clear, however, that he would only stay with his daughter and son-in-law if their house was named as his prison, and he was taken instead to London.[22]

One family within which individuals were deeply divided and where the survival of family papers allows a more detailed consideration of the heart-ache that could result, was the Feilding family of Newnham Paddox in Warwickshire. When Susanna Feilding, Countess of Denbigh, heard in the summer of 1642 that her son Basil intended to oppose Charles I, she was deeply upset. In a letter to him on the eve of the war, she told him:

> I am much troubled to hear the king lay any marks of disfavour upon you, for I desire you should prosper in all things; but at this time, I do more travail with sorrow for the grief I suffer for the ways you take, that the king doth believe you are against him, than ever I did to bring you into the world ... and now give me leave to tell you,

---

[19] Clarendon, *History of Rebellion*, vol. 3, p. 325.
[20] *Verney Memoirs*, vol. 1, p. 282.
[21] HMC *Buccleuch-Whitehall MSS*, vol. 1, pp. 292, 295.
[22] Sir Philip Warwick, *Memoirs of the Reign of Charles I* (London, 1702), pp. 225–6. See also E. S. Cope, *The Life of a Public Man: Edward 1st Baron Montagu of Boughton 1562–1644* (Philadelphia, 1981), pp. 196–7.

you have broke promise, for you did ever assure me that you would never be against the king.[23]

In several subsequent letters written during the summer of 1642, she continued to urge him to join the king. In one, she told him 'you will find that your mother hath dealt more really with you than any other, and I am sure hath suffered more than any other', adding 'I hope you will never take up arms against the king, for that would be too heavy a burden for me to bear.'[24] In August 1642, as hostilities began in earnest, she again begged him to desert Parliament, declaring 'my love puts me to pain for you'.[25] She increased the familial pressure upon her son by involving other relatives in her attempts to persuade him to join the king. At her request, her son-in-law James, Duke of Hamilton, spoke to Charles I about receiving Basil. Hamilton afterwards wrote to Basil, telling his brother-in-law that he himself would be extremely happy to see him, but that if he were thinking of joining the Royalists he should do so as soon as possible, and suggesting that he should journey to York where he would find some of his friends 'who might in some kind prove useful to you here'.[26] Another relative who was recruited to the campaign was Basil's sister Elizabeth; during June 1642 she sent two letters to her brother, in which she spoke of having 'so passionate an affection' for him, and told him to leave Parliament as his name had 'grown odious in print'.[27] The following month she wrote again, warning him that by adhering to Parliament he was risking his life and estates, incurring God's wrath and throwing away his honour. She concluded the letter by declaring that if he continued in his support for Parliament 'I shall leave to be what I am now, your most affectionate sister.'[28]

Despite all these heartfelt appeals from members of his close family, Basil Feilding remained with Parliament and, as we have seen, in the autumn of 1642 he fought against his father, William Feilding, Earl of Denbigh, at the battle of Edgehill. The family's great sorrow at these developments was further heightened the following spring when Basil's father was wounded while attacking Birmingham with Prince Rupert and died a few days later at Cannock. Basil was granted a pass to travel to

---

[23] WRO, Feilding family MSS, CR. 2107, C1, lett. 17. See also HMC *Appendix to Fourth Report*, pp. 259–60, and Cecilia, Countess of Denbigh, *Royalist Father and Roundhead Son* (London, 1915), pp. 169–90.
[24] WRO CR. 2107, C1, lett. 21.
[25] Ibid., lett. 23.
[26] Ibid., lett. 105.
[27] Ibid. C2, lett. 130.
[28] Ibid., lett. 131.

Cannock to see his dying father, but arrived too late. In the months which followed her husband's death, Susanna Feilding, who was now in attendance upon Queen Henrietta Maria at The Hague in Holland, renewed her efforts to persuade Basil, the new Earl of Denbigh, to lay down his arms. After Basil had written to her to comfort her over the old Earl's death, she wrote back: 'I beg of you, my first born, to give me the comfort of that son I do so dearly love, that satisfaction which you owe me now, which is to leave those that murdered your dear father.' She also told him that it was his father's dying wish that God should forgive him and 'touch his heart', and at one point exclaimed:

> O, my dear Jesus, put it into my dear son's heart to leave that merciless company that was the death of his father, for now I think of it with horror, before with sorrow . . . Before you were carried away with error, but now it is hideous and monstrous . . . Let your dying father and unfortunate mother make your heart relent; let my great sorrow receive some comfort.[29]

Over the next few weeks Susanna continued to write to her son, warning him that the Royalists were on the point of victory and telling him 'it is time for you to run to the King upon your knees and crave his pardon.'[30] Finally, in one last despairing attempt to prevail upon him, she declared:

> I have so often written to you to alter your course that I am out of all hope of prevailing; yet my tender and motherly care cannot abstain from soliciting of you to go to the king before it be too late . . . have pity upon me, your poor mother. I have so great a part in you, that you are cruel to deny me any longer. Look up to Heaven, the great God of heaven commands you obey me in this my just desire.[31]

Basil's sister also sent him another plea, assuring him that there was 'more honour in quitting an ill way than in being constant to it'.[32] Once again, however, Basil Feilding refused to respond to his family's emotional entreaties, and he remained in arms for Parliament throughout the war.

In addition to straining normal family relationships by causing anguish and sorrow, divided allegiance also led to serious and sometimes long-

---

[29] Ibid. C1, lett. 24.
[30] Ibid., lett. 26.
[31] Ibid., lett. 28.
[32] Ibid. C2, lett. 128.

term breaches between kin. Edward Moulton of Devon, who had deserted from the Parliamentarian army during the Civil War and joined the Royalists, was later accused of specifically requesting Prince Maurice to sequester his father's estate.[33] In 1653, Thomas Warriner, a dyer from Knaresborough in Yorkshire, informed on his own brother, telling the authorities that during a conversation he had with him some weeks before, his brother had admitted that he had killed a parliamentary soldier during the war and had expressed his continuing support for the exiled king.[34] During the trials of the regicides which followed the Restoration, the judge Sir Thomas Twysden presided at the trial of his cousin, Sir Henry Vane the younger, and narrowly missed hearing the case against his brother-in-law Matthew Thomlinson.[35] Another regicide, William Heveningham of Ketteringham in Norfolk, claimed in his defence in the early 1660s that he had come to the assistance of his Royalist brother, Colonel Arthur Heveningham, after the end of the war, and that following Arthur's death he had cared for his widow and her children. Arthur's widow Jane, however, informed the government that William had in fact fraudulently deprived her of her jointure lands and within two months of Arthur's death had turned them out of his house, so that 'but for friends' they would have been destitute.[36]

A number of examples also exist of individuals depriving relatives of their inheritances because they had fought for the opposing faction during the Civil War. The parliamentary supporter Stephen Hutchinson of Wykeham Abbey in Yorkshire disinherited his son on the grounds that he was a Royalist and 'thereby hath incurred my displeasure'.[37] The regicide John Lisle also disinherited his son William for his Royalism, and his fellow regicide Sir Thomas Mauleverer was accused by his Royalist son Richard of keeping from him an annuity of £500 a year.[38] Colonel John Hutchinson, the parliamentary governor of Nottingham, was left nothing when his father died in 1643, a fact which his Royalist enemies attributed to the father's displeasure at his active support for Parliament.[39] In 1645, Edward Andrew claimed that his father had

---

[33] *Cal. Com. Advance Money*, vol. 2, p. 885.

[34] J. Raine (ed.), *Depositions form the Castle of York Relating to Offences Committed in the Northern Counties in the Seventeenth Century*, Surtees Soc. Publs 40 (1861), 59.

[35] *DNB*, Sir Thomas Twysden (1602–83); F. W. Bennitt (ed.), 'The Diary of Isabella, wife of Sir Roger Twysden, bart.', *Archaeologia Cantiana*, 51 (1939), 115.

[36] *DNB*, William Heveningham (1604–78); CSPD 1660–1, p. 360.

[37] J. T. Cliffe, *The Yorkshire Gentry from the Reformation to the Civil War* (London, 1969), p. 338.

[38] Ibid., p. 338; CSPD 1660–1, p. 341.

[39] *Hutchinson Memoirs*, pp. 134–8.

stopped his allowance and was threatening to disinherit him because he had abandoned his active Royalist stance.[40] When the Royalist Henry Danvers, Earl of Danby, died during the war, he left his lands to his sister, Lady Gargrave, rather than to his Parliamentarian brother, Sir John Danvers. Over the next few years, Danvers engaged in a bitter and protracted legal battle with his sister in an attempt to obtain the estate, claiming that he had been deprived of it 'for his Affection, and adhering to Parliament', and taking advantage of his privileged position as a member of the Council of State to pressurize unsuccessfully for the nullifying of his brother's will.[41] After the death during the Civil War of Lewis Somersall of Grantham in Lincolnshire, his son-in-law, Thomas Hurst of Barrowby in the same county, a staunch Royalist and former chaplain to Charles I, was named executor of the estates. Hurst subsequently attempted to prevent any of the Parliamentarian beneficiaries of the will receiving any money, but when he told his wife's cousin, John Somersall, of his intentions in the summer of 1646, Somersall promptly informed on him to the Committee of Compounding.[42]

On occasions, divergent allegiance could produce still greater hostility and even result in feuds and violence within families. Such problems were particularly evident when individuals acquired property which had been confiscated from Royalist relatives. When the lands of the Lincolnshire Royalist Edmund Cockerill were sequestered, they were obtained by his brother Henry; but another brother, Nicholas, who had also been a Royalist, led a campaign of harassment against Henry and caused disturbances which required the intervention of the trained bands.[43] At the end of the Civil War, Leonard Rawlinson acquired an estate at Marsh Grange in Lancashire which had been sequestered from his Royalist uncle. In the summer of 1648, however, he was forced to abandon it as a Scots army marched south in support of Charles I, and he later informed the parliamentary Committee for Advance of Money that his mother, whom he declared 'plots my destruction', had afterwards invited the 'Cavaliers' on to the property and entertained them as they plundered it.[44]

The political differences created by civil war could also exacerbate and complicate pre-existing family disputes, and act as a cover for more mercenary designs. At the beginning of 1644, the parliamentary army

---

[40] *Cal. Com. Comp.*, vol. 2, p. 882.
[41] Noble, *Lives of Regicides*, vol. 1, pp. 163–70; *Commons Journal*, vol. 6, pp. 211, 232, 304.
[42] *Cal. Com. Comp.*, vol. 2, p. 1310.
[43] Ibid., vol. 3, pp. 1801–2.
[44] *Cal. Com. Advance Money*, vol. 2, p. 890.

officer William Leversage forcibly ejected his uncle, whom he claimed was a Royalist, from his house at Wheelock Hall in Cheshire. Ignoring orders from his commander, Sir Thomas Fairfax, that the uncle should be restored to his property, Leversage continued to hold the house by force until it was eventually captured by parliamentary troops. The Cheshire county committee subsequently testified that the uncle had been a supporter of Parliament, and the uncle himself later claimed that his nephew had been primarily motivated by a desire to acquire his lands.[45] When Francis Charleton of Apsley Castle in Shropshire died during the Civil War leaving a widow and three young children, his Parliamentarian brother Robert attempted to acquire the guardianship of his son, who was heir to the estate. Fearing that Robert might thus gain permanent possession of Apsley, Francis's widow Mary opposed him. With the help of her second husband, she garrisoned Apsley Castle for the king, whereupon her brother-in-law besieged the house, captured it for Parliament and kept Mary and her children in custody. The resourceful Mary, however, later managed to escape with the children to Essex and she resisted all Robert's subsequent efforts to regain control of them.[46] In the early 1650s, the disabled parliamentary soldier, Eyton Crompton, returned from service in Ireland to take possession of Dawley Castle in Shropshire, which he believed his deceased father had bequeathed to him. He was, however, resisted by his stepmother, who he later claimed had attempted to persuade him to side with the king and when he refused, had evicted him and 'clapped a garrison of the enemy on the estate'. Eyton subsequently joined the parliamentary forces which took Dawley by force, but he failed to regain possession of the castle, as his stepmother produced a deed dating from 1637 which showed that it had been conveyed to her and her children, Fulke and Frances.[47]

Divided civil-war allegiance was, then, experienced by many families during the 1640s, and frequently resulted in either deep emotional anguish or estrangement and conflict between kin. However, before we can gauge the overall significance of any damage which the war inflicted upon the family, we need first to assess the relative extent of divided allegiance and to consider whether it always and inevitably produced deep and long-lasting familial animosity.

It is first important to remember that, while it is impossible to give an exact figure for the total number of families actively involved in the civil-war conflicts, in all parts of the country large numbers of people were

[45] *Cal. Com. Comp.*, vol. 2, p. 933; *Cal. Com. Advance Money*, vol. 1, p. 337.
[46] Samuel Clarke, *The Lives of Sundry Eminent Persons in this Later Age* (London, 1683), part 2, pp. 181, 184–9.
[47] *Cal. Com. Comp.*, vol. 4, pp. 3043–4.

clearly anxious to avoid any unnecessary commitment, and, as a result, only a minority of families in the country contained active combatants. Again, among those that did, in addition to the divided families cited above, there are numerous examples of families who exhibited great consistency of political outlook. The records of the parliamentary Committee for Compounding, which was responsible for setting the fines paid by Royalists for the return of their sequestered estates, reveal details of nearly 200 cases where Royalist sympathies were shared by two or more members of the same nuclear unit. Within the Lunsford family of Sussex, for example, three brothers, Thomas, Henry and Herbert, were all Royalists.[48] Similarly, William Sydenham of Dorset and at least four of his sons fought for Parliament, and a report in the newsbook *The Kingdom's Weekly Intelligencer* during September 1644 claimed, 'This may be said of a Fairfax and a Sheffield, that there is not one of either of those names in England but was engaged in the service of Parliament.'[49] It is a far from straightforward task to assess what proportion of the families actively involved in the Civil War experienced divisions in allegiance, but approximate estimates have been arrived at for a number of individual counties. In Lancashire, 292 of the 774 gentry families displayed an active commitment, and, of these, 18 were divided; this represents just over 2 per cent of the whole group, or about 6 per cent of the active minority. In Suffolk, out of a total of 949 gentry families, 135 were active and only 9 divided; here the divided families were less than 1 per cent of the total, and about 7 per cent of the active group.[50] In Yorkshire, out of a total of 679 gentry families, 439 were actively involved and, of these, 69 were either divided in allegiance or changed sides during the war; in this area, the divided families made up about 10 per cent of the total of gentry families, or 16 per cent of those actively committed.[51] In Berkshire in the south-east of the country, of the 38 families in the elite magisterial gentry group, 34 showed some active involvement and, of these, only two had members who supported opposite sides.[52] Another sample which can be considered is the group of families which the *Dictionary of National Biography* records as being actively involved in the civil-war conflicts. Examination of the *Dictionary* has revealed 159 instances where more than one member of a nuclear

---

[48] Blaauw, 'Civil War in Sussex', p. 83.
[49] DNB, Thomas Sydenham (1624–89); *The Kingdom's Weekly Intelligencer*, 17–24 Sept. 1644 (TT).
[50] I am grateful to Gordon Blackwood for providing me with the Lancashire and Suffolk figures by a private communication. The Suffolk totals are only provisional. See also B. G. Blackwood, *The Lancashire Gentry and the Great Rebellion* (Manchester, 1978), pp. 46–7.
[51] Cliffe, *Yorkshire Gentry*, p. 336.
[52] Durston, 'Berkshire', vol. 2, *passim*.

family was actively engaged in the Civil War and of these 33, or about 20 per cent, exhibited division. With regard to the aristocracy, Lawrence Stone has calculated that one in seven families was divided in allegiance; out of a total of 119 noble families, 18 were split within the nuclear group, 13 of them between father and son.[53] The impression given by these admittedly imprecise calculations is that families divided in their allegiance probably made up only between one-tenth and one-fifth of the aristocratic and gentry families which were most actively involved in the war, and a much smaller percentage of the total number of families in the country. Most of the families in England during the 1640s could not, therefore, have been damaged by internecine political divisions, simply because they did not experience them.

There is also considerable evidence to suggest that within the minority of families which did experience division individuals made strenuous efforts to minimize any damage their political differences might cause, and frequently managed to remain on good terms with relatives of an opposed viewpoint. Writing to his wife Dorothy at the beginning of the war, the Royalist Henry Spencer, Earl of Sunderland, told her that he often thought of her uncle, the Parliamentarian Earl of Northumberland, and that he hoped that he was in no danger.[54] A similar concern for relatives on the opposite side of the political fence was exhibited by members of the D'Ewes family. On the eve of the war in June 1642, Richard D'Ewes, who was with the king at York, wrote to his brother Simonds, who was sitting as an MP at Westminster, to urge him to join him. The letter was couched in the friendliest of terms and Richard reassured his brother:

> I daily understand how you stand affected, and what your opinions are, and out of the sincere affection I bear you, I heartily wish you fortunate in their continuance and increase.[55]

Several weeks later, he wrote again to Simonds, telling him 'I should have been most glad to have seen you at York, but since your occasions will not permit, I shall pray for your content where you are.'[56] Richard maintained the correspondence after the war had begun, and later, after he had resigned his commission in the Royalist army, he travelled to

---

[53] Stone, *The Family, Sex and Marriage*, p. 127.
[54] J. Cartwright, *Sacharissa, Some Account of Dorothy Sidney, Countess of Sunderland* (London, 1893), pp. 90–1.
[55] BL Harleian MSS 383, fo. 203; and see J. O. Halliwell (ed.), *The Autobiography and Correspondence of Sir Simonds D'Ewes, Bart.* (2 vols, London, 1845), vol. 2, pp. 290–1.
[56] BL Harleian MSS 379, fo. 192.

London to arrange a secret meeting with his brother.[57] In 1649, Simonds offered to pay the composition fine upon Richard's sequestered estates.[58] Elsewhere too, the emotional links between other politically divided kin survived even a decade of division. When the Sussex parliamentary committeeman George Oglander died in the late 1640s, his Royalist brother, Sir John Oglander of Nunwell on the Isle of Wight, described him as 'a most violent man for the Parliament's cause', but also as 'an honest man' and 'a most loving brother'.[59]

As we have seen, Basil Feilding's decision to adhere to Parliament at the start of the Civil War caused his close relatives considerable distress and sorrow, but despite their differences members of the family managed to remain on good terms with each other. Basil's mother was still writing to him in affectionate terms in the late 1640s; in one letter, probably written in 1647 when Feilding was at Holdenby House in Northamptonshire guarding Charles I for Parliament, she thanked him for looking after his sister Harriet and told him that 'to be deprived of your company and the rest of my children is very troublesome to me.' After asking him to be 'kind' to the king, she gave him her blessing and signed herself 'your loving mother'.[60] In 1649, Basil was asked by his cousin, the prominent Royalist George Villiers, Duke of Buckingham, to help him in his efforts to compound for his confiscated lands, on the grounds that Buckingham knew 'no other man that I can rely upon in this business but Your Lordship'. When Basil's mother also wrote to him on Buckingham's behalf, Basil wrote back expressing his willingness to do what he could, but he also pointed out that recovery of the estate would not be easy and advised her, 'as Your Ladyship tenders the happiness and being of our family', to make sure that her nephew did not engage further against Parliament.[61]

Basil Feilding also remained on friendly terms with his Royalist brother-in-law James, Duke of Hamilton. In April 1647, Hamilton sent a letter to Feilding in which he defended himself against some recent accusations that had been made against him in the English Parliament. He wrote of his disappointment at not having seen him the previous year when he had been at Newcastle in attendance upon Charles I who was a prisoner of the Scots army, and referring to the 'many former obligations Your Lordship hath heaped on me', he expressed his confidence that 'in

---

[57] BL Harleian MSS 379, fo. 197.
[58] *Cal. Com. Comp.* vol. 3, p. 1962.
[59] Bamford (ed.), *A Royalist's Notebook*, p. 112.
[60] WRO CR. 2107, C1, lett. 19.
[61] Winifred, Lady Burghclere, *George Villiers, 2nd Duke of Buckingham 1628–87* (London, 1903), pp. 32–3; HMC *Appendix to Fourth Report*, pp. 256, 281.

that which doth so nearly concern me, your Lordship's endeavours will not be wanting.'[62] The following year, Hamilton led the Scots army which invaded England in support of Charles I, and, after its defeat by Cromwell, he was captured and susequently sentenced to death by Parliament. In the period before his execution, Basil Feilding attempted to intercede for his brother-in-law and, according to the Earl of Clarendon, even as he was being taken to the scaffold, Hamilton still believed that Feilding might be able to save him.[63] After the duke's death, Feilding came to the assistance of his family, and in 1651 he promised his niece, Lady Anne Hamilton, that he would 'use the small power and interest I have to remove such obstructions as by misfortune may fall into the current of Justice.'[64]

Wartime political differences imposed similar strains upon the relationships within the Buckinghamshire Verney family, but here too they failed to overwhelm the strong ties and loyalties of the family. The Royalist Sir Edmund Verney was deeply hurt and distressed when he heard in the summer of 1642 that his eldest son, Sir Ralph, intended to remain with Parliament and, although a great many Verney family letters survive from the early 1640s and father and son had corresponded regularly up until that point, there is no evidence of any communication between the two after the outbreak of war. The Countess of Suffolk, a close friend of the family, informed Sir Ralph that his father was 'much troubled . . . that you declared yourself for Parliament', but she added that he had admitted to her: 'Madam, he hath ever lain near my heart and truly he is there still.' She also told Sir Ralph that she had high hopes that if he and his father could meet, 'one discourse or two will make all well again', and in the meantime she advised him 'not to write passionately to your father, but overcome him with kindness'.[65] Tragically for the Verneys, before any attempt could be made to heal the breach between father and son, Sir Edmund was killed at the battle of Edgehill.

The relationship between Sir Ralph and his younger Royalist brother Edmund was also severely strained by their divergent political stances. At the start of the war, Edmund sent a letter to Sir Ralph, in which he expressed his disappointment at his brother's support for the king's enemies, writing:

---

[62] WRO CR. 2107, C1, lett. 110.
[63] Clarendon, *History of Rebellion*, vol. 4, p. 507; and see Edmund Ludlow, *Memoirs of Edmund Ludlow*, ed. C. H. Firth (2 vols, Oxford, 1894 edn), vol. 1, p. 222.
[64] WRO CR. 2107, C2, lett. 121; see also letters 119, 120.
[65] *Verney Memoirs*, vol. 1, pp. 263–4; and HMC *Appendix to Seventh Report*, p. 440.

Brother, what I feared is proved too true, which is your being with the king; give me leave to tell you, in my opinion, 'tis most unhandsomely done and it grieves my heart to think that my father already, and I who so dearly love and esteem you should be bound in conscience (because in duty to our king) to be your enemy.[66]

Edmund received no reply from Sir Ralph and, at the beginning of 1643, upset at the rift between them, he sent him another letter in which he expressed the hope that their differences would not destroy their friendship, and declared:

> ... I beseech you, Let not our unfortunate silence breed the least distrust of each other's affections. Although I would willingly lose my right hand that you had gone the other way, yet I will never consent that this dispute shall make a quarrel between us, there be too many to fight with besides ourselves ... Though I am tooth and nail for the king's cause and shall endure so to the death, whatsoever his fortune be, yet, sweet brother, let not this my opinion (for it is guided by conscience), nor any report which you can hear of me, cause any diffidence of my true love to you.[67]

Sir Ralph now wrote back, explaining that because Edmund's original letter had been 'so full of sharpness' he had 'chose to forbear answering it (being willing to avoid all matters of dispute) than return such a reply (as the language did deserve) to a brother I love so well.' He went on to thank him for the second, more conciliatory letter and to ask him to 'stick to the resolution you have taken concerning me, and I shall promise to do the like to you.'[68] Thereafter, the correspondence between the brothers continued and their relationship gradually improved; Edmund declared in one subsequent letter 'pray be assured, I have as much affection towards you as any friend you have', and Ralph in return promised him that

> ... though perhaps in some things we may differ in judgement and opinion, yet nothing of that kind shall ever prevail with me to break that knot of true affection that ought to be betwixt us, there are too many others to contend with.[69]

---

[66] *Verney Memoirs*, vol. 1, p. 282, and HMC *Appendix to Seventh Report*, p. 441.
[67] *Verney Memoirs*, vol. 1, p. 283.
[68] Ibid.
[69] Ibid., p. 285.

In both the Feilding and Verney families, then, family relationships survived because individuals were extremely reluctant to allow even the most highly inimical of political stances to estrange them from their close relatives. Within many other families too individuals refused to allow their political affiliations to stand in the way of their familial obligations, but rather on numerous occasions came to the assistance of relatives who were encountering problems as a result of their support for the opposing civil-war faction. Sir Edward Ford, who had garrisoned Chichester for the king during the war and had been imprisoned following the capture of the town, was subsequently released through the influence of his brother-in-law, the New Model Army officer Henry Ireton.[70] Several weeks before the execution of his younger brother Henry Rich, Earl of Holland, the prominent Parliamentarian Robert Rich, Earl of Warwick, petitioned the House of Commons in an attempt to save his life.[71] In 1658, Thomas Belasyse, Viscount Fauconberg, intervened on behalf of his Royalist kinsman Sir Henry Slingsby, who was on trial for his life for plotting against Cromwell, and, as a result of his efforts, Slingsby was spared the usual traitor's death of hanging, drawing and quartering, and was executed by decapitation instead.[72] After the Restoration, Sir Henry Vane the younger was similarly spared the cruelties of a traitor's death following representations from his Royalist relations, and, probably as a result of the intervention of his father-in-law Sir Thomas Herbert, the regicide Robert Phayre was considerably more fortunate and escaped execution altogether.[73] Another regicide, William Heveningham, also appears to have escaped execution through the influence of a Royalist kinsman – in this case his wife's relative, the Earl of Dover.[74]

Another way in which supporters of Parliament could be of particular assistance to their Royalist relatives was in helping them to protect their estates from sequestration, or if their lands were confiscated, in assisting their attempts to compound for them. In 1644, the Royalist John, Viscount Tracy, sought the help of his nephew, the Parliamentarian colonel, Edward Harley, in his attempts to recover his estates, requesting him 'to do me all the right and favour that lies in your power, both for

---

[70] *DNB*, Sir Edward Ford (1605–70); *Cal. Com. Comp.*, vol. 2, p. 869; *Commons Journal*, vol. 6, p. 257.

[71] *Commons Journal*, vol. 6, p. 159.

[72] *DNB*, Sir Henry Slingsby (1602–58); Sir H. Slingsby, *Original Memoirs of Sir Henry Slingsby* (Edinburgh, 1906), pp. xiv–xv.

[73] Rowe, *Sir Henry Vane*, p. 241; *DNB*, Robert Phayre (1619?–82). For Herbert see N. H. Mackensie, 'Sir Thomas Herbert of Tintern: A 'Parliamentary' Royalist', *Bull. Inst. Historical Research*, 29 (1956), 32–86; and G. E. Aylmer, *The State's Servants* (London, 1973), pp. 274–6.

[74] *DNB*, William Heveningham (1604–78); *CSPD* 1660–1, p. 312.

my sister's and my own sake.' After Harley had expressed his willingness to help, Tracy responded:

> I cannot but return my thanks to you for your love towards me. These evil days deny me outward demonstration of love to those I am beholden to; but, if you please to accept of my good will in slender tokens such as are left me, I shall take it as an addition to your kindness.

In a subsequent letter to Edward's father, Sir Robert Harley, Tracy remarked, 'my relation to you makes me confident of your assistance in any business that concerns me', adding 'your son has befriended me to the utmost of his power.'[75]

Many other examples of similar co-operation could be cited. When he attempted to compound for his lands in Kent, Sir Roger Twysden initially received a very unsympathetic response from some members of the local parliamentary committee, but another committeeman, Edward Monings, who was his 'near kinsman', spoke up on his behalf.[76] Robert Sidney, Earl of Leicester, appears to have avoided sequestration through the efforts of his brother-in-law the Earl of Northumberland, who was a member of the parliamentary Committee for Both Kingdoms, and Robert Rich, Baron Rich of Leighs, who had been at Oxford during the war, had his composition fine waived through the influence of his father, the Parliamentarian Earl of Warwick.[77] Even some of the most prominent and committed Parliamentarians were prepared to assist their Royalist kin in this way. In April 1646, the New Model Army commander, Sir Thomas Fairfax, wrote to William Lenthall, the speaker of the House of Commons, asking that his kinsman Lord Paulet be allowed to compound on the articles of surrender at Exeter, and on 2 May, 'according to the wishes of the General', the house agreed.[78] Henry Ireton secured some remission in the fine of his brother-in-law Sir Edward Ford, and in 1647 Sir William Brereton came to the assistance of his Royalist brother-in-law Richard Egerton.[79] In 1650, Colonel Charles Fleetwood paid the first part of the composition fine levied on his brother Sir William, and made clear his willingness to pay the rest; and, in the same year, the

---

[75] HMC *Portland MSS*, vol. 3, pp. 124–7.
[76] 'The Journal of Sir Roger Twysden', *Archaeologia Cantiana*, 1–4 (1858–61), part 4, p. 138.
[77] *DNB*, Robert Sidney (1595–1677), Robert Rich (1587–1658); *Cal. Com. Comp.*, vol. 3, p. 1729.
[78] *Cal. Com. Comp.*, vol. 2, pp. 1052–3.
[79] Ibid., p. 869; vol. 3, p. 1801.

committed republican Henry Marten wrote to the Committee for Compounding on behalf of his relatives, the recusant Blunt family of Mapledurham in Oxfordshire.[80] John Milton also assisted the efforts of his wife's Royalist relations the Powells, to recover their sequestered lands.[81] In October 1646, Oliver Cromwell wrote to a member of the Committee for Compounding on behalf of his distant Royalist relative Thomas, Lord Cromwell of Oakham, declaring 'What favour you show my Lord Cromwell herein, you shall oblige your very loving friend, Oliver Cromwell'; and in July 1649, he secured the waiving of the large composition fine imposed upon his Royalist cousin Henry Cromwell.[82]

Still further evidence of the strength of familial ties is found when one investigates how long the political animosities of the 1640s were allowed to persist; for it then becomes clear that within most families the divisions of the Civil War were very rapidly put aside after 1646. Richard Neville of Billingbear in Berkshire had served as a colonel in the Royalist armies and acted as Royalist sheriff of Berkshire during the war; his brother Henry, however, was a staunch Parliamentarian and advocate of republicanism, who was imprisoned after the Restoration for alleged complicity in a plot against Charles II and subsequently forced into exile in Italy. None the less, the two brothers remained on the friendliest of terms and corresponded regularly in the 1660s, referring to themselves in their letters as 'your loving brother', and when Richard drew up his will in 1661, he named Henry as one of his executors.[83] Even Prince Rupert, who remained in active opposition to the English state throughout the 1650s, was prepared to sink his differences with his elder brother, Charles Louis, who had deserted their uncle, Charles I, at the start of the Civil War. After his brother's defection, Rupert had initially refused to have any contact with him, and although the two brothers met briefly at Oatlands in the final weeks of the war, the breach continued after Charles Louis left England in the late 1640s and returned to the Palatinate, to which he had been restored by the terms of the Peace of Westphalia. In 1654, however, Rupert wrote a conciliatory letter to Charles Louis and a friendly reunion subsequently took place at Heidelberg. While the *rapprochement* may have been to some extent motivated by Rupert's financial difficulties, it nevertheless indicates that

[80] Ibid., vol. 2, p. 1403; vol. 3, p. 2245.
[81] Ibid., vol. 2, pp. 1439–43.
[82] Ibid., vol. 2, pp. 950–1, 978–9; *Commons Journal*, vol. 6, p. 256.
[83] Durston, 'Berkshire', vol. 2, pp. 116–23; and Berkshire Records Office, D/EN F 8/1, D/EN F 8/2, D/EN F/9.

even within the royal family the enmities of the 1640s were already losing some of their vehemence by the mid 1650s.[84]

The speed with which division was healed is also clearly seen in the way in which families which had been politically opposed in the 1640s began to forge new links almost as soon as the fighting had ended. Intermarriage between Royalist and Parliamentarian families began, in fact, even before the war was over. In May 1646, the sister of the Parliamentarian Sir Henry Vane the younger, married the heir of the prominent Royalist Sir Thomas Liddell.[85] Within two years of the end of the war, Jane Meldrum, whose husband John had lost his life in 1645 serving as a colonel in the parliamentary armies, had married her kinsman George Meldrum, who had been a major in the king's forces.[86] Although during the same period several other proposed marriages between individuals whose families had been on opposite sides during the war were forbidden by the families involved, the recent political differences between the families do not seem to have figured among the objections. When Anne Murray, whose family had supported the king, and Thomas Howard, son of the Parliamentarian Lord Howard of Escrick, wished to marry in the late 1640s, Anne's mother vehemently opposed the match, not because of political division between their families, but rather because she believed she could not offer the Howards a large enough dowry.[87] Similarly, although the respective parents of Dorothy Osborne and William Temple put forward a whole range of objections to the pair marrying in the early 1650s, they at no time argued that the earlier political divergence between the families was an obstacle to the match. Indeed, at one point the Royalist Osbornes were considering a possible alternative match between Dorothy and Oliver Cromwell's son Henry.[88]

By the mid-1650s, intermarriage between families which had formerly been enemies was a common occurrence. In 1655, the widow of the regicide Sir Gregory Norton married the Royalist Robert Gordon, Viscount Kenmure, and in the same year Edward Russell petitioned to be exempted from the decimation tax on former Royalists on the grounds that he had married the widow of Sir William Brooke, who had been

---

[84] Patrick Morrah, *Prince Rupert Of the Rhine* (London, 1976), pp. 197, 286–8; Bulstrode Whitelocke, *Memorials of English Affairs* (4 vols, Oxford, 1853), vol. 2, p. 44.

[85] Rowe, *Sir Henry Vane*, p. 90.

[86] *Cal. Com. Advance Money*, vol. 2, p. 952.

[87] J. Loftis (ed.), *Memoirs of Anne, Lady Halket and Anne, Lady Fanshawe* (Oxford, 1981), p. 14.

[88] Kingley Hart (ed.), *The Letters of Dorothy Osborne to Sir William Temple 1652 to 1654* (London, 1968), *passim*, esp. p. 42.

killed in the service of Parliament in the 1640s.[89] The Royalist Sir Thomas Harris married the daughter of the Parliamentarian Thomas Mytten of Shropshire: John Fry of Yarty in Devon, whose father had acted as one of Charles I's judges in 1649, married Anne Napier, daughter of the Royalist Robert Napier of Dorset: and Robert Wright, who had commanded a regiment for Charles I during the Civil War, married Elizabeth Danvers, daughter of the regicide Sir John Danvers.[90] In 1659, the daughter of the Paliamentarian Philip, Lord Wharton, married into the Royalist Bertie family.[91] In 1657, Mary Fairfax, daughter of the former New Model Army commander, Sir Thomas Fairfax, married George Villiers, Duke of Buckingham, a staunch Royalist and close friend of the exiled Charles Stuart. This last match was objected to not by either of the families involved, but by the head of state, Oliver Cromwell, who was furious with Fairfax for allowing the match and sent a troop of soldiers to Yorkshire in an attempt to arrest the bridegroom. Fairfax, who appears to have established a good relationship with his new son-in-law, further infuriated Cromwell the following year when he met him at Whitehall to argue for his release from custody.[92] Shortly after the Restoration, the Parliamentarian John Hutchinson learned that his son had secretly married the daughter of the Royalist Sir Alexander Ratcliffe. According to his wife, Hutchinson was initially 'so discontented that he once resolved to have banished them forever', but once he had met his new daughter-in-law 'his good nature was soon overcome, and he received them into his bosom, and, for the short time he enjoyed her, had no less love for her than for any of his own children.'[93] Such marriages surely indicate that, even within the short space of time between the end of the Civil War and the Restoration, the traditional tidal flow of family life was already beginning to wash away the divisions and animosities of the 1640s.

We have seen, therefore, that the political divisions of the English Civil War had varied effects; in some cases they caused deep animosities, while elsewhere they were quickly submerged beneath older loyalties. Within the Nottinghamshire Hutchinson family both reactions can be seen.

---

[89] E. S. De Beer, *The Diary of John Evelyn* (6 vols, Oxford, 1955), vol. 3, p. 90, n. i; for Norton, see George Edward Cokayne, *Complete Baronetage* (6 vols, London, 1900–9), vol. 1, pp. 257–8; *Cal. Com. Comp.*, vol. 2, p. 846.

[90] *DNB*, Thomas Mytten (1597?–1656), Robert Napier (1611–86) and Robert Danvers (1621?–74).

[91] *DNB*, Philip Wharton (1613–96).

[92] W. C. Abbott (ed.), *The Writings and Speeches of Oliver Cromwell* (4 vols, Cambridge, Mass., 1937–47), vol. 4, pp. 623, 869; Noble, *Lives of Regicides*, vol. 1, pp. 226–7.

[93] *Hutchinson Memoirs*, p. 338.

While Colonel John Hutchinson acted as governor of Nottingham for Parliament during the war, his cousin, Sir Richard Byron, served as the Royalist governor of nearby Newark. Despite their close family relationship, the two were bitter enemies. After Byron had captured the town of Nottingham and trapped his cousin in the castle, Hutchinson led a counter-attack into the town, telling his men to shoot Byron on sight and to cut his legs off rather than let him escape. John's wife Lucy later commented that her husband had been more antagonistic towards Byron than to any of the other governors of Newark, remarking 'Whether it were that the dissension of brethren is always most spitefully pursued... it is true they were to each other, the most uncivil enemies that can be imagined.'[94]

Yet Hutchinson was not consistent in his attitude to his Royalist kin, for towards his wife's brother, Sir Allen Apsley, he showed great friendship and kindness. Apsley, who had been Royalist governor of Barnstaple in Devon until its surrender in April 1646, stayed with the Hutchinsons at Nottingham for some time after the end of the war, and John assisted his brother-in-law when he encountered difficulties in compounding for his estates, being, according to Lucy, 'no less concerned in the injustice done to him, than if he had suffered it himself'.[95] As a result of this active support for his brother-in-law, Hutchinson came under suspicion from his fellow Parliamentarians, but the close family relationship persisted and Apsley in turn came to Hutchinson's aid when he was in trouble after the Restoration.[96] The explanation for John Hutchinson's apparently contradictory attitudes towards those kin to whom he was politically opposed must surely lie in the nature of the pre-war family connection. Where tensions and resentments had pre-dated the Civil War, or where kinship links had been purely formal and obligatory, family ties were liable to be further eroded by the partisan loyalties of civil conflict. But where they had been close and affectionate and reinforced by feelings of friendship and love, they remained of greater weight and importance than any loyalties to the political factions of the 1640s.

The fears of some contemporaries that the Civil War might destroy family ties were, therefore, largely unfounded. There were indeed numerous occasions during the 1640s and 1650s when individuals found that their political beliefs conflicted with their family loyalties, and sometimes they resolved these dilemmas by renouncing their families. More frequently,

[94] Ibid., p. 134; see also pp. 138, 143.
[95] Ibid., pp. 243–4.
[96] Ibid., pp. 326, 329, 360.

however, familial loyalty overcame ideological fervour; most individuals were anxious to do all they could to retain the friendship of relatives with whom they were at odds during the Civil War, and once open hostilties ceased in 1646 there was a general desire to bury animosities and recommence normal family life. Familial relationships were undoubtedly strained by the pressures of revolution, but because large numbers of English men and women agreed with Sir Ralph Verney that the connection with kin was a 'knot of true affection', the English family survived the severe buffeting it received during the turbulent years of the mid-seventeenth century, and remained a healthy and highly valued social institution.

4
Marriage

For any society which is founded upon the institution of the family it is vital that there should be a constant supply of new nuclear units, initiated through the processes of courtship and marriage. Individuals in early-modern England were encouraged to leave the parental home and to establish their own separate households with a married partner both by social pressure and by their own emotional and sexual drives, and every year thousands of men and women formed the cores of new families in marriage. During the seventeenth century, it was widely believed that the most successful marriages were those in which the partners had been drawn together by mutual affection, and the great majority of those who were considering marriage were allowed considerable freedom in their choice of spouse. Those aged under twenty-one, however, were strongly advised to obtain parental consent when they married, and even amongst older people there was a widespread reluctance to marry against the wishes of parents. Although war and revolution brought no fundamental changes to the normal procedures of courtship and pre-marital negotiation, the social and economic disruption which accompanied the war did introduce some temporary distortions into the marriage market. The physical mobility of the civil-war soldiers, for example, created new marriage opportunities both for themselves and for the women of the communities upon which they were billeted, and the economic problems experienced by many families, particularly those within the landed classes, sometimes made it difficult for them to make the customary financial provisions for children who wished to marry. However, the most drastic change in matrimonial procedure resulting from the war and its aftermath concerned the marriage ceremony itself. The Puritan governors of Interregnum England were determined to bring greater order and uniformity into the procedures for solemnizing marriages, and in 1653 the members of Barebone's Parliament replaced the church wedding with a new secular ceremony conducted by a justice of the peace and declared that marriages conducted in churches would no longer be considered legally binding.

Throughout the seventeenth century, most English men and women believed that the perfect match was one in which the firm affection of the intended spouses was complemented by the approval of both sets of parents. Reality, however, often fell short of this ideal. On many occasions, one or both sets of parents objected to a proposed marriage, causing either the abandoning of the project or an elopement and secret marriage. In other instances, parents suggested as potential spouses men or women whom their children either viewed without any real affection or positively disliked; sometimes such proposed marriages would go ahead regardless, but frequently a daughter would exercise a right of veto and prevent the match. For the most part, this normal pattern of matrimonial preliminaries remained largely unaffected by the political upheavals of the 1640s and 1650s. Young men and women continued to defy their parents and marry those of whom they disapproved; in October 1649, Sir John Oglander, a landowner from the Isle of Wight, recorded in his commonplace book:

> Know all men that I do . . . acknowledge that the match between Sir Robert Eaton's son and my daughter Bridget was never with my approbation or good liking. It was her importunity that induced me to give way unto it, and she was resolved to have him whatever became of her and gave me so much under her own hand before marriage . . . I beseech God to bless them and to make her happy, which I much doubt.[1]

Many other young women continued to reject any marriage which failed to meet with the approval of their parents. When Thomas Howard, son of Lord Howard of Escrick, proposed marriage to Anne Murray in 1644 and the match was opposed by their parents, Howard tried to persuade Anne to marry him secretly. She made it clear, however, that she considered such a course of action as 'the highest act of ingratitude and disobedience that children could commit', and she told him:

> he need never expect that I should marry him without his father's and my mother's consent. If that could be obtained, I should

---

[1] Bamford (ed.), *A Royalist's Notebook*, p. 130.

willlingly give him the satisfaction he desired, but, without that, I could not expect God's blessing either upon him or me, and I would do nothing that was so certain a way to bring ruin upon us both.[2]

But while she would not consider being a party to a clandestine marriage, Anne was prepared to promise Thomas that she would never allow her mother to force her to marry someone else, declaring that 'though duty did oblige me not to marry any without my mother's consent, yet it would not tie me to marry without my own.'[3]

A similar approach was adopted in the early 1650s by Dorothy Osborne, whose wish to marry William Temple was also opposed by both of their families. While telling Temple that she could not consider defying her parents and advising him that he should abandon his suit and look elsewhere for a wife, she at the same time rejected a stream of alternative suitors and refused to contemplate any marriage which was not founded upon real affection. In one letter to Temple, she told him: 'seriously, I find I want courage to marry where I do not like . . . and I have not faith enough to believe a doctrine that is often preached, which is that, though at first one has no kindness for them, yet it will grow strangely after marriage.'[4] Eventually Dorothy's and Temple's persistence wore down their parents' objections and they were married in 1654.

In one particularly despairing letter to Temple, Dorothy Osborne described their proscribed relationship as 'a country wasted by a civil war, where two opposing parties have disputed their right so long till they have made it worth neither of their conquests, 'tis ruined and desolated by the long strife within it to that degree as 'twill be useful to none.'[5] Apart from providing this powerful metaphorical image, however, the abnormal political conditions of the 1640s and 1650s appear to have had little direct bearing upon Dorothy Osborne's matrimonial difficulties. Nor do they seem to have substantially affected the circumstances of Bridget Oglander or Anne Murray. Elsewhere, however, the complicated process of negotiating and contracting a marriage was significantly affected by the war and its aftermath. In a number of cases, the unusual external conditions which existed during these years produced greater freedom and opportunities for those wishing to marry. Large numbers of soldiers met their future brides when travelling round England in the 1640s with the various civil-war armies,

[2] Loftis (ed.), *Memoirs of Halket, Fanshawe*, pp. 14, 18.
[3] Ibid., p. 15.
[4] Hart (ed.), *Letters of Dorothy Osborne, passim*, esp. p. 24.
[5] Ibid., p. 138.

and sometimes marriages grew out of the most inauspicious circumstances. In the summer of 1644, the parliamentary soldier Jeremiah Abercromby was married to Susan Denton, whom he had met only a few days earlier while taking part in the sacking of her home, Hillesden House in Buckinghamshire.[6] Perhaps equally surprisingly, some of the parliamentary troopers who crossed to Ireland with Cromwell's expeditionary force in 1649, later married into the native Irish population and settled in the reconquered colony.[7]

In addition, where the war and its attendant political problems resulted in the separation of parents from their children, young people could find that they were less constrained by parental interference in their romantic attachments and marriage plans. In October 1646, Penelope Verney, whose father had been killed at Edgehill and whose eldest brother, Sir Ralph, was in exile in France, married without waiting for her family's approval; another brother, Henry, later told Sir Ralph that Penelope had deliberately avoided consulting him 'lest you put a stop to it'.[8] Similarly in 1652, William Clarke's sister Elizabeth secretly arranged her marriage while her brother was in Scotland with the parliamentary army, and William only learned of the match when a friend later wrote to him that

> Your sister, Betty, is married and hath gotten a husband. They were greatly in league one with the other, and I thought there would be a great deal of ill-conveniency to part them . . . I would very gladly [have] had your approbation, but that it is so you was so far remote. I hope you shall have no cause to dislike of it.[9]

One further development during these years which may also have increased the freedom which individuals could exercise when choosing a marriage partner was the abolition in 1646 of the Court of Wards. Despite some reform of the court's procedures during James I's reign, on the eve of the Civil War the Crown's ancient feudal right to the custody of the estates of minors remained both a lucrative royal enterprise and one of the most grievous complaints of landed society. Courtiers paid large sums of money to purchase wardships from the Crown, and often set about recouping their financial outlay through systematic exploita-

---

[6] *Verney Memoirs*, vol. 1, pp. 318–19.
[7] Patrick J. Corish, 'The Cromwellian Regime 1650 to 1660', in T. W. Moody, F. X. Martin and F. J. Byrne (eds), *A New History of Ireland* (9 vols, Oxford, 1976), vol. 3, p. 373.
[8] *Verney Memoirs*, vol. 1, pp. 426–7.
[9] HMC *Leybourne-Popham MSS*, p. 103.

tion of their charges' estates. In addition, in order to retain an interest in the estate after the heir or heiress had reached the age of maturity, they often made strenuous efforts to marry them off to a member of their own family. As the court was abolished in 1646 and not brought back in 1660, this pressure upon heirs and heiresses was permanently removed, with the result that some minors and their mothers may have found themselves with more freedom to decide between prospective spouses.

However, while some found that the climate of the 1640s and 1650s allowed them greater opportunities and freedom to arrange marriages, others discovered that the abnormal environment of these years involved them in added difficulties, restrictions and delays. Some contemporary observers believed that the employment of large numbers of young men on military service and the premature deaths caused by the fighting had significantly reduced the supply of marriageable males and thus had a serious adverse effect upon women's marriage prospects. The early months of 1643 saw the appearance of several pamphlets which complained of the scarcity of potential marriage partners in London since the beginning of the war. *The Widows' Lamentation* claimed that, because of the war, widows could no longer hope to find a 'young, lusty husband', and *The Virgins' Complaint for the Loss of their Sweethearts* argued that the absence of the soldiers was depriving the capital's young girls of 'the benefit which creation made us for, to be a helper to man in his necessities, which it is impossible for us to do, except we betroth ourselves to frosty-bearded usurers, that are as cold in their constitutions and performance as they are in their charities.'[10]

In September 1647, after the end of the first Civil War, another pamphlet, *Hey-Hoe for a Husband, or the Parliament of Maids*, also suggested that women who wished to marry were suffering from a shortage of eligible men; outlining the legislation which could be expected from an imaginary parliament of women, it included measures to prevent widows from enticing young men into marriage and the proposal that every tenth man in a parish should be forced to marry every tenth woman, irrespective of looks.[11] Finding suitable marriage partners for his sisters was certainly a major worry for Sir Ralph Verney, who was in exile in France during the 1640s, and on several occasions his friends and relatives referred in their letters to the particular difficulties that the war had created in this area. In 1644, his Aunt Isham wrote that 'if these times hold up, I think there will be no men left for women', and Lady

---

[10] *The Widows' Lamentation*, p. 6; *The Virgins' Complaint for the Loss of their Sweethearts* (London, 1643), p. 3 (TT).

[11] *Hey-Hoe for a Husband or the Parliament of Maids* (London, 1647), *passim* (TT).

Sussex later warned him 'I am afraid in these bad times you will not match your sisters as you desire.'[12]

Such evidence may not, however, be entirely reliable, for the comments of Sir Ralph Verney's correspondents are contradicted by remarks found in other collections of letters. Writing to Thomas Knyvett in 1650, Elizabeth Hampden declared 'there is no scarcity of wives nor portions for I never heard of so great marriages as are now, both of men and women.'[13] The pamphlets mentioned above may also give a misleading impression; light and humorous in tone, they reflect a prurient male interest in the sexual appetites of women, and as their message was that the fighting should end and the parliamentary soldiers should return to London, they may have been the work of Royalist sympathizers who wished to undermine the morale of those of the capital's menfolk who were fighting for Parliament. As London contributed far more young men to the civil-war armies than many other communities in the country, any problems which occurred in the capital would not necessarily have been experienced elsewhere. In addition, as the civil-war fighting was limited in scale and the resultant mortality relatively low, any adverse long-term impact upon the numbers of marriageable males was probably only slight.

In order to obtain a more quantitative asssessment of the impact of war and revolution upon marriage prospects in the 1640s and 1650s, one must turn to the estimates of yearly marriage totals recently calculated by Wrigley and Schofield, and included in their *Population History of England 1541–1871*. They suggest that, from an average of just under 43,000 marriages a year in the ten years before the Civil War, the annual figure dropped to 32,184 in 1643 and to 31,085 in 1644. It then recovered in the final two years of the war to the pre-war levels of 42,714 in 1645 and 42,938 in 1646, before returning to a particularly low level between 1647 and 1653, when the average annual total was only just over 34,000. The lowest level of all was recorded in 1648, when according to their calculations only 28,607 marriages took place.[14] Interpretation of these figures is far from straightforward, the recovery in the latter part of the war being particularly difficult to explain. As the totals are estimates, arrived at through the use of computer back-projection, rather than actual recorded marriages, there must be a

---

[12] *Verney Memoirs*, vol. 1, pp. 418–9; Miriam Slater, *Family Life in the Seventeenth Century: The Verneys of Claydon House* (London, 1984), p. 81.

[13] B. Schofield (ed.), *The Knyvett Letters 1620–1644*, Norfolk Records Soc. Publs, 20 (1949), 44.

[14] E. A. Wrigley and R. S. Schofield, *The Population History of England 1541–1871* (London, 1981), pp. 497–8. The averages are mine from their yearly totals.

suspicion that they do not represent the reality entirely accurately. However, if the broad trends they suggest can be trusted, they would seem to indicate that the absence of men during the actual fighting may have been a less serious obstacle to marriage than the economic dislocation which was produced by the conflict and which persisted after the hostilities had ceased in 1646. Certainly, during 1648, when the number of marriages contracted was the lowest annual figure for the whole of the seventeenth century, the country was suffering from an acute post-war economic depression complicated by serious harvest failure.

Such grave economic problems could reduce the number of marriages contracted, both by lengthening the time it took those without substantial assets to save up sufficient money to establish themselves in their own home, and by making it more difficult for the wealthier families of landed society to make the customary financial provision for young people who wished to marry. In normal times, brides from landed families brought their husbands a substantial dowry, or portion, usually in the form of land or cash, and the groom's family in return bestowed upon the couple jointure lands, property which would come to the woman on the death of the husband to sustain her in her widowhood. As a result of the war-induced financial difficulties of the 1640s, however, some parents clearly struggled to find the resources to make financial settlements for their children, who therefore had either to delay their marriages or to wed without a secure financial future. Writing to his wife from prison in 1644 about his children's marriage prospects, Thomas Knyvett of Ashwellthorpe in Norfolk remarked: 'I should be as glad to see my children disposed of for their advantage in that way as you or any parent living, but I see much impossibility of effecting any such thing in these times and in the present condition we are now in.'[15]

After Anne Harrison and Richard Fanshawe had met and fallen in love in Oxford during the Civil War, they were married in May 1644 in a quiet ceremony at Wolvercote church, a few miles north of the city. Anne's family offered Fanshawe the large dowry of £10,000, but he had to agree to wait for the money, and Anne later reflected that she and her new husband 'might truly be called merchant adventurers, for the stock we set up our trading with did not amount to £20 betwixt us.'[16] Financial difficulties also created problems for the Verney family. When Sir Ralph Verney's sister Susan married Richard Alport at the end of the war, her dowry had to be paid in instalments, and when several months

---

[15] Schofield (ed.), *Knyvett Letters*, p. 150.
[16] Loftis (ed.), *Memoirs of Halket, Fanshawe*, pp. 111–12.

later her sister Penelope rushed into marriage, her brother Henry attributed her haste to awareness that 'her portion lay in a desperate condition'.[17] Again, on the marriage of Margaret Lucas to William Cavendish, Duke of Newcastle, at the end of the war, Margaret's mother was obliged to write to the duke to explain that 'the state of the kingdom is such that her mother cannot give unto her that which is hers, nor can I show my love and affection towards my daughter as I would, in respect of the great burdens we groan under.'[18]

Such financial constraints upon marriages continued to cause problems in the early 1650s. In September 1651, John Percival wrote to his uncle, Beverley Usher, to outline his assessment of his marriage prospects. He told him that much of his family's property was in Ireland and that,'because of the calamity of the times', had yielded no revenue during recent years; consequently, he could only consider marrying a woman who would bring him a substantial portion which he could then use to provide dowries for his sisters.[19] When, the following year, one of these sisters, Judith, wished to marry a Royalist, Colonel Randal Clayton, John was very worried about Clayton's meagre estate, which was still under sequestration and of which he commented 'a poor subsistence for a family in the best of times; what must it be in the worst?'[20] His misgivings delayed the match for some time, but Judith's determination to marry Clayton eventually overcame his reservations and the couple were wed in early 1654.[21]

If some people's marriage prospects were diminished by the unfavourable economic climate of these years, others found that their freedom to choose a spouse was severely restricted by political and religious pressures. In at least one case, political exigency was directly responsible for compelling a woman to marry against her wishes. In the late 1640s, the Yorkshire parliamentary committeeman Richard Darley offered to help the family of the Royalist George Wandesford to compound for their sequestered lands, but only on condition that George's sister Alice agreed to marry his relative, William Thornton. Alice's uncle agreed to the bargain without even consulting his niece or her mother, and when Alice subsequently expressed her unwillingness to go through with the match, Darley threatened to ruin her family. For the sake of her relatives, Alice was obliged to go ahead with the marriage, but she later

---

[17] *Verney Memoirs*, vol. 1, pp. 418–19, 426–7.
[18] HMC *Portland MSS*, vol. 2, p. 137.
[19] HMC *Egmont MSS*, vol. 1, pp. 500–2.
[20] Ibid., p. 512; for the marriage negotiations see pp. 502–39.
[21] Ibid., p. 539.

commented in her memoirs that this 'manner of persuasion to a marriage, with a sword in one hand, and a compliment in another, I did not understand.'[22]

Another group of individuals whose choice of spouse was constrained by ideological considerations were the members of the various sectarian gathered churches which grew up in the freer religious climate of the late 1640s and 1650s. Difficulties frequently arose when members of these gathered congregations decided to defy the elders of their churches and marry non-members. One congregation within which the choice of marriage partners was a particular problem throughout the 1650s was the Baptist church at Fenstanton in Huntingdonshire. In 1655, the whole of the congregation met together to discuss whether members should be permitted to marry outside the church, and 'after much debate' it was decided that such marriages were not permissible.[23] None the less, a number of the Fenstanton Baptists continued to find that their matrimonial plans conflicted with their religious duties, and on such occasions the desire to marry often proved the stronger consideration. The elders of the Fenstanton church frequently examined fellow Baptists who were accused of consorting with non-members, but they found that most of them were unrepentant, refusing to accept that they were committing any sin and remaining determined to go ahead with their planned marriages. When they visited Anne Johnson in 1658, she told them that the man she intended to marry was 'one that did all that was required', and she refused to come to the church to justify her choice before the congregation.[24] In 1656, the Fenstanton elders wrote to their counterparts at Royston, declaring: 'Oh, how many ways doth he [Satan] labour to destroy the church of God; amongst which we have taken notice greatly of his wicked device, in persuading many members of the congregation to join themselves in marriages with those that are without.'[25]

Several individuals seem to have been allowed to remain in the congregation after contracting marriages with non-members, but at least five members of congregation were excommunicated during the 1650s for marrying out.[26] Similar problems were experienced by the neighbouring Baptist congregation at Warboys, where four members of the congregation were excommunicated for marrying out and one of the

---

[22] C. Jackson (ed.), *The Autobiography of Mrs Alice Thornton of East Newton, co. York*, Surtees Soc. Publs, 62 (1873), 44–7, 61–2.
[23] E. B. Underhill (ed.), *Records of the Churches of Christ Gathered at Fenstanton, Warboys and Hexham 1644–1702*, Hanserd Knollys Soc. Publs (London, 1854), p. 147.
[24] Ibid., pp. 246, 249.
[25] Ibid., p. 185.
[26] Ibid., pp. 9, 24, 158, 163, 172–9, 181–2, 184, 191, 211.

elders, William Dunne, was deposed from office after being accused of 'countenancing and encouraging mixed marriages'.[27]

The abnormal conditions of the period 1640 to 1660 had, then, some limited effect upon the degree of opportunity and choice available to those planning to marry. They had, however, a much more dramatic impact upon the way any resulting marriages were regulated and solemnized, for, in their determination to put an end to the notorious confusion in the way that marriages were contracted, the Puritan regimes of the Interregnum considered major reforms in this area, and in 1653 they introduced a civil marriage ceremony and established it as the only legally binding form of marriage service.

The regulations governing the solemnization of marriage had undoubtedly caused some confusion in the period before 1640; as Lawrence Stone has pointed out, marriage in early-modern England was 'an engagement that could be undertaken in a bewildering variety of ways'.[28] By the late-sixteenth and early-seventeenth centuries, most people were married in church and it was widely believed that the presence of a minister was necessary for the valid contracting of a marriage. This belief was, however, mistaken. According to the canon law of the established Anglican church, a perfectly valid marriage could be contracted through 'spousals', the simple exchange of vows before witnesses. Spousals took the form of either a declaration that the couple considered themselves to be man and wife or a promise to marry at some future date, and, when they were followed by cohabitation, the couple involved were validly married. In practice, few marriages were based solely upon spousals and indulgence in sexual relations before the solemnization of marriage in church was considered highly irregular; nevertheless, it remained technically possible to contract a legal marriage without setting foot in church.

A further complication was that many of the marriages carried out by clergymen failed to comply with the detailed instructions for the conducting of church weddings laid down by the ecclesiastical authorities. Archbishop Bancroft's canons of 1604 had stipulated that weddings should be performed only in the morning in the parish of residence of one of the contracting parties and that, when one of the parties was under twenty-one, parental consent should be obtained. Some unscrupulous

---

[27] Ibid., pp. 241, 274–5.
[28] Stone, *Family, Sex and Marriage*, p. 30. An earlier version of the following discussion of the Barebones Marriage Act appeared in vol. 31 of the *Historical Journal* (1988), pp. 45–59, under the title '"Unhallowed Wedlocks": The Regulation of Marriage during the English Revolution'. I am grateful to the editors of that journal for permission to reproduce the material here.

clerics, however, had ignored these injunctions and engaged in a brisk and highly lucrative trade in quick, 'no questions asked', marriages. Such marriages were particularly easily obtained in some of the London parishes, and were often performed in secret, and without the parental consent which the 1604 canons had required for marriages where one of the parties was under twenty-one. Marriage by licence was also available to those who wished to avoid the inconvenience of the publishing of banns and could afford the higher fee involved.[29]

There was already, then, considerable matrimonial irregularity in early seventeenth-century England, and, after the outbreak of war in 1642, the confused conditions opened the way to still more abuse. In particular, the difficulties of travel and communication and the interruption of the normal administrative procedures allowed greater scope to those who wished to contract illegal marriages. Some of the soldiers who had left home to fight during the 1640s subsequently abandoned their existing families, settled in other parts of the country and contracted second, bigamous marriages. Others returned home after a long absence, only to find that they had been presumed dead and that their wives had remarried.[30] In 1650, the MPs of the Rump Parliament attested to the seriousness of the problem caused by the physical separation of wives and husbands during the 1640s, by including in their notorious Adultery Act a clause protecting from conviction women who had remarried after not hearing from a previous husband for three years, or whose husbands were believed dead 'by common fame'.[31] Quarter sessions records from various parts of the country contain regular indictments for bigamy during the 1640s and 1650s, and according to the newsbook *The Moderate Intelligencer*, in 1653 one Mr Gibson was executed at Southampton after being convicted of having the astonishing total of twenty-seven wives.[32] Anne Murray only narrowly avoided marrying a man whose wife was still alive. Proposing marriage to her in the late 1640s, Joseph Bamfield told her that his previous wife was dead; over the

---

[29] Stone, *Family, Sex and Marriage*, pp. 30–5.

[30] For examples see G. R. Quaife, *Wanton Wenches and Wayward Wives: Peasants and Illicit Sex in Early Seventeenth Century England* (London, 1978), pp. 46, 49, 126; and J. A. Sharpe, *Crime in Seventeenth Century England* (Cambridge, 1983), p. 68.

[31] C.H. Firth and R. S. Rait (eds), *Acts and Ordinances of the Interregnum 1642–1660* (3 vols, London, 1911), vol. 2, pp. 387–9.

[32] B. Cunnington (ed.), *Records of the County of Wilts.* (Devizes, 1932), pp. 210–11; J. Bennett and J. Dewhurst (eds), *Quarter Sessions Records of the County Palatine of Chester*, Lancashire and Cheshire Records Soc. Publs, 94 (1940), 166; Raine (ed.), *Depositions from the Castle of York*, p. 43; B. C. Redwood (ed.), *Quarter Sessions Order Book 1642–9*, Sussex Records Soc. Publs, 54 (1954), 140; J. C. Atkinson (ed.). *Quarter Sessions Records*, North Riding Records Soc. Publs, 5 (1887), 110, 151, 154; and *The Moderate Intelligencer*, 17–24 July 1653 (TT).

following months, Anne heard persistent reports that his wife was in fact still living, but for several years she was quite unable to discover the truth, and it was not until the spring of 1653 that she eventually found out that Bamfield was indeed still married.[33]

Puritan opinion in England had long been affronted by such matrimonial irregularities, and had also objected strongly to certain elements of the Anglican marriage ceremony which they regarded as 'popish', including the use of the ring and the husband's declaration 'with my body I thee worship'. During the 1630s, some Puritans had also been opposed to the Laudian injunction that couples should receive communion on their wedding day, and in the early 1640s those who drew up the Root and Branch Petition calling for the abolition of episcopacy included amongst their criticisms of the Laudian episcopal bench the favouring of marriage by licence without the publication of banns.[34] Once the Puritans who had voiced these criticisms acquired some real power after 1642, initiatives for matrimonial reform soon followed. The MPs of the Long Parliament first took the reform of the marriage laws into consideration in October 1643, when the House of Commons requested the committee which was liaising with the Westminster Assembly of Divines 'to consider some course to prevent the mischiefs that happen by clandestine marriages, and by the marrying of people by laymen'.[35] Fifteen months later, the Westminister Assembly incorporated a revised form of marriage service into its *Directory of Public Worship*, which was to form the liturgical basis of the new Presbyterian state church. The *Directory* declared that 'Marriage be no Sacrament, nor peculiar to the Church of God, but common to mankind', but it deemed a church service necessary in order that couples could be given religious instruction and receive God's blessing. The new Presbyterian marriage ceremony was much shorter than that laid down in the Anglican *Book of Common Prayer*, and dispensed with the ring and the husband's statement that he would worship his wife with his body. The Westminster divines also outlined regulations for the publishing of banns and the securing of parental consent, which, for those aged under twenty-one, was essential in all first marriages and desirable in any remarriages.[36]

The failure, however, of this Presbyterian attempt to reform and regularize the marriage service and to eradicate malpractice was made clear in September 1646, when, now that peace had returned, Parliament

---

[33] Loftis (ed.), *Memoirs of Halket, Fanshawe*, pp. 27–82.
[34] R. L. Greaves, *Society and Religion in Elizabethan England* (Minneapolis, 1981), pp. 184–5; J. P. Kenyon, *The Stuart Constitution* (Cambridge, 1986 edn), p. 156.
[35] *Commons Journal*, vol. 3, p. 288.
[36] Firth and Rait (eds), *Acts and Ordinances*, vol. 1, pp. 599–601.

decided to appoint another committee to consider ways to prevent clandestine and incestuous marriages.[37] The mounting political crisis of 1647 and 1648 delayed any further progress until after the execution of the king and the establishment of the republic, but in July 1649 the Rump of the Long Parliament felt it necessary to set up another committee to draft legislation against secret marriages.[38] The following March, the matter was entrusted to the committee preparing legislation against incest and adultery, but, apart from incorporating into its 1650 Adultery Act a list of relatives with whom marriage was forbidden, this group also failed to act.[39] In January 1651, the Rump appointed yet another committee 'to bring in an act to avoid abuses in marriage', and instructed it to meet daily.[40] It was not, however, until over a year later that Lord Commissioner Whitelocke finally, in March 1652, presented to the MPs a bill 'concerning marriages, registering thereof and births and burials'.[41] The Rumpers referred this bill back to the committee and no further progress had been made by the time Oliver Cromwell terminated their proceedings in April 1653.

It was left, therefore, to the more industrious members of Barebone's Parliament to bring in legislation to reform the marriage ceremony. They discussed the question at some length during August 1653, and, on the 24th, eventually passed the 'Act touching Marriages and the Registering thereof', abolishing the church wedding and replacing it with a civil ceremony before a justice of the peace.[42] The new legislation stipulated that all couples wishing to marry after 29th September following had to submit their own and their parents' names to a parish register (i.e. registrar) at least twenty days before their wedding, so that this new official could publish their intent to marry on three separate occasions, either in the parish church after the Sunday service, or in the nearest market-place on market day. Having thus publicized the proposed marriage, the parish register would then provide them with a certificate which, along with proof of parental consent if either party were under twenty-one, they would take to a local JP. The justice would then marry them in a simple, secular ceremony, during which the man would promise to be a 'loving and faithful husband', and the woman to be a 'loving, faithful and obedient wife'. If anyone objected to the proposed match, the register was instructed to make a note of this on the certificate

[37] *Commons Journal*, vol. 4, p. 678.
[38] Ibid., vol. 6, p. 263.
[39] Ibid., p. 385; Firth and Rait (eds), *Acts and Ordinances*, vol. 2, pp. 387–9.
[40] *Commons Journal*, vol. 6, p. 522.
[41] Ibid., vol. 7, p. 107.
[42] Ibid., pp. 297–301, 308–10, 312–13, 316–17.

and refer the matter to the justice for investigation. The Act also raised the age of consent for marriage to sixteen years for a man and fourteen years for a woman. In an attempt to achieve uniformity in marriage solemnization, the legislation stipulated that 'no other marriage whatsoever after 29th September . . . shall be held or accounted a marriage according to the laws of England.'

The new parish registers were to be elected before 22 September by a majority of those who contributed towards the parish poor rate, and subsequently approved by a justice. Where parishes were especially small, the justices were empowered to amalgamate them for registration purposes. The registers were required to keep a book 'of good vellum or parchment', in which to record all marriages, births (rather than baptisms) and burials. Their charges were laid down as 12*d*. for registering a marriage, and 4*d*. for a birth or burial. As the marriage certificate also cost 12*d*., the total cost of the new form of marriage was 2 shillings. During the debates on the bill's final reading, a motion to reduce these fees for 'labouring people' had been defeated, but the Act did allow them to be waived for those in receipt of poor relief. In an effort to reduce abductions and forcible marriages, the Act also declared that anyone convicted of kidnapping a minor would be sentenced to seven years hard labour and forfeit all their property.[43] The members of the assembly were anxious that the provisions of the Act should be widely publicized, and over the next few weeks its full text was printed in five of the weekly newsbooks.[44]

That this clear and straightforward legislation failed, however, to bring about the regularization of marriage practice that its authors had been seeking is made clear by some subsequent incidents which will be discussed below. It was also obvious to some of the MPs of Oliver Cromwell's two Protectorate Parliaments. In September 1654, shortly after the meeting of the first of these Parliaments, some MPs expressed fears that, because the Act's requirements for a valid marriage were particularly stringent, it might give rise in the future to a great many disputes about legitimacy and inheritance. They requested the House to consider the impact that the marriage legislation had had in the year since its introduction, and the matter was referred to a committee.[45] Two years

---

[43] Firth and Rait (eds), *Acts and Ordinances*, vol. 2, pp. 715–18.

[44] These were *The Perfect Diurnal*, 22–29 Aug. 1653 (TT); *Several Proceedings of Parliament*, 23–30 Aug. 1653 (TT); *Mercurius Politicus*, 25–31 Aug. 1653 (TT); *A Perfect Account*, 24–31 Aug. 1653 (TT); and *Several Proceedings of State Affairs*, 25 Aug.–1 Sept. 1653 (TT).

[45] J. T. Rutt (ed.), *The Diary of Thomas Burton 1656–1659* (4 vols, London, 1828), vol. 1, pp. xxxix–xl.

later, at the start of the second Protectorate Parliament, yet another committee was instructed to prepare a bill for the 'settlement of marriage',[46] and in early 1657 further discussion of the Barebones Marriage Act revealed serious disagreements among the MPs as to whether civil marriage should continue. In the spring of 1657, Parliament offered Cromwell the crown in the document 'The Humble Petition and Advice', and, while he considered the offer, negotiations took place over which of the legislative measures of earlier assemblies would be confirmed under an amended constitution. The Barebones Marriage Act was discussed at the end of April, and after much heated debate and a series of confused and narrow divisions, the MPs voted to extend it for a further six months. Still worried, however, about the legal status of those marriages that had been contracted during the previous four years without a strict adherence to all the Act's provisions, they dropped from the legislation the clause invalidating all alternative forms of ceremony. While this was, no doubt, a sensible, pragmatic move, it further confused the situation, and one MP was particularly disturbed that they might as a result have validated all marriages contracted since 1653 without parental consent.[47]

When the MPs assembled for the second session of Parliament in January 1658, they took into consideration new legislation to replace the Barebones Act which had technically lapsed the previous October, but before any new proposals could be acted upon the House was dissolved at the beginning of February. During the final months of the Interregnum, the legal position regarding the solemnizing of marriage remained extremely unclear, and at the Restoration the reigning confusion and the great importance of an issue with such a direct bearing on the descent of property prompted swift action from the government. The Convention Parliament turned its attention to the question in July 1660, and in January 1661 Charles II gave his assent to an Act which legalized all marriages 'had or solemnized in England since 1st May 1642 before any JP or pretended JP'.[48]

Among the prime objectives of those who were responsible for the reform of the marriage laws were simplification and standardization. However, because they were unable to enforce the new uniformity, they in fact created still more confusion and an even greater variety of marriage ceremonies. During the mid-1650s, many couples did, of

---

[46] *Commons Journal*, vol. 7, pp. 428, 441, 454.
[47] Ibid., pp. 526–7; Rutt (ed.), *Burton Diary*, vol. 2, pp. 38, 44, 67–74; Firth and Rait (eds), *Acts and Ordinances*, vol.2, p.1139.
[48] *Commons Journal*, vol. 7, pp. 581, 591; vol. 8, pp. 105, 114, 155, 222, 225; Rutt (ed.), *Burton Diary*, vol. 2, pp. 337–8, 344; BL E.1075.27, pp. 121–4.

course, marry in accordance with some or all of the requirements of the Barebones Act, but many others continued to wed in church. Throughout the Interregnum, Presbyterians remained attached to the *Directory* format, and many Anglicans, like the Kentish gentleman Sir Edward Dering, continued to be married according to the *Book of Common Prayer* service.[49] This diversity of ceremony can be observed even within Cromwell's own family. During November 1657, the month after the Barebones Act had lapsed, two of the Protector's daughters were married within a few days of each other: Frances married Robert, Lord Rich, in a civil ceremony which was followed by lavish festivities, while Mary married Lord Fauconberg in a quiet church service performed at Hampton Court by the Royalist divine, Dr Hewitt, who would shortly afterwards lose his life for plotting against the government.[50]

Some even devised their own, hybrid ceremonies; at Earls Colne in Essex in 1655, a couple were married in a ceremony attended by both the minister, Ralph Josselin, and a local justice of the peace, and in July 1656 John Simmonds and Margery Gunhill were similarly married both by a minister and the mayor of Basingstoke.[51] Some members of the radical religious sects further complicated this confused situation by ignoring the official regulations altogether and marrying by simple declarations before their gathered congregations. In *Gangraena*, published in 1646, Thomas Edwards denounced one sectary for declaring he would 'be hanged rather than married by a priest.'[52] Statements of intent to marry made before witnesses constituted valid spousals and thus rendered the resultant marriages canonically valid and, outside the period 1653–7, legally binding. Some gathered congregations, like the Baptist church at Fenstanton, even kept their own registers of those married in this way.[53]

Despite the efforts of those in authority to publicize the details of the new matrimonial legislation, there appears to have been widespread ignorance and misapprehension about the nature of the changes. When two couples from Portbury in Gloucestershire were questioned by a justice in Somerset in August 1654 about marrying in a chapel at Shirehampton, they claimed to have had no knowledge of the new law.[54] Ignorance of the new legislation also seems to have led to some couples,

---

[49] Bennitt (ed.), 'Diary of Isabella Twysden', p. 123.
[50] Abbott (ed.), *Writings and Speeches of Cromwell*, vol. 4, pp. 661–2.
[51] A. Macfarlane (ed.), *The Diary of Ralph Josselin 1616–83* (London, 1976), p. 346; W. A. Fearon and J. F. Williams (eds), *Parish Registers and Parochial Documents in the Archdeaconry of Winchester* (London, 1909), p. 70.
[52] Edwards, *Gangraena*, part 3, p. 24; see also Bod. Lib. Rawlinson MSS D.828, fo. 5.
[53] Underhill (ed.), *Fenstanton Records*, pp. 18–19.
[54] E. Harbin (ed.), *Quarter Sessions Records for the County of Somerset* vol. 3, Somerset Records Soc. Publs, 28 (1912), xlviii.

who were cohabiting after contracting what they believed to be valid marriages, being indicted by the authorites for fornication. At the quarter sessions held at Kirbymoorside in January 1656, the justices for the North Riding of Yorkshire convicted a couple from the parish of Sinnington as fornicators. At the same time, however, they dismissed the register of Sinnington, Robert Henley, for 'betraying his trust and abusing the register books committed unto him, and deceiving the people', and fined John Storr, a clergyman from Malton, 20 shillings for illegally marrying William Hardwick and Mary Smith of Sinnington.[55] If, as seems highly likely, Smith and Hardwick were the couple accused of fornication, they were probably cohabiting in the belief that they had been properly married by Henley and Storr. The following July at Thirsk, another couple were presented before the justices as fornicators as a result of irregularities in the way that the register of Malton had publicized their intention to marry.[56]

The plight of the confused or unaware was on occasions worsened by the activities of unscrupulous clerics and laymen who took advantage of the new uncertainties to trick their more gullible neighbours. When, in February 1655, John Denman was reported by the register of Somerton in Somerset to a local justice for being married in a church, he told the magistrate that he had been assured by the minister that marriages performed by clerics were now permitted.[57] In March 1655, Henry Page and Anne Reeves of Banwell in Somerset travelled the twelve miles to Wells to be married by the justice, William Smith. They failed to find Smith, but met with one Owen Willoughby, who informed them that a proclamation issued the previous week had made marriages by clergymen legal. He then introduced them to a minister, Richard Donne, who charged the large sum of five shillings to marry them.[58] Confusion could also result from couples' attempts to avoid the new procedures. In August 1654, William Pinckney and Mary Knight of Russell, Wiltshire eloped and were married by a minister in Hampshire. On their return, they were examined by the Wiltshire justices, who declared the marriage invalid; Pinckney then left Mary, remarried and settled in Berkshire, whereupon the same justices issued a warrant for his arrest as a bigamist.[59]

There was clearly also some confusion about the legal position regarding marriages with relatives. The 1650 Act against adultery and

---

[55] Atkinson (ed.), *Quarter Sessions Records*, pp. 203, 206.
[56] Ibid., p. 218.
[57] Harbin (ed.), *Quarter Sessions Somerset*, p. xlix.
[58] Ibid., p. xlviii.
[59] HMC *Various Collections*, vol. 1, pp. 129–30.

incest had included a list of relatives with whom marriage was forbidden; this table of affinity was closely based upon the rules outlined in the Old Testament book of Leviticus, and it outlawed as incestuous marriage with one's grandparents, parents, siblings, children, grandchildren, aunts and uncles, sons and daughters-in-law, and step-parents and children. Although these regulations were very similar to the earlier Anglican ones outlined by Archbishop Parker in a Table of Kindred and Affinity published in 1563, some were clearly unsure of their detailed provisions. In January 1654, the register of Middlewich in Cheshire wrote to a local JP, asking for guidance in the case of a proposed marriage between Francis Banne of Shropshire and his uncle's widow, Anne Banne of Drayton in Cheshire. The magistrate was also uncertain about how to proceed, and he ordered that the 1650 Act be examined before any decision were taken.[60] The following year, however, the Wiltshire justices were much more decisive in their treatment of John Tily of Hullavington. Tily wished to marry his deceased wife's sister, by whom he had already fathered a child, but the justices forbade the marriage and ordered that Tily should be whipped and his intended bride sent to a house of correction for a year.[61]

In some areas magistrates also scrutinized existing marriages to see whether they complied with the new regulations. In 1653, a west-country gentleman, Edward Jenkins, was bound over to appear before an assize judge on a charge of marrying his dead brother's wife.[62] Later the same year, the unfortunate William Frodsham also found himself in serious trouble after admitting to marrying his stepdaughter, 'not knowing any law or thing to the contrary'. Frodsham was brought before the Cheshire justices and, in accordance with the 1650 Act, sentenced to death for committing incest. His execution was, however, deferred several times, at first by the Cheshire bench and later by the Council of State, and in September 1653 he petitioned Barebone's Parliament for a pardon on the grounds that he had been 'ignorant of transgressing any law in that behalf, or that he had been within the compass of the act of the late Parliament made for Incest etc.' His request was supported by several Cheshire justices and the sheriff of the county, who wrote to the assembly to inform them, 'We do believe that his fault was meetly through ignorance, which we are the rather induced unto because he never denied the fact, as thinking it lawful; neither was there any evidence or prosecution against him, but his own confession.'[63] Frodsham's sub-

[60] Bennett and Dewhurst (eds), *Quarter Sessions Chester*, pp. 160–1.
[61] Cunnington (ed.), *Records Wilts.*, p. 230.
[62] F. A. Inderwick, *The Interregnum* (London, 1891), p. 36.
[63] *Several Proceedings of State Affairs*, 15–22 Sept. 1653 (TT); *CSPD* 1652–3, p. 322.

sequent fate is unclear, but the absence of any mention of an execution in the newsbooks of the day suggests that his petition was successful. How his case came to the attention of the authorities is also a puzzle, but the fact that he was condemned to death by some Cheshire JPs and supported in his plea for clemency by others, would seem to indicate that there were serious differences of opinion within the Cheshire bench about how to proceed in cases of matrimonial irregularity. In the same year, another couple from Essex were found guilty of contracting an incestuous marriage; they too were sentenced to death, but were also later reprieved.[64]

Given all this uncertainty about the legal position and the threat of severe punishment for transgressors, it is hardly surprising that some decided it was safer to cover themselves by marrying by more than one method. In 1655, Roger Wiseman and Sarah Barratt were married both by a justice of the peace at Longparish in Hampshire and also in a second religious ceremony, and in 1656 Elizabeth Horler and her husband admitted to a Somerset magistrate that, following their civil ceremony, they had been married a second time by a minister in Chepstow.[65] In 1656, Anne Murray and Sir James Halket were also wed both by a justice and a minister 'that they might object nothing against our marriage'.[66] Speaking during the 1657 debate in Parliament about whether to extend the Barebones Act, Sir John Glynn quoted the comment of the Nottinghamshire gentleman, Sir Gervase Clifton, who, when asked how many wives he had had, replied that 'he had had seven wives, but he had been ten times married, viz. three times to his last wife.'[67] That these were far from isolated examples may be suggested by some of the demographic figures compiled by Wrigley and Schofield. Their calculations seem to indicate that the period following the passing of the Civil Marriage Act saw a dramatic increase in the number of marriages contracted in England, from an average of 35,900 a year in the period 1651 to 1653, to an average of 56,872 a year between 1654 and 1656.[68] However, in view of the continuing economic depression of the 1650s and the apparent unpopularity of the new civil arrangements, rather than signifying an increase in the numbers of single people marrying, the higher totals may be the result of large numbers of couples deciding to

[64] PRO ASSI 35/94/2/2–3, quoted by Sharpe in *Crime*, p. 69.
[65] Harbin (ed.), *Quarter Sessions Somerset*, p. 306; Fearon and Williams (eds), *Parish Registers*, p. 70.
[66] Loftis (ed.), *Memoirs of Halket, Fanshawe*, pp. 84–5.
[67] Rutt (ed.), *Burton Diary*, vol. 2, p. 68.
[68] Wrigley and Schofield, *Population History*, pp. 264, 498. The figures are my averages from their yearly totals.

follow Clifton's example and to remarry their spouses in a second ceremony.

The new matrimonial legislation of the 1650s clearly, then, caused considerable short-term confusion; but did it at least compensate for this by bringing about some improvement in the regulation of marriage and the elimination of the worst abuses that had prompted it? Quarter sessions records for the 1650s from all parts of the country reveal that magistrates frequently delayed marriages in order to investigate objections, which were usually lodged on the grounds that one of the parties was pre-contracted following an earlier exchange of vows.[69] The justices in north Yorkshire certainly appear to have taken this part of their new work seriously; in October 1655 they instructed all the registers of parishes in the North Riding:

> to take notice that, as often as any exceptions shall be made against any intended marriage, that they advise and direct those that shall offer any exceptions against any marriages to repair to the next JP to enter security to make good their exceptions at the Sessions next following, and the sheriff to cause this to be published in all market towns in the North Riding.[70]

In many cases, however, objectors failed to appear, and the magistrates also frequently dismissed claims of pre-contract, perhaps partly because they wished to play down the significance of informal undertakings. In 1657, for example, the Wiltshire justices granted the petition of a man who asked to be released from a vow he had made to a girl five years before when, aged only fifteen, he had declared the devil might take him if he married any but her.[71] Cases of under-age marriage were also brought to the attention of the justices: in October 1657 the Middlesex justices nullified the marriage of Anthony Lowther to Bridget Fleetwood on the grounds that Anthony had not reached the age of consent.[72]

The authorities also frequently indicted and fined clergymen who conducted illegal marriages,[73] and they dealt severely with those accused in cases of marriages contracted through deception and without parental consent, or which involved forcible abduction. In 1655, Thomas

---

[69] For examples see Harbin (ed.), *Quarter Sessions Somerset*, pp. 253, 256, 265; Bennett and Dewhurst (eds), *Quarter Sessions Chester*, pp. 163–4; Atkinson (ed.), *Quarter Sessions Records*, pp. 175, 184, 197, 206; and S. Ratcliff and H. Johnson (eds), *Quarter Sessions Order Book 1650–1657*, Warwick County Records, 3 (1937), 276.
[70] Atkinson (ed.), *Quarter Sessions Records*, p. 197.
[71] Cunnington (ed.), *Records Wilts.*, pp. 231–2.
[72] J. C. Jeaffreson (ed.), *Middlesex County Records*, OS 3 (London, 1954), 264.
[73] For examples see Atkinson (ed.), *Quarter Sessions Records*, pp. 97, 116, 179, 203, 226.

Reynolds, a clothier from Colchester, complained to the Middlesex justices that his son Thomas, who was apprenticed to a woollen draper in London, had been enticed into a marriage with one Susanna Graunt. Graunt and her friends had taken Thomas by coach to a minister in Paddington, who had married them and arranged for the union to be subsequently 'cried' in Westminster market and legitimized by Colonel Grosvenor, one of the Middlesex bench. The marriage, in which the younger Reynolds may well have been a far more willing agent than his father claimed, clearly failed to fulfil the provisions of the 1653 Act, and was thus declared null by the magistrates.[74] In the same year, the judges of Doctors' Commons nullified the marriage of a rich heiress, Joan Hele, upon her complaint that she had married one Chamberlain believing him to be a nobleman, when he was in fact an impoverished vintner's son.[75]

Following a particularly notorious case of abduction in 1649, the Rump Parliament gave women the right to appeal to the courts for the nulling of marriages which they claimed they had been forced into. In the autumn of 1649, Jane Puckering was abducted from Greenwich Park by Joseph Walsh, who took her to Flanders and forced her to marry him there. Pressure from the Council of State brought about her eventual release in June 1650, and Walsh and his accomplices were later indicted as felons.[76] The following January, the Rump authorized the Commissioners of the Great Seal to examine the case and, if abduction were proved, to declare the marriage invalid, adding that any other woman that 'hath been or shall be by force seized on or carried away against her will, or hath or shall have words wrested from her', could similarly appeal to the commissioners.[77] One woman who took advantage of this offer was Anne Blount, daughter of Mountjoy Blount, Earl of Newport. During 1654, she petitioned both the commissioners and Oliver Cromwell for an end to harassment by William Blount, who was claiming to be contracted to her, and Cromwell subsequently ordered the appointment of a committee 'for freeing her from all futher pretence of contract and from all molestation of the said William Blount.'[78] The following year Anne Blount's matrimonial affairs were once more the subject of investigation by the authorities, although on this occasion she probably found their intervention far less congenial. In July 1655, her father successfully petitioned the Middlesex justices for the nulling of her marriage to Endymion Porter's son Thomas, with whom she had eloped

---

[74] Jeaffreson (ed.), *Middlesex Records*, pp. 233–4.
[75] Inderwick, *Interregnum*, p. 44.
[76] Ibid., pp. 40–3.
[77] Firth and Rait (eds), *Acts and Ordinances*, vol. 2, pp. 496–7.
[78] CSPD 1654, p. 105. There is no suggestion that Anne and William were related.

and to whom she had subsequently been married at an inn in Southwark.[79]

These examples show that, when abuses were brought to the attention of the authorities, they were prepared to exercise their new powers in an attempt to correct them. They also reveal, however, that malpractice had not been eradicated by the new legislation. Those cases which came before the courts may well, in fact, have represented only the tip of an iceberg of continuing matrimonial irregularity. Informal and illegal practices clearly persisted and the authorities struggled to control or to prevent them. When questioned by magistrates in Wiltshire some months after the passing of the Barebones Act, Thomas Earle, minister of Shorncott, admitted he had officiated at a wedding ceremony which had taken place during a drinking party in a private house, though he claimed he had viewed the incident as a joke.[80] In 1655, three men from Preston Plunkett in Somerset declared before the justice, George Sampson, that they had been married by a 'wandering person', whose name they did not know and who had given them no certificates.[81] In 1659, a married woman, Jeanette Jones, persuaded Henry Gill of Crowcombe in Somerset to go through a form of marriage ceremony with her and thus acquired part of the lease of his cottage.[82]

The failure of the authorities to prevent such incidents must partly be attributed to the natural limitations upon the power and effectiveness of early-modern English government. Regulating the procedures for tens of thousands of marriages throughout the country was a tall order for the limited central and local bureaucracies of the seventeenth century. Nor did the new registers, who had been appointed to supervise the new arrangements at parish level, always prove reliable instruments. One initial problem was that by 29 September, the date upon which registration was supposed to begin, many parishes had neglected to appoint their register;[83] in January 1654, for example, twelve Norfolk parishes which had failed to hold elections were amalgamated with Swaffham Market for registration purposes.[84] Of those parishes which did appoint the official, some simply entrusted the new duties to the local minister, while those which appointed a layman chose either the local landowner or someone of lower social status who combined the

---

[79] Jeaffreson (ed.), *Middlesex Records*, p. 237.
[80] HMC *Various Collections*, vol. 1, pp. 127–8.
[81] Harbin (ed.), *Quarter Sessions Somerset*, p. xlviii.
[82] Ibid., p. 353.
[83] Rutt (ed.), *Burton Diary*, vol. 2, p. 44.
[84] D. E. Howell James (ed.), Norfolk *Quarter Sessions Order Book 1650–7*, Norfolk Records Soc. Publs, 26 (1955), 65.

registration duties with his previous employment as a tailor, inn-keeper etc.[85]

The Barebones Act had stipulated that the elections of registers should be held in the presence of a majority of those in the parish who contributed towards the poor rate, and that those chosen should be 'able and honest'. In some parishes, however, neither of these requirements seems to have been met. During the quarter sessions for Shropshire which followed the passing of the Act, objection was made to the election of George Whittingham as register for Whitchurch parish, on the grounds that he kept a disorderly alehouse and was one 'disaffected to the state', who had been chosen by 'a particular interest'.[86] In June 1655, the inhabitants of Staplegrove in Somerset complained to the justices about their register, William Pomeroy, who they claimed had been elected by only four people 'without the approbation of the rest of the same parish', and whom they decribed as 'a most desperate malignant, a common drunkard and a man of most lewd life'. As a result, Pomeroy was removed from office and new elections ordered.[87] The following year, malpractice amongst the registers in Essex was presented to the grand jury of the shire as a serious problem for that county's inhabitants.[88] In 1657, Abraham Barton, register of All Saints parish in Northampton, was accused of issuing false certificates 'to the evil example of others, and against the public peace'.[89] The charges of corruption against the two North Riding registers, Robert Henley of Sinnington and Robert Blackwell of Malton, have already been noted, and evidence of corrupt practices by the magistrates themselves also exists; in 1655, the Lincolnshire justice, John Hobson, was accused of frequenting alehouses and taking 'large sums' for marriages.[90] Registration abuses were frequent enough to cause concern to central government; when Parliament was considering revised marriage legislation in January 1658, Sir John Maynard expressed serious misgivings about the registration system, claiming, 'There was a case where, by [e]rasing of a register book, a lawful marriage was vitiated and a bad marriage ratified. It is of

---

[85] Bennett and Dewhurst (eds), *Quarter Sessions Chester*, pp. 163–4; Atkinson (ed.), *Quarter Sessions Records*, p. 218; J. Wake (ed.), *Quarter Sessions Records for the County of Northampton*, Northants. Records Soc. Publs, 1 (1928), 132; and O. Wakeman and R. S. Kenyon (eds), *Shrophire County Records* (Shrewsbury, 1905), pp. 7–8.

[86] Wakeman and Kenyon (eds), *Shropshire Records*, pp. 7–8.

[87] Harbin (ed.), *Quarter Sessions Somerset*, pp. 270–1.

[88] K. Wrightson, 'The Nadir of English Illegitimacy', in P. Laslett, K. Osterveen and R. Smith (eds), *Bastardy and its Comparative History* (London, 1980), p. 184.

[89] Wake (ed.), *Quarter Sessions Northampton*, p. 132.

[90] *CSPD 1655*, p. 398.

great necessity to prove descents and the like, which is the foundation of property etc., and not fit to be trusted in a loose hand.'[91]

However, if the authorities were hampered by the bureaucratic corruption and inefficiency endemic in early-modern England, a more fundamental reason for their failure to achieve uniformity in marriage practice was the unpopularity of the civil legislation and the refusal of large numbers to accept its provisions. In his sermon *The Marriage Ring*, which was published in May 1653 just a few weeks before the introduction of the civil ceremony, the conservative divine, Jeremy Taylor, argued that marriage should be 'in Christ and the church', and counselled those intending to marry to 'see that Christ and His church be in at every of its periods, and that it be entirely conducted and overruled by religion.'[92] With regard to the wedding ceremony, there seems to have been a widespread desire to follow his advice. In London, where quick marriages had long been available, many of the inhabitants avoided the new secular ceremony by marrying during the five-week interval between the passing of the Act in late August 1653 and the date when it came into force at the end of September. The newsbook *Mercurius Democritus*, a popular scandal sheet which specialized in stories of the sexual exploits of the capital's inhabitants, reported that over 500 Londoners had married in one week in September, with the result that the city seamstresses had been unable to cope with the demand for bridal gowns, and the goldsmiths had been reduced to coating flax with gold to provide rings for all the ceremonies. It also claimed that young girls were particularly keen to wed in church 'because their tender consciences will not permit them to be married after the new way'.[93] These stories were confirmed by the more reliable *Kingdom's Weekly Intelligencer*, which reported at the end of September:

> Sure the sign is now in Gemini; there were yesterday twenty marriages in one church, and five and twenty in another. There is a poor blind alley hard by me (one would think it impossible that love should be there, but that love is blind) not above eight houses in all, and in four of them the Parties are agreed and, above two hours ago, are gone to the Parson to be married.[94]

Some, like the minister John Machin, were wed on the 29th itself, the last opportunity for a legally binding religious ceremony.[95] Wrigley and

---

[91] Rutt (ed.), *Burton Diary*, vol. 2, pp. 337–8.
[92] Eden (ed.), *Whole Works of Jeremy Taylor*, vol. 4, p. 212.
[93] Successive issues of *Mercurius Democritus*, 14 Sept.– 5 Oct. 1653 (TT).
[94] *The Kingdom's Weekly Intelligencer*, 20–7 Sept. 1653 (TT).

Schofield have calculated that a total of 9,884 marriages were contracted in England during September 1653; this compares with only 1,401 in August and the extremely low figure of 714 in October, which was normally one of the most popular months for marriages. The figure for September 1653 is the highest total for any month during the 1650s, and more than double the average monthly total for the decade.[96]

Once the new Act had come into force, many retained their attachment to the old forms and resisted the innovations. When Dorothy Osborne first read of the changes in the marriage service in the autumn of 1653, she wrote to William Temple that they 'would fright the country people extremely, for they apprehend nothing like going before a justice.' Although she was herself desperate to marry Temple, she added: 'they say no other marriage shall stand good in law. In conscience, I believe the old one is better; and, for my part, I am resolved to stay till that comes in fashion again.'[97] Later, however, her eagerness to become Temple's wife overcame her objections to the civil ceremony, and, after a series of obstacles to the match had eventually been removed, the couple were married by a Middlesex JP in 1654.[98] Judith Percival, who was also contemplating marriage in the autumn of 1653, reacted to the introduction of the new civil ceremony in a similar manner to Dorothy Osborne; in a letter to her brother at the beginning of September, she declared: 'If I must enter into that condition, I protest it shall never be (without the other) in that manner.'[99] Another woman who was married during the mid-1650s was Anne Murray; she later gave a detailed account of her attitude to the civil ceremony in the following passage from her memoirs:

> Upon Saturday 1st March 1655/6, Sir James and I went to Charlton and took with us Mr Gaile, who was chaplain to the countess of Devonshire, who preached (as he sometimes used to do) at the church the next day; and after supper he married us in my brother Newton's closet, none knowing of it in the family or being present, but my brother and sister and Mr Neale . . . after the evening sermon, my sister, pretending to go to see Justice Elkonheed who was not well, living at Woolwich, took Sir James and me with her in the coach, and my brother and Mr Neale went another way afoot

---

[95] Clarke, *Lives of Eminent Persons*, part 1, p. 85.
[96] Wrigley and Schofield, *Population History*, p. 521.
[97] Hart (ed.) *Letters of Dorothy Osborne*, pp. 93–4.
[98] K. Parker (ed.), *Dorothy Osborne: Letters to Sir William Temple* (Harmondsworth, 1987), p. 6.
[99] HMC *Egmont MSS*, vol. 1, p. 525.

and met us there; and the Justice performed what was usual for him at that time, which was, only holding the Directory in his hand, asked Sir James if he intended to marry me. He answered 'Yes'; and asked if I intended to marry him. I said 'Yes'. 'Then' says he 'I pronounce you man and wife'. So, calling for a glass of sack, he drank and wished much happiness to us, and we left him, having given his clerk money, who gave us in parchment the day and witness and attested by the Justice that he had married us. But, if it had not been more solemnly done afterwards by a minister, I should not have believed it lawfully done.[100]

The antipathy these women felt towards the civil ceremony was shared by many of their contemporaries. Throughout the country, clergymen continued to conduct marriages using the *Book of Common Prayer*, even though this frequently led to their indictment before the magistrates,[101] and they found a stready stream of customers who, like William Pinckney and Mary Knight, wished to be

ritely and canonically joined one to and with the other in holy wedlock, and pronounced ... man and wife together, in the name of the Father and of the Son and of the Holy Ghost, with all other due and decent ceremonies to such solemnity belonging as to the ministerial office thereof, according to the known, ancient and solemn service used in the Church of England, rightly and reverently observed and performed.[102]

In Cheshire, Cromwell's major-general for the north-west of the country, Charles Worsley, waged a concerted campaign against the large numbers who attempted to circumvent the Barebones Act. In February 1656, he informed John Thurloe that he had imprisoned 'a great number' of laymen for being married in church, along with some of the ministers who had officiated at religious marriage ceremonies.[103] Yet resistance to the new Act remained widespread. Even Ralph Josselin, the timorous minister of Earls Colne in Essex, flouted the ban on church marriages. After marrying a couple in May 1655, he commented in his diary that

---

[100] Loftis (ed.), *Memoirs of Halket, Fanshawe*, pp. 84–5.
[101] For examples see Harbin (ed.), *Quarter Sessions Somerset*, pp. xlviii, xlix, 287, 306; Atkinson (ed.), *Quarter Sessions Records*, pp. 97, 116, 179, 203, 226; and Jeaffreson (ed.), *Middlesex Records*, pp. 233–4, 237.
[102] Cunnington (ed.), *Records Wilts.*, p. 228.
[103] John Thurloe (ed.), *A Collection of the State Papers of John Thurloe* (7 vols, London, 1742), vol. 4, p. 523. I owe this reference to Geoffrey Goulbourne.

this was the first wedding he had 'intermeddled with' since the passing of the civil legislation, but he afterwards conducted several more illegal ceremonies.[104] Captain John Pickering, a justice in the West Riding of Yorkshire, performed civil marriages at regular intervals between 1653 and 1657, but many of the couples who came before him had already been married in a religious service, and, after the return of legal church weddings in April 1657, the numbers resorting to him dropped dramatically and he performed his last service in December 1657.[105] Opposition to the 1653 Act may also have accounted for the refusal of the inhabitants of Kenilworth in Warwickshire to pay fees to their register for some months after his appointment.[106]

The civil ceremony was also ridiculed in one of the popular ballads of the day, which labelled the members of Barebone's assembly as 'pitiful clowns' and exclaimed of the justices, 'the devil take 'um'.[107] In addition, civil marriage was denounced in several more substantial literary works. September 1653, the month in which the Act was passed, saw the publication of *Sad and Serious Thoughts or a Sense and Meaning of the late Act Concerning Marriages*, which was written by C. C., perhaps Charles Churchill, rector of Feniton in Devon who was ejected by triers in 1656.[108] The author referred to the new Act as 'so great and . . . unnecessary an innovation', and argued that the new legislation was no real improvement on the old procedures, asserting:

> . . . and mended I think few wise men will judge it; except they shall call that mending that makes the stipulation more loose and the terms more general. Of which, what use may be made by ungodly and crafty wits to the nullifying of the engagement, I wish time may not to the sorrow of some hereafter discover.[109]

An even more swingeing attack came from the pen of the conservative divine, John Gauden, whose *Christ at the Wedding* appeared in February 1655. Gauden wrote the tract in October 1654 and addressed his remarks to the newly assembled MPs of Cromwell's first Protectorate Parliament. He described the new marriage ceremony as a 'mushroom of yesterday' and a 'Gourd of a night's growing, under whose shadow some

[104] Macfarlane (ed.), *Josselin Diary*, pp. 346, 357, 366, 430, 432.
[105] 'Justice's Note Book of Captain John Pickering, 1656–1660', Thoresby Soc. Publs, 11 (1900–4), 69–100; 15 (1909), 71–80.
[106] Ratcliff and Johnson (eds), *Quarter Sessions Order Book*, p. 217.
[107] Bradford District Archives, Hopkinson MSS, 32D86/17.
[108] A. G. Matthews, *Walker Revised* (Oxford, 1948), p. 110.
[109] C.C., *Sad and Serious Thoughts or a Sense and Meaning of the Late Act Concerning Marriages* (London, 1653), pp. 1–3 (TT).

peevish spirits fancy great refreshings'. Calling for the rapid repeal of the Act, he argued that it had caused widespread confusion and anxiety, and that individuals had been forced to travel long distances only to find that the justices conducted the ceremony 'in a hasty and huddled manner'. He declared to the MPs: '. . . you cannot but see and daily hear from all parts how much vexation, trouble, pains, defeats, charges and inconveniences are brought upon the people by this new and exotic mode of marrying far beyond what was formerly ever felt while ministers worthily officiated.'[110] Gauden's pamphlet was, of course, a piece of conservative propaganda and thus open to accusations of exaggeration; in the light, however, of the other reactions noted above, he may well have been articulating a general frustration with the new form of marriage.

In April 1657, during the debate in Parliament on the proposal to extend the Barebones Marriage Act, the MPs of Cromwell's second Protectorate Parliament surveyed the impact that the legislation had had over the previous four years. Lord Broghill argued that, as the new arrangements had been introduced by an unelected assembly – 'another authority than the people usually entrust' – they were 'never looked upon as a law'. Another MP claimed that the eminent in the land would never submit to the new way of marrying, and two members declared that not one in a hundred marriages had been contracted fully in accordance with the Barebones provisions.[111] It was clear to many of the MPs that the new initiative had foundered, and to some that it had done so on the rock of the nation's preference for traditional ways.

In this respect, the civil marriage issue can be seen as a microcosm of the conflicts within revolutionary England. For ranged against this widespread attachment to custom and tradition was the reforming zeal of a minority of Puritan politicians and soldiers, whose ideals were order, standardization and greater moral probity. The new wedding ceremony had been introduced by an unrepresentative assembly which, while no longer considered by historians to have been peopled by a fanatical lunatic fringe, did contain a powerful leaven of revolutionary Fifth Monarchism. According to both John Gauden and the author of *Sad and Serious Thoughts*, the Marriage Act was the product of Barebone's assembly's rampant anticlericalism, and its primary aim was to undermine and demoralize the public ministry.[112] Its anti-clerical features would certainly have helped the Act to find favour with one of the revolution's most enthusiastic supporters, John Milton. In October 1656, Milton married his second wife, Katherine Woodcock, before the

---

[110] Gauden, *Christ at the Wedding, passim*, esp. pp. 1–2, 25.
[111] Rutt (ed.), *Burton Diary*, vol. 2, pp. 38, 44, 67–74.
[112] Gauden, *Christ at the Wedding*, pp. 8–12; C.C., *Sad and Serious Thoughts*, pp. 5–8.

London magistrate Sir John Dethick, and in his *Considerations Touching the Likeliest Means to Remove Hirelings out of the Church*, which was published in 1659, he wrote:

> As for marriages, that ministers should meddle with them, as not sanctified or legitimate without the celebration, I find no ground in Scripture, either of precept or example . . . Our divines deny it to be a sacrament, yet retained the celebration, till prudently a late parliament recovered the civil liberty of marriage from their encroachment, and transferred the ratifying and registering thereof from the canonical shop to the proper cognizance of civil magistrates.[113]

Ralph Josselin may have identified another reason for the attraction of civil marriage for some millenarian radicals in the mid-1650s, when he reflected in his diary that the forbidding of marriages was one of the features of the last days referred to in St Paul's epistle to Timothy.[114]

Radical attachment to the new form of marriage is also clearly seen during the 1657 parliamentary debate, in which the secular service was staunchly defended by army officers such as Francis White, William Goffe, Thomas Kelsey and John Desborough. When Nathaniel Fiennes proposed the amendment to legalize church weddings, these radicals objected strongly and Desborough declared that he had no interest in what happened to the legislation if alternative forms of service were once more to be allowed.[115] When the moderates nevertheless proceeded to reinstate the religious ceremony, it was clear that the revolutionary tide was ebbing away. Six months later, during the Parliament's troubled second session, it was the radical 'Anabaptist', Anthony Nichols, who chaired the committee which once again considered the question of matrimonial reform, until Cromwell's dissolution brought their discussions to an abrupt end.[116] Within two years, Nichols's revolution was over and Charles II restored church weddings by the *Book of Common Prayer*, and perpetuated the confusion in the sphere of marriage regulation. Effective reform in this area would only come with the passing of Hardwick's Marriage Act on the centenary of the Barebones Act in 1753.

During the autumn of 1653, Margaret Harlakenden defiantly ignored all the pressure for a modest civil ceremony. In November 1657, much to

---

[113] W. R. Parker, *Milton, A Biography* (2 vols, Oxford, 1968), vol. 1, p. 480; Wolfe (ed.), *Complete Prose Works of Milton*, vol. 7, pp. 299–300.
[114] Macfarlane (ed.), *Josselin Diary*, p. 327.
[115] Rutt (ed.), *Burton Diary*, vol. 2, pp. 67–74.
[116] Ibid., p. 344.

her father's chagrin, she spent the huge sum of £120 on clothes for her wedding and in December, six months after church weddings had once more become legal, she was married to John Eldred in the priory at Earls Colne by the minister Ralph Josselin. The wedding reception lasted three days and was described by Josselin as 'an action mixed with piety and mirth'.[117] Margaret Harlakenden's rejection of civil marriage was shared by many hundreds of other brides in England during the 1650s, revealing that, while matrimonial reform may have been sorely needed, it was not wanted. In introducing a secular form of marriage, the leaders of the revolution had launched a frontal assault upon an important aspect of the traditional culture of English men and women. But by 1660 they had discovered that this traditional rite of family life was a stronger force than the power of governments, and that their revolutionary zeal had been unable to overcome the people's attachment to their 'old and received customs', which, as the author of *Sad and Serious Thoughts* explained, 'have very great force with men and are fixed with so strong a root'.[118] The English Revolution had, therefore, some limited impact upon the fortunes of those seeking husbands and wives in mid-seventeenth-century England, and a greater effect upon the way in which those who were successful in their search solemnized their unions. But what is made clear, both by the reluctance of some of the Fenstanton Baptists to allow any interference from their co-religionists in their marriage plans, and by the refusal of thousands to abandon the religious wedding, is the strength and tenacity of the traditional concerns and rites of family life, and their ability to survive in the face of considerable external pressure for their curtailment.

[117] Macfarlane (ed.), *Josselin Diary*, pp. 410, 413.
[118] C.C., *Sad and Serious Thoughts*, p. 2.

5
Wives and Husbands

Throughout the early-modern period, women in England occupied a generally subservient role both in the family and in society in general. By the state, they were excluded from most forms of public activity, political, economic, religious and cultural; as wives, they were sometimes given limited responsibility for the daily household budget and the supervision of children, but any power they exercised was subject to the ultimate authority of their husbands. The unparalleled events of the period 1640–60 by no means transformed this situation overnight, but the extraordinary conditions which prevailed during these twenty years did have a dramatic effect upon the lives of many English women. For a short while at least, both single and married women were offered unprecedented freedoms and reponsibilities, and as a result some came to re-evaluate their self-image and to question the assumption of their male-dominated society that the female sex was 'the weaker vessel'. Such a reassessment could hardly fail to affect relationships between husbands and wives within the patriarchal family, but the nature of its impact varied; in some cases it resulted in an increase in tensions and divisions between spouses, while in others it led to the creation of more harmonious and co-operative marital relationships.

The quarrels which resulted in armed conflict in England during the 1640s had arisen within an exclusively male political nation and, as in all other wars, the active participants in the civil war and the revolution which followed were also overwhelmingly male. Indeed, the general contemporary male view was that the conflict was of little or no relevance to women; it was exemplified by the dismissive comment of Captain Thomas Gardiner, who remarked in a letter to Mary Verney in the early months of the war 'I believe that neither king nor Parliament have any quarrel against women, who never did any hurt except with their tongues.'¹ The overwhelming majority of wives adopted without question the religious and political opinions of their husbands, and if any temporary differences of outlook did develop they were most often resolved by the wife's submission. On hearing that her husband, the Yorkshire gentleman Sir Hugh Cholmley had transferred his allegiance from Parliament to the king, Elizabeth Cholmley, who had been away in London, was initially very upset that he had deserted the side for which she was 'very earnest and firm'. However, after Sir Hugh had taken her aside and 'unmasked to her the Parliament's intent', she abandoned her previous position and fell into line with him.² Similarly, when the wife of the Presbyterian minister Samuel Winter was considering joining a Baptist congregation in the 1650s, her husband 'took much pains with her to reclaim and settle her in the Truth', and she subsequently abandoned the plan.³

Some women, however, did uphold their own strongly felt political and religious opinions, and considerable numbers of them became actively involved in a variety of ways in the conflicts of the Civil War years. Women, for example, were frequently involved in petitioning. In his Royalist satire *Hudibras*, Samuel Butler commented that in the early 1640s, the oyster-women of the capital had 'locked their fish up, and trudged away to cry no bishop.'⁴ A group of London women did indeed petition Parliament in favour of the abolition of episcopacy in early February 1642, and the following years saw a number of other female petitions on a wide range of political and religious topics.⁵ In the late 1640s, some women in London petitioned and demonstrated in suppport of the radical political campaign of the Levellers. In one such petition presented to the House of Commons in May 1649, a number of women expressed their anger at the execution of the radical army mutineer, Robert Lockyer, and claimed an equal say with men in the political debate, arguing:

> ... since we are assured of our Creation in the image of God, and of an interest in Christ equal unto men, as also of a proportionable share in the Freedoms of this Commonwealth, we cannot but

---

[1] *Verney Memoirs*, vol. 1, p. 243.
[2] H. Cholmley, *Memoirs of Sir Hugh Cholmley Knt. and Bart.* (Malton, 1870), p. 41.
[3] Clarke, *Lives of Eminent Persons*, part 1, p. 106.
[4] Quoted by A. Fraser in *The Weaker Vessel: Woman's Lot in the Seventeenth Century* (London, 1984), p. 228.
[5] Ellen McArthur, 'Women Petitioners and the Long Parliament', *English Historical Review*, 24 (1909), 698–709; and Patricia Higgins, 'The Reaction of Women, with Special Reference to Women Petitioners', in B. Manning (ed.), *Politics, Religion and the English Civil War* (London, 1973), pp. 179–224.

wonder and grieve that we should appear so despicable in your eyes as to be thought unworthy to Petition or represent our Grievances to this Honourable House.⁶

Many examples of women who conspicuously displayed their own political opinions could be cited. Elizabeth Lady Windham of Kensford in Somerset, Jane Prichard of Uffington in Lincolnshire, Katherine Moore of Grantham in the same county, Katherine Mayo of Bodenham in Herefordshire, Elizabeth, countess of Essex (the estranged wife of the parliamentary general Robert Devereux) and the countess of Derby, all had their estates confiscated for Royalist activities.⁷ In 1647, Dame Amy Clarke claimed that after she had married Sir Henry Clarke of Pleshey in Essex in the middle of the Civil War, her arguments had persuaded her new husband to withdraw from his attendance upon the king at Oxford.⁸ One anonymous woman, widely suspected to be Lady Anne Fairfax, wife of the New Model Army commander, Sir Thomas Fairfax, interrupted Charles I's trial in 1649 by shouting from the public gallery that most of the country was opposed to the proceedings against the king and that Oliver Cromwell was a traitor.⁹ Later the same year, the widow of Rowland Langhorne, who had been executed for his involvement in a Royalist uprising in Pembrokeshire in 1648, was reported to be 'constantly railing against Parliament'.¹⁰ Anne Monck, wife of the chief architect of Charles II's return to England in 1660, George Monck, was also a resourceful woman of strong opinions and was generally believed by contemporaries to have had a great deal of influence over her husband, particularly in the months which preceded the Restoration.¹¹

Some women's involvement in the Civil War went far beyond the mere expression of political opinion. In the early months of the conflict, Queen Henrietta Maria was advised by some of her attendants to establish a fund for female contributions towards the Royalists' financial needs; a number of prominent ladies at court gave £100 each, and the organizers hoped to raise £10,000 by contacting wealthy women, 'as well wives as widows', throughout the country.¹² The Parliamentarians also thought it important to canvass female support; in his sermon *The Glorious Name*

---

⁶ *To the Supreme Authority, The Commons. The Petition of Diverse Women of the Cities of London and Westminster* (London, 1649) (TT); see also *A Remonstrance of the She Cityzens of London* (London, 1647) (TT).
⁷ *Cal. Com. Comp.*, vol. 2, pp. 1105, 1373; vol. 3, pp. 1663–4, 1676, 1828, 2228.
⁸ Ibid., vol. 2, p. 1212.
⁹ C. V. Wedgwood, *The Trial of Charles I* (Harmondsworth, 1983 edn), pp. 154–5.
¹⁰ *Cal. Com. Advance Money*, vol. 2, p. 876.
¹¹ *DNB*, George Monck (1608–70).
¹² Cecilia, Countess of Denbigh, *Royalist Father and Roundhead Son*, pp. 165–6.

of God, the Lord of Hosts, which he delivered in London in the early months of the Civil War, Jeremiah Burroughs urged wives not to dissuade their sons and husbands from joining the parliamentary forces, citing Sarah and Deborah as biblical examples of women who had courageously assisted their menfolk through wartime difficulties. In his eagerness to strengthen the resolve of women, Burroughs even went so far as to deny the almost universal belief that they were inferior to men, quoting the words of an Old Testament female warrior, who, he claimed, had declared:

> Cease to accuse . . . the fragility of the feminine sex. What, are we not made of the same matter that men are? Yea, after God's image are we made as well as they. God did not use flesh to make women of in token of infirmity: we are bone of his bone, in token we must be strong in the living God.[13]

In a number of parliamentary centres, including London, Coventry, Norwich and Canterbury, women involved themselves in fund-raising activities: at London and Bristol they helped to construct the city fortifications: at Nottingham they patrolled the streets, and at Nantwich they assisted in putting out fires.[14] Women were also frequently used as emissaries or to gather intelligence; Jane Whorwood was active in the underground Royalist network in the late 1640s, and Anne Murray helped to organize the escape of Charles I's son James, Duke of York, from parliamentary custody in 1648.[15] The commitment of some women stretched as far as active involvement in military operations. Judith Barrington, wife of Sir Thomas Barrington, a parliamentary committee-man in Essex, helped to organize the parliamentary effort in that county in 1643.[16] A number of other women, such as Blanche Arundell at Wardour Castle, Charlotte, Countess of Derby at Lathom House, Lady Mary Bankes at Corfe Castle, Lady Brilliana Harley at Brampton Bryan Castle, Lady Anne Savile at Sheffield Castle and the Countess of Portland at Carisbrooke Castle, were responsible, in the absence of their husbands, for defending their homes against attacks and sieges by hostile troops.[17]

If the numbers of women thus involved in the front line of the civil-war

---

[13] Jeremiah Burroughs, *The Glorious Name of God, the Lord of Hosts* (London, 1643), pp. 79–80.
[14] Fraser, *Weaker Vessel*, pp. 180–4.
[15] Ibid., p. 186; Loftis (ed.), *Memoirs of Halket, Fanshawe*, pp. 23–30.
[16] HMC *Appendix to Seventh Report*, pp. 552, 564.
[17] Fraser, *Weaker Vessel*, pp. 163–84; DNB, George Savile (1633–99).

fighting was relatively small, the lives of many hundreds of others were significantly affected by the involvement of their husbands and sons in the conflict. In particular, many wives were subjected to frequent, and sometimes long, separations from husbands who were either actively engaged in fighting elsewhere, or in prison or exile. One immediate and dramatic result of such absences was that a much greater number of women than in the pre-war period were required to shoulder powers and responsibilities relating to the running of the family. Within the landed classes, many wives found themselves in overall control of the family estates, sometimes for a period of years. For most of the period from 1642 to 1644, Sir Robert Harley of Brampton Bryan in Herefordshire was away from home, serving as a Long Parliament MP at Westminster. In his absence, his wife, Lady Brilliana, took charge of the Harley family estate. She undertook her new responsibilities with some trepidation, complaining to her son Edward in 1642 that 'now your father is away, you know I have nobody I can speak to.'[18] She was, none the less, convinced that it was her duty to protect the family's interests, and assured Edward that she had 'no desire that a stranger should come to look to your father's business'.[19] Lady Brilliana's views on the best course of action for the family during these troubled months sometimes differed from those of her husband, nor was she always in agreement with Sir Robert about the best way to organize their affairs. In June 1642, she told him that he would be better advised to borrow money rather than melt down the family plate, on the grounds that the plate might be more valuable at a later date when it was no longer possible to borrow; on another occasion she informed Edward:

> ... and what is done in your father's estate pleases him not, so that I wish myself with all my heart at London, and then your father might be a witness of what is spent; but if your father think it best for me to be in the country, I am well pleased with what he shall think best.[20]

Once actual hostilities had broken out in Herefordshire, Lady Brilliana found her separation from her Parliamentarian husband and isolation in a largely Royalist county increasingly irksome, but, in accordance with Sir Robert's wishes, she resisted the temptation to come to London and remained at Brampton Bryan. She subsequently defended her home

---

[18] T. Taylor Lewis (ed.), *The Letters of Lady Brilliana Harley*, Camden Soc. Publs, 58 (1854), 150–1.
[19] Ibid.
[20] Ibid., p. 167.

against a number of Royalist attacks, but her exertions and anxieties during these months severely taxed her both physically and mentally, and probably contributed substantially to her premature death in 1644.

Similar responsibilities were assumed by Thomas Knyvett's wife Katherine, and by the women of the recusant Blundell household of Crosby Hall in Lancashire. While the Royalist Thomas Knyvett was held in custody by the Parliamentarians at Norwich, Cambridge and Windsor during the first half of the Civil War, Katherine Knyvett was left in control of the family estate at Ashwellthorpe in Norfolk. In March 1642, Sir Thomas wrote to her, assuring her 'I know I cannot have a better steward than thyself to manage our affairs.'[21] Similarly, when the Roman Catholic William Blundell left home to fight for Charles I at the end of 1642, his wife Anne remained at home with her sisters-in-law Winifred and Frances, and was left in sole charge of the family estate and of William's young son Nicholas. Blundell fought for the king until 1645, when, following the crushing defeat of the Royalists at the Battle of Naseby, he took refuge first in Wales and subsequently on the Isle of Man. After a five-year absence, he returned to Crosby in 1647 to find the greater part of his estate sequestered for his recusancy and delinquency. Over the next few years, his residence with his family was further interrupted by frequent bouts of imprisonment. He later described Anne as 'the Ark who hath saved our little cockboat at Crosby from sinking in many a storm', and acknowledged that she had been largely responsible for keeping the family from complete ruin during these years.[22] Two other women who also took upon themselves the running of their husbands' estates, were the wives of the Parliamentarian soldier Luke Lloyd, and the committed republican politician, Sir Henry Vane the younger. Amongst the difficulties Mrs Lloyd encountered was the unwillingness of at least one of her husband's tenants to accept that she had the authority to collect rents; in February 1644, she was forced to write to Luke that 'Thomas Roe questions your man when I send him for your rent, whether I have commission to receive it. I desire he may be satisfied in a line or two, for it comes very slowly from him.'[23] According to his fellow republican, Algernon Sidney, Sir Henry Vane the younger was 'as solicitous for the public good as he was negligent of his own private interest, leaving the care of his domestic affairs entirely to his wife.'[24]

[21] Schofield (ed.), *Knyvett Letters*, p. 110.
[22] M. Blundell (ed.), *Cavalier; The Letters of William Blundell to his Friends* (London, 1933), pp. 10, 54.
[23] HMC *Kenyon MSS*, p. 62.
[24] Rowe, *Sir Henry Vane the Younger*, p. 279.

This role of estate manager could, of course, be assumed by women within the landed classes only, but some women of lower social rank also found greater freedoms and opportunities in the 1640s and 1650s, their principal forum being the radical religious sects which proliferated in England during these years. Women joined the gathered churches of the Independents, Baptists, Quakers and other sects in great numbers, sometimes outnumbering the male members of these congregations. In addition, within some sects they were allowed to take an active role in the organization of church affairs. The radical sectary Katherine Chidley was one of the earliest contributors to the heated literary controversy over the merits of the gathered churches, and other women like Martha Simmonds and Elizabeth Calvert actively supported their husbands' attempts to popularize radical religion in the 1650s and early 1660s.[25] The leaders of the Quaker movement accorded women a full equality with men in church affairs, and Quaker women were allowed to testify during services. In the 1650s, several Quaker meetings for women were established in London, and regular women's monthly meetings spread throughout the country from the 1670s.[26] Some Quakers also offered women an unprecedented freedom in marriage; when the Quaker leader George Fox married Margaret Fell in the late 1660s, he promised that she could retain complete control over her own property.[27] According to the arch-enemy of these radicals, Thomas Edwards, some sectarian women went so far as to argue that it was wrong to attend services conducted by men; Edwards claimed in *Gangraena* that 'there are some women, ten or eleven in one Town or vicinity, who hold it unlawful to hear any man preach either publically or privately, because they must not be like those women in Timothy, ever learning and never coming to knowledge of truth.'[28] As a proportion of the total female population, the numbers of women who joined the sects was small; none the less, for those that did become involved in their activities, the years of civil war and revolution in England must have been a heady experience, and one which could hardly have failed to have had profound repercussions for their families.

The impact of changes in the *mentalité* of societies has always been notoriously difficult to quantify, and any speculation about the effect upon contemporaries of the presentation of such new expectations and possibilities to women can only be tentative. Patricia Crawford and

---

[25] R. L. Greaves and R. Zaller (eds), *A Biographical Dictionary of British Radicals in the Seventeenth Century* (3 vols, Brighton, 1982), vol. 1, pp. 119, 139–40; vol. 3, pp. 175–6.
[26] W. C. Braithwaite, *The Second Period of Quakerism* (London, 1919), pp. 270–2, 286–8.
[27] Hill, *World Turned Upside Down*, p. 252.
[28] Edwards, *Gangraena*, part 1, p. 31.

Lawrence Stone have both argued that one consequence of the wartime dislocation and frequent separations of spouses in England during the 1640s was a marked increase in the amount of writing by women.[29] For most women, any such efforts were restricted to letters written to friends and relatives, but some, like Margaret Cavendish, Duchess of Newcastle, were responsible for more extensive literary productions.[30] According to Patricia Crawford, 69 new works by women were published during the late 1640s, the highest total for any half-decade in the seventeenth century.[31]

Again, both contemporaries and historians have suggested that some women grew more self-sufficient as a result of the war. In 1645, James Strong claimed in his *Joanereidos* that 'to most 'tis known, the weaker vessels are the stronger grown',[32] and Lawrence Stone has argued that, through their new experiences in the 'crucible of war', some women developed 'a strong, if ephemeral sense of independence'. As evidence of a change in attitudes among post-revolutionary women, Stone cites the remarks made by the heroine of Edward Ravenscroft's Restoration comedy *The Careless Lover*, who declares: 'But uncle, it is not now as it was in your young days. Women then were poor, sneaking, sleepish creatures. But in our age, we know our own strength, and have wit enough to make use of our talents.'[33]

If some women did acquire a greater sense of independence and a heightened awareness of their potential as a result of the English Revolution, this could hardly have failed to have had a substantial effect upon their attitude towards marriage, and upon their subsequent relations with their husbands. Dorothy Osborne certainly had strong views about the nature of the marital relationship; rejecting an unwelcome offer of marriage in the early 1650s, she declared of her suitor: 'I could not have flattered him into a belief that I admired him to gain more than he and all his generation are worth.'[34] She also made clear to William Temple, the man she hoped to marry, that she would never allow a husband to destroy her personality or individual 'humour', warning him that:

> ... though it might be reasonably enough expected that I should

---

[29] Stone, *Family, Sex and Marriage*, p. 228; Patricia Crawford, 'Women's Published Writings 1600–1700', in Mary Prior (ed.), *Women in English Society 1500–1800* (London, 1985), pp. 211–82.
[30] *DNB*, Margaret Cavendish (1620?–74).
[31] Crawford, 'Women's Writings', p. 265.
[32] Quoted by Fraser in *Weaker Vessel*, p. 161.
[33] Stone, *Family, Sex and Marriage*, pp. 277, 307.
[34] Hart (ed.), *Letters of Dorothy Osborne*, p. 129.

conform mine to their's, (to my shame be it spoken), I could never do it. And I have lived so long in the world, and so much at my own liberty, that whosoever has me must be content to take me as they find me, without hope of ever making me other than I am.[35]

Within some marriages, tensions were undoubtedly exacerbated by the adoption of new attitudes by wives. The new climate of religious freedom, in particular, was responsible for causing a number of disputes between spouses. During the late 1640s, a woman named Goodsone, who attended John Goodwin's Independent church at Coleman Street in London, became 'aggrieved' that her husband, who was a member of a sectarian congregation in the city led by David Brown and Samuel Chidley, was refusing to 'communicate with her in spiritual worship'. In August 1648, the two churches held a conference to discuss the Goodsones' problems, in the course of which the husband, who was a sea-captain, declared that he could not worship with his wife because he was 'joined to a separated congregation', whereas 'Mr Goodwin's people's practice was to preach and hear in the parish churches of England.'[36] Similarly, one Mr Willis, who was master of a school at Isleworth in Middlesex during the 1640s and 1650s, was a staunch Presbyterian, but was married to a 'furious' Independent. According to one of his pupils, Francis North, the couple's differences 'conjured up a spirit of opposition betwixt them, so that they hated each other more than either the bishops or even papists themselves'. North added that Mrs Willis 'thinking it a sin . . . would scarce let her carnal husband have conjugal intimacy with her'.[37]

An almost inevitable corollary of such marital friction was the calling into question of the husband's right to command his wife. In her *Justification of the Independant Churches of Christ*, published in 1641, Katherine Chidley quoted Christ's comment that 'a man's foes shall be they of his own household' and claimed that husbands had no authority over their wives in religious matters.[38] In the summer of 1652, an itinerant Quaker woman, Jane Holmes, appeared at Malton in Yorkshire and began to denounce the established minister and to hold her own religious services in the fields near the town. Numbers of women soon

---

[35] Ibid.
[36] David Brown, *Two Conferences Between Some of Those that are Called Separatists and Independents* (London, 1650), pp. 9–11 (TT); see also Ian Gentles, 'London Levellers in the English Revolution: The Chidleys and Their Circle', *Journal of Ecclesiastical History*, 29 (1978), 289.
[37] Roger North, *Lives of Francis North, Dudley North and John North*, ed. A. Jessopp (3 vols, London, 1890), vol. 1, p. 16.
[38] Chidley, *The Justification of the Independant Churches*, pp. 25–6.

began to resort to her, sometimes in defiance of their husbands. Thomas Dowsley later complained to the magistrates that, as a result of Jane Holmes's influence, his wife had started to stay out all night and had told him that he had no more authority over her than any other man, and one Major Baildon testified that

> the said Jane hath by delusion drawn the affection of his wife from him, so as he cannot keep her at home for this Jane, but she doth delude and draw her away, and he hath wanted her many days and one night, and often she hath come into his house at unseasonable times at night home; and she sayeth that she ought not to own him any more than any other man; He went to Roger Hebden's house and found the said Jane and his wife amongst a hundred people and he desired his wife to go home and she said she would not go, neither could she go.[39]

The following year, under examination by two of the elders of the Fenstanton Baptist church, the wife of Robert King of Kingston near Caxton in Cambridgeshire, declared that 'she never received anything from the teachings of any man that did stick by her.' The elders further reported that, when asked whether she believed it was her duty to obey her husband, she 'made no pertinent answer, but spake many things which savoured of Rantism.'[40] The new enhanced status for women which the Quaker leaders were advocating also caused some conflict between spouses; in the 1670s, Nathaniel Coleman of Slaughterford in Wiltshire, objected 'in rage and passion' to the idea of separate meetings for women and told George Fox that 'he would rule over his wife.'[41] Some of the gathered congregations also challenged the traditional authority of the husband by interfering in marital disputes. In 1657, the Fenstanton elders rebuked Thomas Bedford for beating his wife in public.[42] When, the following year, they questioned one of their number, Jane Adams, about why she had absented herself from church services, Jane told them that her husband 'would not suffer her' to come; she added that he had sworn an oath that he would prevent her attending, and that 'being minded to seek her place' she was reluctant to force him to break it. The elders responded, however, that, unless her husband forcibly restrained her from attending services, her absence was a 'great

---

[39] Raine (ed.), *Depositions from York Castle*, pp. 55–6; see also Barry Reay, *The Quakers and the English Revolution* (London, 1985), pp. 69–70.
[40] Underhill (ed.), *Fenstanton Records*, p. 73.
[41] Nickalls (ed.), *Journal of George Fox*, pp. 666–7.
[42] Underhill (ed.), *Fenstanton Records*, p. 211.

fault' and a breach of the promise she had made to the congregation. They subsequently held a debate in the church on the question, and the congregation confirmed their ruling that the opposition of a husband was insufficient grounds for absence.[43] In 1663, the neighbouring Baptist church at Warboys excommunicated John Christmas for 'not loving Anne, his wife, as he ought, and for speaking hateful and despising words against her, giving her occasion to depart from him by his unkindness.'[44]

On the eve of the civil war, a radical woman preacher, Joan Bauford of Faversham in Kent, was accused of telling her female audiences that 'husbands, being such as crossed their wives' wills, might lawfully be forsaken.'[45] In a number of cases over the ensuing years, ideological differences did ultimately lead to separations of husbands and wives. Writing in 1648 to her husband Sir Ralph, Mary Verney informed him: 'Your cousin, James Fiennes, and his wife are parted; and they say the reason is because they cannot agree in disputes of conscience, and that she doth not think him holy enough; but, in my opinion, there is very little conscience in [wives] parting from their husbands.'[46]

At Colchester in 1649, John Alexander and Mary Pickis, two members of a local gathered congregation who had been accused of deserting their lawful spouses and living as man and wife, told the Essex magistrates that they had been given to each other by God, and thus no longer considered their marriages valid.[47] In *Gangraena* Thomas Edwards accused two London sectaries, William Jenney and Mrs Attaway, of abandoning their lawful spouses and cohabiting, and claimed that Jenney had justified their action by arguing that 'when a man's wife was not a meet help, he might put her away and take another.'[48] Edwards also asserted that a woman whose Baptist husband had deserted her, had been abused by his fellow sectaries whenever she tried to contact him, and that they had told her 'she is an unbeliever and of the world, what have they to do with her.'[49] One of the Royalist soldiers who had been part of the garrison at Wallingford in Berkshire during the Civil War was accused of deserting his wife under the influence of sectarian ideas, and in 1653 a Quaker woman admitted to the authorities in Yorkshire that she had

---

[43] Ibid., p. 242.
[44] Ibid., p. 278.
[45] *A Discoverie of Six Women Preachers* (London, 1641), p. 4 (TT).
[46] *Verney Memoirs*, vol. 1, pp. 394–5.
[47] Sharpe, *Crime*, p. 68.
[48] Quoted by Thomas in 'Women and the Civil War Sects', p. 50.
[49] Edwards, *Gangraena*, part 3, p. 113.

deserted her 'husband in the flesh', John Williamson, and that she loved John Harwood 'so far as Christ was in him'.[50]

Several other individuals who came under the influence of antinomian ideas also decided that they had received divine commissions for the desertion of their wives. In the late 1640s, William Francklin claimed that God had told him to separate from his wife and to cohabit with Mary Gadbury, the woman whom He had marked out for him. Shortly after meeting Gadbury, Francklin had told her: 'as for the woman, his wife, he owned her so to be his wife while he carried about that body in which he was so joined to her, and he then also owned his children to be the children of that body, but now they were no more to him than any other woman and children.'[51] When Mary Gadbury was later examined by the justices of the peace in Hampshire about her husband, she was reported to have replied that 'she had now no husband according to the flesh, but that her Maker was her husband.'[52] According to the Wiltshire justice, Edward Stokes, another man, whom he referred to as J.O., had under the influence of Ranter opinions deserted his wife and run away to Kent with his neighbour's daughter. John Robins, who shared many of the Ranters' beliefs, was also accused of abandoning his wife and giving his followers permission to change their spouses.[53]

All such ad hoc marital separation occurred despite the continuation of the official ban on divorce. As we have seen, John Milton had campaigned vigorously during the mid-1640s for freer divorce laws, and the introduction of new regulations was discussed by Parliament on a number of occasions during the 1640s and 1650s. In 1653, the members of Barebone's assembly considered incorporating into their Civil Marriage Act a clause making divorce available to husbands and wives on proof of their spouse's adultery; the proposal gained a second reading but was rejected without a division.[54] No subsequent divorce legislation was forthcoming, but it nevertheless remained virtually impossible to prevent desertion and informal separation. In addition, some contemporaries believed that the clause in the Rump's 1650 Adultery Act, which permitted wives whose husbands had deserted them to remarry, was an active encouragement to *de facto* divorce; shortly after the passing of the

---

[50] Humphrey Ellis, *Pseudochristus* (London, 1650), pp. 46–7 (TT); Raine (ed.), *Depositions from York Castle*, p. 64.
[51] Ellis, *Pseudochristus*, p. 11.
[52] Ibid., p. 41.
[53] Edward Stokes, *The Wiltshire Rant* (London, 1652), p. 7 (TT); Hill, *World Turned Upside Down*, p. 253.
[54] *Commons Journal*, vol. 5, p. 478; vol. 6, pp. 211, 263, 274–5, 348; vol. 7, pp. 213, 246, 249; A. Woolrych, *Commonwealth to Protectorate* (Oxford, 1982), p. 291. For Milton's campaign see ch. 2.

Act, the admittedly hostile Royalist newsbook *Mercurius Pragmaticus* declared that the clause was 'a fine, cleanly way of divorce for such who love not their wives, or such wives who will blaze abroad their Husband's deaths, because they love them not; and pretend no knowledge that they are living.'[55] Whether or not the authorities were, therefore, unwittingly to blame for some separations, the numbers of married couples splitting up during these years were sufficient to cause some concern within traditional circles; writing to William Temple in the early 1650s about several conspicuous cases of marital strife and separation, Dorothy Osborne commented: 'What an age do we live in, where 'tis a miracle if, in ten couples that are married, two of them live so as not to publish to the world that they cannot agree.'[56]

Following the Restoration, legislation was considered as a remedy for marital breakdown, the MPs of the Convention Parliament discussing in November 1660 a bill 'for prevention of voluntary separation and living apart of married Persons'. Some MPs appear to have been concerned that numbers of wives had deserted their husbands but continued to make financial demands upon them; in a letter to Sir Richard Leveson dated 10 November 1660, Edward Gower commented: 'This day was a bill brought into the House to provide against women that separate themselves from from their Husbands and after claim alimony, and take up things upon their score. It was, after much debate whether it should be thrown out of the House or no, at last referred to a committee.' The committee reported back to the House at the end of November, but no legislation resulted.[57]

John Milton's own unhappy marriage to Mary Powell, which had undoubtedly been a strong motivation behind his campaign in favour of divorce, did in fact survive, but it was certainly not helped by the political problems of the 1640s. The match seems to have been ill advised from the start; the courtship was rapid, and Mary, who was half the poet's age, appears to have had little in common with her intense and cerebral husband. Nevertheless, the disturbed political environment did nothing to increase their chances of developing a successful relationship. As the Powells were a Royalist family, the poet and his wife were ideologically, as well as temperamentally, incompatible, and only a few weeks after the marriage had taken place Mary deserted her new husband and returned to her parents' home at Forest Hill in Oxfordshire. As Forest Hill was only a few miles from the king's headquarters at Oxford, subsequent

---

[55] *Mercurius Pragmaticus*, 14–21 May 1650 (TT).
[56] Hart (ed.), *Letters of Dorothy Osborne*, p. 120.
[57] *Commons Journal*, vol. 8, pp. 181, 183, 195; HMC *Appendix to Fifth Report*, p. 200.

contact was difficult and the pair hardly communicated during the next two years. In 1645, Mary returned to London and the couple's married life recommenced, but the following year, after their Oxfordshire lands had been sequestered for their Royalism, the rest of the Powell family also came to live with the poet in London. Milton was obliged to accommodate his homeless in-laws for the next two years in his small London house, and to pay the composition fine imposed upon their Oxfordshire lands before they could eventually return home.[58]

In some instances, therefore, the revolutionary events of the years 1640–60 imposed additional strains and tensions upon marriages, and caused animosities and sometimes even marital breakdown. In many other cases, however, these same events either had no noticeable adverse effect, or actually contributed to a strengthening of the marital bond.

Friction and estrangement were not the inevitable results of political and religious disagreements between spouses, for some couples managed to coexist amicably despite deep ideological differences. In 1640, Mrs Hazzard, the wife of an Anglican minister in Bristol, decided to join a radical Baptist congregation in the city. Her desertion from her husband's church caused both her and her husband great anguish and imposed a severe strain upon the marriage, but despite their continuing religious divisions, the couple remained together until the minister's death nearly thirty years later.[59] When the devout Anglican Alice Wandesford was pressurized during the late 1640s into a marriage with the Presbyterian William Thornton of East Newton in Yorkshire, she was initially extremely worried that their divergent religious outlooks would make a good married relationship impossible. However, after she had confronted her prospective husband with her fears and warned him that she had no intention of altering her religious affiliation, Thornton accepted the situation and, as Alice later related in her memoirs, assured her that: 'he was well satisfied with my opinion and religion and all things else concerned me, being much above his hopes, desert or expectation . . . and that I should enjoy my own conscience as I desired.'[60] The marriage subsequently went ahead and proved generally harmonious. In 1652, Margaret Fell and most of her household at Swarthmoor Hall in Cumberland were converted to Quakerism by George Fox while her husband was absent in Wales. On his return, Judge Thomas Fell was understandably shocked and disturbed by the transformation that had come over his family, but despite the fact that his wife's conversion had

[58] Parker, *Milton*, vol. 1, pp. 226–341.
[59] R. Hayden (ed.), *Records of a Church of Christ in Bristol 1640–1687*, Bristol Records Soc. Publs, 27 (1974), 89, 93.
[60] Jackson (ed.), *Autobiography of Alice Thornton*, pp. 78–9.

placed him, as an MP and assize judge, in a particularly embarrassing position, he came to terms with the situation within a few days and the marriage survived. Although he declined to become a Quaker himself, Thomas Fell subsequently gave the group his protection and allowed his house to be used as a centre of their activities.[61]

There are also many examples from the 1640s and 1650s of husbands and wives giving strong and enduring support to each other in the face of great external adversity, and of this joint shouldering of affliction resulting in a deepening of the marital bond. During the Civil War, some wives refused to seek refuge from the fighting and chose instead to remain with their husbands, sometimes in the face of considerable personal danger. When Dorothy Shaw, wife of the Parliamentarian minister, John Shaw of Hull, died in the late 1650s, one published tribute described her as: 'a special help to her husband for saving his life and liberty in these troublesome times, and a cheerful sufferer with him, to the hazarding both of her health, liberty and life in the time of the Wars and since.'[62] Sir Hugh Cholmley's wife Elizabeth remained with her Royalist husband throughout the twelve-month siege of Scarborough Castle, a period during which, according to her husband, she showed 'a courage even above her sex'. When the parliamentary beseigers threatened to put the garrison to the sword if the castle were not surrendered, she told Sir Hugh he must not let her presence affect his reply. She later crossed the north-Yorkshire moors on foot to take possession of the family house at Whitby which had been evacuated by parliamentary troops, and, after spending some months in exile with Sir Hugh on the Continent, she returned to England in 1649 to pay the first instalment of his composition fine. No doubt partly as a result of these exploits, Sir Hugh held Elizabeth in high regard. Imprisoned in Leeds Castle in Kent during the Scottish invasion in 1651, he found 'a great miss of her company', and, after her death in 1655, he was no longer able to live at Whitby, 'being indeed not able to endure the sight of those rooms and places in which I had used to enjoy her company'.[63] Another woman who shared considerable wartime inconvenience with her husband was Sir Richard Fanshawe's wife, Lady Anne; during the 1650s, she followed her Royalist husband into exile on the Continent, enduring constant discomfort and frequent danger as Sir Richard worked for the return of Charles II.[64]

[61] W. C. Braithwaite, *The Beginnings of Quakerism* (Cambridge, 1955 edn), pp. 102–4.
[62] *Mistress Shaw's Tombstone* (London, 1658), pp. 19–20 (TT).
[63] *Cholmley Memoirs*, pp. 42–50.
[64] Loftis (ed.), *Memoirs of Halket, Fanshawe*, pp. 127–40; and see HMC *Marquis of Bath MSS*, vol. 2, p. 89.

Some wives whose husbands had been imprisoned after falling foul of the political authorities joined them in their gaols. When the Leveller leader, John Lilburne, was imprisoned in the Tower of London by the House of Lords in 1646, he was deeply distressed at the prospect of being separated from his wife Elizabeth, and complained to the House of Lords that 'my wife is all the earthly comfort that now in this world I have left unto me', adding that: 'truly, God hath so knit in affection the hearts and souls of me and my wife, and made us so willing to help to bear one another's burdens, that I profess, as in the sight of God, I had rather you should immediately beat out my brains than deprive me of the society of my wife.'[65] As a result of this appeal, Elizabeth was allowed access to her husband some weeks later. Katherine Lunsford also joined her Royalist husband Thomas in the Tower of London between 1645 and 1647,[66] and after Susan Verney had joined her Royalist husband Richard Alport in prison, she informed her brother, Sir Ralph, that 'It is no prison to me. I live as well here as ever I lived anywhere in all my life, and dare compare husbands with her that has the best.'[67] For some months during 1655, the wife of the radical Fifth Monarchist John Rogers was allowed to share her husband's imprisonment in Windsor Castle, and when the pair were subsequently separated, John was deeply upset.[68] According to Samuel Clarke, Margaret Baxter also readily joined her husband Richard in gaol after the Restoration and 'did much to remove the removeable inconveniences of prison'.[69]

Perhaps the highest tribute paid to a wife during these years, however, was that which resulted from Lady Anne Waller's devotion to her husband, Sir William. Waller was arrested by New Model Army soldiers during their purge of Parliament in December 1648, on suspicion of having instigated the Scottish invasion of the previous summer, and for the next three years was kept in custody at Denbigh Castle in north Wales. After discovering his whereabouts, Lady Anne disguised herself and undertook the long and hazardous journey to join her husband, 'thinking it the duty of the wife to risk all things for the satisfaction of her husband'. Sir William later recollected that: 'she seemed, when she discovered herself to me, to be like the Angel who appeared unto Peter in like circumstances; she did not indeed bid my prison gates fly open, but in

---

[65] Gregg, *Free-Born John*, pp. 142–3.
[66] Blaauw, 'Civil War in Sussex', pp. 82–3.
[67] *Verney Memoirs*, vol. 1, p. 425.
[68] E. Rogers, *Some Account of the Life and Opinions of a Fifth Monarchy Man* (London, 1867), pp. 245–6.
[69] Clarke, *Lives of Eminent Persons*, part 2, p. 186.

her sweet converse and behaviour, she made those things seem light which were before heavy, and scarce to be borne.'[70]

In many instances, the assumption by wives of unaccustomed powers and responsibilities led not to increased rivalry and conflict but rather to greater co-operation and mutual appreciation between spouses. One way in which wives could be particularly supportive to their husbands was in assisting their efforts to compound for their sequestered estates. In August 1646, Sir Ralph Verney, who was in exile in France, was informed by his neighbour, Dr Denton, that it was becoming a common practice to send wives to negotiate with the parliamentary composition committee at Goldsmiths' Hall in London; Denton assured him that 'women have never been as useful as now', and added:

> though you should be my agent and solicitor of all the men I know . . . yet I am confident, if you were here, you would do as our sages do, instruct your wife and leave her to act it with the committees; their sex entitles them to many privileges and we find the comfort of them more now than ever.[71]

Many instances of women taking a prominent role in composition cases could be cited; among some of the most active on their husbands' behalfs were Anne Fanshawe, Margaret Cavendish, Mary Verney and Isabella Twysden. In 1646, Sir Richard Fanshawe, who was in attendance upon the Prince of Wales in the Channel Islands, sent his wife, Lady Anne, to England to initiate his composition proceedings. Anne took lodgings in Fleet Street and, with the help of a Parliamentarian contact of the family, obtained permission for Sir Richard to come to England to compound. She later told her son that 'this was the first time that I had taken any journey without your father, and the first manage to business he ever put into my hand.'[72] Presumably impressed by her success, Sir Richard sent Anne back to England from the Continent on several subsequent occasions to obtain money. Later, when Sir Richard was imprisoned following the battle of Worcester in 1651, Anne successfully pleaded with Cromwell for his release on bail, on the grounds of his ill health.[73]

When Margaret Cavendish, Duchess of Newcastle, returned to England from the Continent in the early 1650s in an attempt to secure a

---

[70] William Waller, *Recollections*, printed as an appendix to H. Cowley (ed.), *The Poetry of Anna Mathilda* (London, 1788), pp. 164–5.
[71] *Verney Memoirs*, vol. 1, p. 342.
[72] Loftis (ed.), *Memoirs of Halket, Fanshawe*, p. 119.
[73] Ibid., pp. 122, 135, 140.

fifth of her husband's confiscated estate for her own maintenance, she too found that women had become 'pleaders, attornies, petitioners and the like, running about with their several causes'; she remained in the country for eighteen months before admitting defeat and returning to her husband in Antwerp.[74] Although pregnant, Mary Verney also returned to England in late 1646 and, after more than a year of negotiation, she finally obtained an order for the lifting of the sequestration upon her husband's lands.[75] In the early 1640s, Sir Roger Twysden of Roydon Hall in Kent was imprisoned and had his lands sequestered for petitioning Parliament for the retention of bishops. His wife, Lady Isabella, whom he described as 'a wise and temperate solicitrix', was left alone with the task of recovering the family estate which, according to Sir Roger, involved her in 'unspeakable trouble, vexation and charge'. She became embroiled in a series of jurisdictional disputes between the Goldsmiths' Hall committee and the local sequestration committee, and was obliged to make constant journeys between London and Kent to argue her case. On one occasion, she rose from her bed just a few days after giving birth and journeyed on horseback to London to protest against the local committee's proposal to cut down much of the timber on the family's estate. As a result of these exertions on his behalf, Sir Roger held Isabella in great esteem; he later commented in his journal that when he had on occasions expressed regret at the trouble he had caused her, she had replied that 'she would endure much more for my sake.'[76]

Other wives laboured tirelessly on behalf of impoverished or imprisoned husbands. As a result of his support for Parliament, the London merchant Daniel Searle suffered heavy losses during the early stages of the Civil War, and was subsequently forced to abandon his family and leave the country to avoid his creditors. After spending three years putting his case before Parliament, his wife Mary eventually succeeded in 1648 in obtaining some financial help for the family.[77] When Sir John Oglander of Nunwell on the Isle of Wight was imprisoned in London in 1644, his wife obtained his release by 'mediation and solicitation', and when, to her husband's great sorrow, she died soon afterwards of smallpox, Sir John was convinced that the illness was the result of her 'overheating her blood in procuring my liberty'.[78] After the failure of Sir

---

[74] Margaret Cavendish, *The Life of William Cavendish, Duke of Newcastle*, ed. C. H. Firth, (London, 1886 edn), pp. 298–300, 304.
[75] *Verney Memoirs*, vol. 1, pp. 345–98.
[76] 'The Journal of Sir Roger Twysden', part 4, pp. 137–201.
[77] *Cal. Com. Advance Money*, vol. 2, p. 714.
[78] Bamford (ed.), *A Royalist's Notebook*, p. 107.

John Penruddock's western rising in 1655, his wife Lady Arundell mounted a vigorous campaign on behalf of her condemned husband, and travelled to London to plead in vain with Cromwell for his life.[79] Another Royalist wife, Elizabeth Mordaunt, was more successful than Arundell Penruddock; when her husband John, Viscount Mordaunt, was imprisoned and put on trial for his life in 1658 for plotting against Cromwell, she was tireless in her efforts to save his life. She advised John not to antagonize his captors by disputing their authority and organized the escape of a vital prosecution witness, and as a result was largely responsible for his eventual acquittal.[80] When the Parliamentarian John Hutchinson was imprisoned after the Restoration, at first in the Tower of London and later in Kent, his wife Lucy also campaigned vigorously for his release or for an improvement in his prison conditions.[81]

In 1659, shortly after Elizabeth Mordaunt had secured her husband's acquittal, Edward Hyde wrote to her, expressing his hope that 'God will preserve you from all sorts of enemies and that you will long enjoy each other, with a comfortable and a pleasant remembrance of the killing fears, apprehensions and separations you have passed through, and even mastered by an unexampled courage.'[82] In suggesting that a frequent consequence of spouses offering each other strong mutual support in the face of external difficulties was the creation of deeper and more appreciative marital relationships, Hyde was undoubtedly correct. There is, in addition, little doubt that the hearts of many husbands and wives living in England during these years also grew fonder as a result of the frequent separations occasioned by the war and its aftermath. Embroiled in the disturbing events of the early months of the Long Parliament, the MP Thomas Knyvett wrote in early 1641 to his wife who was at home in Norfolk, telling her that he wished that they could retire to 'a little house by ourselves ... where we may spend the remainder of our days in religious tranquil';[83] and when Sir Roger Twysden was imprisoned at the start of the Civil War, he wrote to his wife that he 'never knew what it was to be parted from you till now.'[84] In 1642, George Coke, Bishop of Hereford, spent some months in prison in the Tower of London; in May, he wrote to a relative about his fears for his wife, who was in poor health and facing problems from their children which, he declared 'she cannot

---

[79] W. W. Ravenhill, 'Records of the Rising in the West A.D. 1655', *Wiltshire Archaeological Magazine*, 13–15 (1872–5): 13, 132; 14, 62–5.

[80] M. Coate (ed.), *The Letter Book of John, Viscount Mordaunt 1658–1660*, Camden Soc. Publs, 3rd Series, 69 (1945), xi.

[81] *Hutchinson Memoirs*, pp. 352–82.

[82] Coate (ed.), *Letter Book of John Mordaunt*, p. 101.

[83] Schofield (ed.), *Knyvett Letters*, p. 98.

[84] Bennitt (ed.), 'Diary of Isabella Twysden', p. 114.

so well wield alone as by my help, and which I fear is a great occasion of her sickness.' He added that his wife was 'the only stay and support of that whole poor family, which, without her, I can by no other well wield.'[85]

The particularly acute anxiety felt by some wives whose husbands were actively involved in the civil-war fighting is revealed in some of the correspondence and memoirs which have survived from the war years. In February 1644, Mrs Lloyd wrote to her Parliamentarian husband, begging him: 'as thou tenders the life of thy poor desolate wife', to return home.[86] Similarly, although the Essex clergyman Ralph Josselin spent only very brief periods away from his family while serving as an army chaplain during 1645, his wife was also deeply disturbed by his absences. After his return to Earls Colne in June 1645, he commented in his diary: 'abundance of love made my wife grieve, for which I must the more respect and love her'; and coming home in September, he found her 'indifferent cheerful, only in my absence she was wondrous sad and discontented.'[87] The letters written by Elizabeth Feilding to her husband, Basil Feilding, Earl of Denbigh, who fought for parliament throughout the civil war, are especially touching. The couple were married in July 1641, and had thus been together for only a year before Basil left home in the summer of 1642. During the early months of the war, Elizabeth sent Basil a stream of increasingly impassioned and desperate letters, in which she repeatedly enquired after his welfare and pleaded with him to visit her. She also referred constantly to her great love for him and her 'disquiet' at his absence, exclaiming in one letter: 'You cannot imagine what I would give to see you. If I had you, to gain ten thousand worlds you should not go from me. Oh, dear God, what would I give to see you, for God's sake, write to me and come as soon as may be.'[88]

Across the top of another letter, in which she obviously felt she had expressed her feelings too strongly, she wrote: 'I am transported with grief, I know not what I wrote.'[89] By 1644, Elizabeth was beginning to worry that the enforced separation might be damaging their relationship, and in one letter written to Basil while he was at London, she remarked: 'I know in London you may have many mistresses to please your fancy which far surpass me', adding later: 'dear heart, pardon my ill-longing, for this is the first letter I ever writ in this way.'[90] Several months later, in

---

[85] HMC *Cowper MSS*, vol. 2, p. 315.
[86] HMC *Kenyon MSS*, p. 62.
[87] Macfarlane (ed.), *Josselin Diary*, pp. 41, 45.
[88] WRO Feilding Family MSS CR. 2107, C2, lett.152. The whole collection is at CR. 2107, C2, letters 149–71.
[89] Ibid., lett. 150.
[90] Ibid., lett. 166.

early July 1644, she wrote to him again to ask whether he would be able to return home for their third wedding anniversary, telling him:

> I should have been glad to have been with you the 8th July, because it is our wedding day, but, if it be not my good fortune to attain that happiness, my Lady Su. Hambleton and I will have three cherry pies and drink your health and think of you all day long and wish myself with you . . . I desire to live chiefly because I love thee, and to enjoy thy dear company.[91]

While engaged during the autumn of 1643 in the siege of Gloucester, Henry Spencer, the Royalist Earl of Sunderland, wrote a number of times to his wife Dorothy; on 25 August, he told her that her recent letter which he had received as he was coming out of the trenches 'gave me so much satisfaction, that it put all the inconveniences of the siege out of my thoughts'; he added that their corrrespondence was 'the most pleasant entertainment that I am capable of in any place; but especially here, where, but when I am in the trenches . . . I am more solitary than ever I was in my life.' He concluded the letter by telling Dorothy: 'how infinitely more happy I should esteem myself quietly to enjoy your company at Althorp, than to be troubled with the noises and engaged in the actions of the Court, which I shall ever endeavour to avoid.'[92] A few weeks later, he was killed during the first Battle of Newbury. When Sir Richard Fanshawe was sent from Oxford to Bristol on the king's business in March 1645, the prospect of separation from his new wife who had just given birth to their first child, caused him great distress. Lady Anne Fanshawe later recalled that

> as . . . it was the first time we had parted a day since we married, he was extremely afflicted even to tears, though passion was against his nature. But the sense of leaving me with a dying child, which did die two days after, in a garrison town, extreme weak, and very poor, were such circumstances as he could not bear with . . . And, for my part, it cost me dear, that I was ten weeks before I could go alone.[93]

During the late 1640s and early 1650s, Sir Richard Fanshawe's activities in support of the defeated Royalist cause continued to keep him apart from Anne for long periods, and consequently to cause her great anxiety;

---

[91] Ibid., lett. 168.
[92] Cartwright, *Sacharissa*, pp. 94–5, 99.
[93] Loftis (ed.), *Memoirs of Halket, Fanshawe*, p. 114.

following the defeat of Charles II's forces at the Battle of Worcester in 1651, Anne claimed she 'neither ate nor slept, but trembled at every motion', until she had heard news that, although he had been captured, he was safe.[94]

For many others too, separations continued beyond the ending of the fighting in 1646. During the time she was residing in London in an attempt to organize her husband's composition, Mary Verney clearly missed Sir Ralph deeply. When she heard in January 1647 of his plans to move to another French town, she wrote to him:

> ... believe me my dear heart, so I have but thy company, I care not in what town it is, or whether I have any other company or not. For if it please God to bring me to thee again, I assure thee it should be a very strange occasion could ever make me go from thee again ... for, truly my heart, I find myself very unable to bear such a separation ... I am most impatient to be with thee for, though everybody here is very jolly, yet I never had so sad a time in all my life.[95]

Similarly, Margaret Cavendish claimed that her separation from her husband, the Duke of Newcastle, during the early 1650s, when she too was petitioning the parliamentary authorities for the return of some of their confiscated property, made her mind 'so restless as it did break my sleep and distemper my health'.[96] Edward Hyde, who travelled extensively through France and Spain in the service of the exiled Charles II during the late 1640s and 1650s, also corresponded regularly with his wife, who had remained at Antwerp. When she wrote in the autumn of 1649 that she had heard reports that he was to be based at Madrid for the next three years, he replied that the rumour was untrue, but added that

> I wish with all my heart it were true, for if it were, upon my life, I would not stir from this place till thou camest to me, and we would learn Spanish together; and be confident, if I find myself at any time fixed in one place for a third of that time, I will not live without thee.[97]

In another letter from Madrid in March 1650, Hyde temporarily abandoned his political aspirations and declared to his wife: 'I have no

---

[94] Ibid., p. 134; see also pp. 121, 133, 135–6.
[95] *Verney Memoirs*, vol. 1, p. 351.
[96] Cavendish, *Life of William Cavendish*, p. 304.
[97] HMC *Marquis of Bath MSS*, vol. 2, p. 83.

ambition, but to be with thee, and to live and die with thee in any condition.'[98]

Any precise evaluation of the impact of war and revolution upon the nature of married life in mid-seventeenth-century England is, then, extremely difficult to make. As we have seen, the abnormal events of these years produced a wide variety of different responses. Many couples, especially those within the lower orders who managed to avoid involvement in the quarrels within landed society, were able to a large degree to insulate themselves from any unusual external developments which might have altered the nature of their married lives. The relationships of some other married couples were clearly damaged by the added pressures of ideological discord and economic dislocation. Others again, however, responded to the new hazards and uncertainties of the revolutionary environment by turning all the more to their spouses for support and solace, and many of these found that their husbands and wives could be sources of great comfort, and their homes welcome refuges from the vagaries of public life. While for some, therefore, the pressures of political and religious upheaval weakened the marital relationship, for many others a greater appreciation of the importance and benefits of family life was a lasting legacy of their experience of revolution.

[98] Ibid., vol. 2, p. 88; see also pp. 80, 82, 84, 86–7, 92.

6
Parents and Children

Another sphere of family life which was substantially affected by the revolutionary upheavals of the mid seventeenth century was the pivotal relationship between parents and their children. This generational nexus, as fundamental to the family as the bond between husbands and wives, came under pressure from forces which challenged it at every stage in its development, from pregnancy and childbirth to the growing emancipation and eventual independence of the adolescent child. Wartime dislocations increased the already extreme risks faced by women in childbirth, and revolutionary Puritan governments were responsible for introducing major changes to the long-established religious rite of baptism, by which a new child was formally accepted into the Christian community. The widespread dissemination during the revolutionary years of a wide range of conflicting political and religious beliefs enhanced the likelihood of ideological conflict between parents and their older children, and, in addition, the assault upon the patriarchal authority of the father of the state, Charles I, may have led some children to question the absolute authority of their own natural fathers. However, if within some families the potential for discord was heightened by the events of the revolution, within others these same disturbing events appear to have led to a greater appreciation of the mutual solace inherent in the symbiosis of parent and child.

Pregnancy and childbirth were experiences extremely familiar to most married women in early-modern England, for it was not uncommon for a wife to spend a large part of her fertile years pregnant and to give birth to seven or more children. The familiarity of such events, however, did little to lessen the extreme dangers which they presented for women. Throughout the early-modern period, the primitive state of obstetric knowledge rendered any abnormal pregnancy or delivery potentially fatal for both mother and child, and parturitional complications were a major cause of both infant and female mortality. No political developments could, of course, have any decisive impact upon this essentially medical problem, but there is some evidence to suggest that the disruptions which the Civil War brought to England during the 1640s may have added to the risks involved in these already hazardous ordeals, rendering them both more frightening and more physically exhausting.

Among the factors that increased the risks involved in pregnancy and childbirth were the anxieties created by political uncertainty, the shouldering of additional burdens and responsibilities by women who were pregnant or had recently given birth, the more frequent absences during pregnancy and labour of husbands and midwives, and the unsuitable environments in which some were forced to give birth. Lucy Hutchinson attributed the physical weakness of her eldest daughter born in 1642, and the child's subsequent death at the age of only three, to her own and her nurse's 'griefs and frights in those troublesome times'.[1] She also related in her memoirs how, when the quarter-master of the parliamentary forces in Nottingham Castle came under investigation by the local parliamentary committee in 1644, his pregnant wife was so alarmed that she suffered a miscarriage from which she almost died.[2] Mary Springett, the wife of the Sussex gentleman Thomas Springett, also believed that her health had been adversely affected during her pregnancy in the autumn of 1643 by her anxieties over the safety of her husband, who was serving as a Parliamentarian soldier, and that it improved dramatically after she had heard that he had survived the first Battle of Newbury. The threats to this particular pregnancy, however, did not end there. Several months later, when Thomas was taken seriously ill at Arundel Castle, Mary undertook a hazardous midwinter journey to join him, during the course of which she was subjected to a throw from her coach into a ditch, a boat trip through flooded countryside and a walk of several miles. When she reached Arundel, she sat with Thomas for forty-eight hours despite the risk of infection. Shortly after her arrival, Thomas died from his illness, but, perhaps surprisingly, Mary and her child both survived.[3]

Throughout her pregnancy in the middle of the Civil War, Lady Isabella Twysden was engaged in strenuous efforts to secure the lifting of the sequestration on the lands of her imprisoned husband, Sir Roger Twysden. In the course of her negotiations with the parliamentary authorities, she was obliged to make frequent journeys between London and Kent and was

[1] *Hutchinson Memoirs*, p. 100.
[2] Ibid., p. 206.
[3] Blaauw, 'Civil War in Sussex', pp. 69–70, 373.

subjected to long delays by unsympathetic parliamentary committees. Her husband, Sir Roger, later commented that, perhaps as a result of 'her many journeys on my errands' or of 'an unhappy midwife', she experienced 'a very ill time after being delivered and indeed never recovered her former strength during all her life'.[4] Another Royalist spouse whose pregnancies were made more dangerous by wartime exigencies was Lady Anne Fanshawe. While pregnant in 1645, she journeyed to the Isles of Scilly and Jersey with her husband Sir Richard, who was in attendance upon the Prince of Wales, arriving 'almost dead' after a rough crossing. She was again pregnant in 1649 when she was caught up in a disturbance in Cork in Ireland and was forced to walk 10 miles on foot to rejoin Sir Richard at Kinsale. Although pregnant for much of the 1650s too, she continued to accompany her husband on his travels on the Continent in the service of the Stuarts. The frequent discomfort and dangers they faced on these journeys may have contributed to the early deaths of several of her children; in a sad aside in her memoirs, she later noted that she had buried children in Lisbon, Madrid and Paris, as well as Oxford, Yorkshire, Hertfordshire and Kent.[5]

In 1646, a pregnant Mary Verney was forced to leave her husband, Sir Ralph, in France and to travel alone to London to treat with the parliamentary Committee for Compounding. She later wrote to Sir Ralph, telling him that 'to lie[-in] without thee is a greater affliction than I fear I shall be able to bear.'[6] In 1645, the parliamentary authorities refused the imprisoned Royalist Sir Lewis Dives permission to visit his wife who was about to give birth; both mother and child later died during the delivery, and the Royalist newsbook *Mercurius Academicus* subsequently blamed the king's opponents for the deaths, claiming that Lady Dives had become convinced that she would die unless she saw her husband before her confinement.[7] Wartime dislocation also deprived some women of the services of midwives. In 1644, the parliamentary forces besieging Sheffield Castle refused to allow a midwife to pass through their lines to attend Lady Anne Savile, the pregnant widow of the governor, Sir William Savile, who had died some weeks before. Notwithstanding, Lady Anne refused to surrender the castle and held out until August, when a mutiny among the garrison's soldiers forced her to capitulate. Her child was born the following day.[8] In addition, because

[4] 'Journal of Sir Roger Twysden', part 4, p. 146.
[5] Loftis (ed.), *Memoirs of Halket, Fanshawe*, pp. 107, 118–24.
[6] Quoted by Fraser in *Weaker Vessel*, p. 218.
[7] H. G. Tibbutt (ed.), *The Life and Letters of Sir Lewis Dives 1599–1669*, Bedfordshire Historical Records Soc. Publs, 27 (1946), 80–1.
[8] *DNB*, Sir George Savile (1633–99).

some pregnant women had joined their imprisoned husbands in gaol during these years, a number of children were born in prison, and several were given christian names which testified to their inauspicious beginnings; two of John and Elizabeth Lilburne's children were born in the Tower of London, one of them being named Tower, and when the wife of the Fifth Monarchist John Rogers gave birth in Windsor Castle in 1655, the parents named the child Prisonborn.[9]

Not even those of the very highest social rank were able to avoid the added childbirth complications which the war created. In April 1644, when a parliamentary siege of the Royalist headquarters at Oxford appeared imminent, a pregnant Queen Henrietta Maria was forced to leave her husband and journey to Bath and then Exeter in an attempt to find a safe place for her confinement. Charles I meanwhile sent an urgent note to her former physician, Sir Theodore Mayerne, who was living in retirement at London, imploring him 'pour l'amour de moi, allé trouver ma Femme.' Mayerne and another doctor, Sir Matthew Lister, reached Exeter just in time, and in mid June, after a very difficult and painful delivery, the queen gave birth to a daughter, Henrietta Anne.[10] Several weeks later, however, with the Earl of Essex's parliamentary army marching westwards towards her, she was forced to leave the child at Exeter and flee into Cornwall. Francis Bassett, who saw her at this time, commented in a letter to his wife: 'Here is the woefullest spectacle my eyes ever looked on, the most worn and weak pitiful creature in the world, the poor queen shifting for an hours life longer.'[11]

Describing in her autobiography how her sister, Lady Danby, had died during the Civil War several months after giving birth to her sixteenth child, Alice Thornton blamed the fatality upon an unfortunate combination of the above circumstances, stating:

> The troubles and distractions of those sad times did much afflict and grieve her, who was of a tender and sweet disposition, wanting the company of her husband, Sir Thomas, to manage his estate and other concerns. But he, being engaged in his king's service was not permitted to leave it, nor come to Thorpe but seldom, til she fell sick. These things, added to the horrid rudeness of the soldiers and Scots quartered then among them which, vexing and troubling her much with frights, caused her to fall into travail sooner than she expected,

---

[9] Fraser, *Weaker Vessel*, p. 267; Rogers, *Life and Opinions of a Fifth Monarchy Man*, pp. 245, 331–2. I owe the first reference to Peter Hammond.
[10] Patrick Morrah, *A Royal Family; Charles I and His Family* (London, 1982), pp. 77–8.
[11] Quoted by Cecilia, Countess of Denbigh in *Royalist Father and Roundhead Son*, p. 235.

nor could she get her old midwife, being then in Richmond, which was shut up for the plague was exceeding great there.[12]

In the absence of comprehensive and reliable registration data from the seventeenth century, it is difficult to estimate how widespread such misfortunes were, or to what extent the confused and disturbing political climate of the period 1640–60 dissuaded couples from bringing children into the world. As the civil-war fighting was localized and sporadic in nature, the pregnancies of many thousands of women would have remained virtually unaffected by the conflict, and from her study of the effects of the war upon the women of the Buckinghamshire Verney family, Miriam Slater has concluded that there is little evidence to suggest that 'any of the principals of childbearing age retreated from parenthood'.[13] She has also pointed out, however, that when Nathaniel Hobart's wife Anne found that she was to have a child in 1645, her husband reacted to the news by commenting that it was an 'unseasonable blessing', and the reaction of another relative was to remark to Mary Verney: 'God hath blest you in keeping you so long without one.'[14] At the beginning of April 1645, Ralph Josselin referred in his diary to the additional hazards of wartime pregnancy, remarking:

> My wife was now even confident she was breeding and supposed it a daughter, the Lord give us thankful contented spirits, the times, our neglected condition in the town, and the ruinous coldness of our house, and the time of year in the depth of winter are some discouragements, but God's mercy is above all these.[15]

In addition, several pamphlets published in London during the war years suggested that the capital's midwives were complaining about a decline in their trade, and that the war had left London 'thin of people'.[16]

In an attempt to form a more general picture, we must turn again to the computer calculations of Wrigley and Schofield, outlined in their *Population History of England 1541–1871*. These suggest that, although the level of fertility in England did not decline as an immediate consequence of the civil-war hostilities, it did fall sharply between 1646 and 1651 and remained at an abnormally low level for the next three

---

[12] Jackson (ed.), *Autobiography of Alice Thornton*, pp. 49–50.
[13] Slater, *Family Life*, pp. 123–4.
[14] Ibid.
[15] Macfarlane (ed.), *Josselin Diary*, p. 37.
[16] *The Midwives' Just Petition* (London, 1643), unpag. (TT); and see Fraser, *Weaker Vessel*, pp. 440–1.

decades. From a pre-war average of 158,732 births per annum in the period from 1630 to 1642, the average annual total actually rises slightly to 166,397 during the civil-war years, but then drops to an average figure of 144,877 per annum for the period between 1647 and 1660.[17] Wrigley and Schofield admit that this apparent drop in fertility in the post-civil-war period might simply be a result of the greater imperfections of the registration records during the revolutionary period, but point out that the low levels persist beyond the Restoration in 1660 when the records once more improve. Their tentative conclusion is that there was a real fall in fertility, occasioned by a later age of marriage and increased male emigration; these are developments which may, in turn, have been encouraged by the war-induced economic depression of the late 1640s, and the continuing political uncertainty of the 1650s.

For the vast majority of the many thousands of men and women who did bring children into the world during the middle decades of the seventeenth century, it was extremely important that the new member of their family should be received into the Christian community at an early age through the ceremony of baptism. A central rite of the Christian church throughout its history, baptism had been one of the few Catholic sacraments retained by the Protestant reformers of the early sixteenth century, but, in the century following the Reformation, considerable debate and conflict had arisen within the European Protestant churches over the exact form the rite should take. There was, in particular, a great deal of controversy about whether the sacrament should be administered to young children or delayed until adulthood, when those receiving it could testify to their own conscious desire to join the Christian church. Radical 'Anabaptist' groups which advocated the latter approach were viewed as extremely subversive of both the ecclesiastical and secular order and were ruthlessly persecuted throughout Europe.

During the period 1560–1640, small groups of English men and women also began to reject infant baptism in favour of the baptism of adult believers. The first English Baptist church was established at Spitalfields in London in 1612, by a group of religious radicals who had returned to England from exile in Amsterdam, and during the next few years other Baptist churches were founded in a number of provincial towns. The Baptist movement later became divided over the doctrine of predestination; the Particular Baptists upheld the Calvinist view of the existence of immutable groups of the saved and the damned, while the General Baptists acknowledged the possibility of a general salvation. On

---

[17] Wrigley and Schofield, *Population History*, pp. 229–33, 497–8, 528. The totals are my averages from their yearly figures.

the eve of the Civil War, the Particular Baptists decided that, in order to symbolize the death and rebirth of the recipient, adult believers' baptism should involve total immersion.[18]

Such extreme opinions were confined to a small radical minority, but these same years also witnessed a protracted controversy within the established English church over the exact form that the sacrament of the baptism of infants should take. The 1552 *Book of Common Prayer*, published at the height of the radical Protestant reforms of Edward VI's reign, contained a new baptismal service which dispensed with a number of features of the Roman Catholic ceremony, such as the exorcism of the devil and the anointing of the child with chrism. This 1552 ceremony provided the model for the baptismal service which was included in Elizabeth I's 1559 Prayer Book, the liturgical basis of the established church for the following eighty years, but elements of Puritan opinion remained firmly opposed to certain aspects of the Anglican ceremony. Some Puritans believed that, in order to make the rite as public as possible, baptisms should be carried out at the front of the church before the whole congregation, rather than at the font. Others objected to the participation of godparents, or 'gossips', believing that their involvement encouraged the abdication of parental responsibility. Opposition to the use of the 'popish' sign of the cross was also widespread, and in 1604 the conservative Archbishop of Canterbury, Richard Bancroft, felt it necessary to include a lengthy justification of the practice in his ecclesiastical canons.[19]

After the outbreak of the Civil War in 1642, the controversy over whether young children should be baptized assumed considerable prominence. In the freer publishing environment of the revolutionary years, many of the rival theorists found it relatively easy to discuss their views in print, and well over a hundred tracts dealing with the topic of infant baptism were collected by the London bookseller, George Thomason, during the 1640s and 1650s.[20] Debate between the supporters and opponents of child baptism was often acrimonious, with conservative writers such as Daniel Featley and Thomas Edwards accusing the 'Dippers' of a wide range of subversive opinions and practices.[21] According to Edwards, at Yaxley in Huntingdonshire in the 1640s a

---

[18] Michael Watts, *The Dissenters* (Oxford, 1978), vol. 1, pp. 7, 13, 44–5, 49–50, 65–6. For the early Baptists, see also B. R. White, *The English Baptists of the Seventeenth Century* (London, 1983), *passim*.

[19] S. B. Babbage, *Puritanism and Richard Bancroft* (London, 1962), pp. 84–5.

[20] For a list of these titles see G. K. Fortescue (ed.), *A Catalogue of Pamphlets, Books . . . Collected by George Thomason 1640–1661* (2 vols, London, 1908), vol. 2, pp. 468–71.

[21] Edwards, *Gangraena*, parts 1–3, *passim*; and Daniel Featley, *The Dippers Dipped* (London, 1645), *passim* (TT).

group of parliamentary soldiers forcibly prevented the baptism of a child, and subsequently urinated in the font and enacted the mock baptism of a horse.[22] The anonymous author of the pamphlet *Bloody News From Dover*, which appeared in 1647, even claimed, rather implausibly, that an Anabaptist mother from Dover, who had quarrelled with her husband over whether their child should be baptized, had actually cut off the infant's head and presented it to him, declaring that he could baptize the head without the body. The author's propaganda purpose was revealed in the comment, 'Thus may we see that, where division and controversy doth arise, sad effects will suddenly follow.'[23] The issue also appears to have been widely discussed at a local level; the Essex minister Ralph Josselin held a number of conferences and discussion meetings on the topic in the late 1640s and early 1650s with both his parishioners and other local clergymen, and in February 1652 he took part in a public disputation on the issue with Robert Nichols, a Quaker from a neighbouring parish.[24] Richard Baxter was also involved in a similar day-long discussion with a Quaker about baptism before 'a crowded congregation' at Kidderminster in the 1650s.[25]

As the 1640s progressed, a small, but growing, number of English men and women were persuaded by the arguments of the Anabaptists and decided not to baptize their children. When John and Lucy Hutchinson were considering baptism for their child born in 1646, they consulted both the Bible and a number of local ministers before deciding not to proceed with the ceremony. As a result of their decision, they were reviled as fanatics and Anabaptists by their fellow worshippers who, according to Lucy, 'conceived implaccable malice against them upon this account.'[26] Despite such violent conservative opposition, hundreds of other sectarian parents subsequently joined the Hutchinsons in their repudiation of child baptism. In 1654, the radical sectary, John Webster, told one gathered congregation in London that child baptism was a Satanic ordinance, and that salvation could not be won through 'washings, nor disciplines nor any external rules'.[27] Infant baptism was also totally rejected during the 1650s by the rapidly growing Quaker movement, which regarded it as a 'Babylonish and heathenish' ordinance.[28]

Those parents who rejected child baptism always remained a small minority, but within the much larger group which continued to approve

---

[22] Quoted by Watts in *Dissenters*, p. 114.
[23] *Bloody News From Dover* (London, 1647), unpag. (TT).
[24] Macfarlane (ed.), *Josselin Diary*, pp. 101, 105, 109–10, 122, 271.
[25] *Reliquiae Baxterianae*, p. 96.
[26] *Hutchinson Memoirs*, pp. 242–3.
[27] Quoted by Watts in *Dissenters*, p. 184.
[28] Ibid., p. 192.

of the sacrament, pre-war disagreements over the way the service should be conducted continued and intensified. When the wife of the Sussex landowner, Thomas Springett, gave birth to a child in 1642, her husband refused to allow the midwife who had attended the delivery to recite the usual formal prayers: several days later, he took the child to a Puritan preacher who baptized it in the presence of a number of 'the professing people round about'. His wife later claimed that Thomas had been the 'first of quality' in Sussex not to nominate godparents for his child, and that his decision to present it himself had caused 'much gazing and wonderment'.[29] Three years later in 1645, the *Directory of Public Worship*, which contained the liturgy of the new Presbyterian state church which Parliament intended to impose upon the country, outlined a simplified baptismal service reformed in line with the long-standing Puritan objections to the Anglican ceremony. The new Presbyterian service was to be carried out by a minister as soon as was convenient after the child's birth, and was to take place at the front of the church, 'where the people may most conveniently see and hear', rather than 'in the places where Fonts in the time of Popery were unfitly and superstitiously placed'. The sign of the cross and a number of the Anglican prayers were dispensed with, and the minister was enjoined to sprinkle water on the infant's face 'without adding any other ceremony'. Godparents were also outlawed, the child being presented for baptism by its father.[30]

This service remained the official form of baptism until the Restoration. When Lady Isabella Twysden's sister-in-law gave birth to a daughter in September 1647, it was christened the same afternoon 'without gossips, the new way', and Lady Isabella referred in her diary to several subsequent christenings which were also conducted according to the Presbyterian format.[31] At Crondall in Hampshire in 1648, in order to comply with the new regulations, the parishioners built a small marble font at the front of the church to replace the 'polluted papist font'.[32] After the birth of Ralph Josselin's first child, Mary, on the eve of the Civil War in April 1642, four witnesses attended her christening, and the celebrations after the service cost Josselin more than £6. Similarly, the baptism of his second child, Thomas, in January 1644 was attended by two witnesses. After the publication of the *Directory*, however, Josselin

---

[29] H. Dixon (ed.), 'An Original Account of the Springett Family', *Gentleman's Magazine*, 36 (1851), 367.
[30] Firth and Rait (eds), *Acts and Ordinances*, vol. 1, pp. 594–6.
[31] Bennitt (ed.), 'Diary of Isabella Twysden', pp. 121, 127, 132.
[32] Fearon and Williams (eds), *Parish Registers*, p. 68.

began to use the new service. In August 1645, he had his first experience of officiating at a baptism where a child was presented by its father, and thereafter, when recording in his diary instances of baptisms at Earls Colne during the remainder of the 1640s and 1650s, he made no mention of the involvement of witnesses or godparents.[33]

Nevertheless, like many of the other requirements of the *Directory*, the new baptismal service was by no means universally observed. Throughout the 1640s and 1650s, some parents remained attached to the Anglican rite and continued to attempt to baptize their children using the *Book of Common Prayer*, and to follow the ceremony with the traditionally lavish celebrations. At Beeston Regis in Norfolk in 1648, a fight broke out after the incumbent minister refused to admit to the church one William Feezer who wished to have his child baptized at the font by an ejected cleryman.[34] John Evelyn's wife gave birth to several children during the 1650s and, rather than take them to church to be baptized according to the new formula, the Royalist diarist had them christened privately at home according to the old Anglican rite. In September 1652, the Royalist clergyman, Mr Owen, christened Evelyn's eldest son Richard at his house at Sayes Court near Deptford, with a number of his relatives acting as 'susceptors' or godparents. In October 1653 and February 1655, the same minister conducted further private christening ceremonies for Evelyn's younger children 'according to the rite of the Church of England', and in February 1657 Evelyn's fourth son was baptized at Sayes Court, on this occasion by the influential Royalist divine, Jeremy Taylor. At frequent intervals during these years, Evelyn also attended private christenings of his friends' and relatives' children; he sometimes acted as a godparent, and in November 1648 he spent the large sum of £18 on a christening present for his new niece Mary. When one of Evelyn's servants gave birth to a child in 1656, it too was christened at a private ceremony at Sayes Court, which Evelyn and his friends attended.[35]

The Evelyns' rejection of the new public form of baptism was shared by a number of other parents. Philip, Lord Lisle's son born at Salisbury House in London in January 1647, was christened there privately three days later with the Earls of Northumberland and Salisbury and the Countess of Leicester acting as godparents.[36] Later the same year, in a

---

[33] Macfarlane (ed.), *Josselin Diary*, pp. 12, 14, 42, 44, 112, 400.
[34] John Morrill, 'The Church in England 1642–9', in John Morrill (ed.), *Reactions to the English Civil War* (London, 1982), p. 108.
[35] De Beer (ed.), *Diary of John Evelyn*, vol. 2, pp. 78, 544, 567; vol. 3, pp. 19, 63, 75, 89, 147, 166–7, 194, 218.
[36] The Journal of the Earl of Leicester in Blencowe (ed.), *Sydney Papers*, p. 4.

letter to his pregnant wife Mary, who was in London, the exiled Sir Ralph Verney discussed arrangements for the christening of the child she was carrying. He instructed her: 'Have a parson ready to christen the child (any way will satisfy me so it be christened), the best way to prevent all danger and avoid all trouble will be to dispatch it as soon as it is born, and that as privately as may be.' In her reply, Mary Verney expressed her distaste at the new ceremony and the suppression of godparents, and told Sir Ralph that she would ask a minister to perform a private service in her lodgings 'in the old way'. She concluded the letter by remarking: 'Truly, one lives like a heathen in this place.'[37] By the mid-1650s, such unauthorized private baptism ceremonies may have been very common; in 1656, Ralph Josselin remarked in his diary how rare public baptisms were becoming in Earls Colne.[38]

Throughout the years of revolutionary upheaval in England, then, many men and women continued to see the baptism of children as an important and meaningful sacrament. A strong cultural attachment to this rite of passage can be found even within the ranks of those radical Baptist congregations that had apparently set their faces so firmly against it. During 1652, John Epping and his wife of Sutton near Ely in Cambridgeshire, who were both members of the Fenstanton Baptist church, had two of their children baptized by the local parish minister. When the officials of their Baptist congregation later questioned them about the matter, they refused to acknowledge that they had done any wrong; the wife told them that she did not believe her children to be any the worse for their baptism, and John Epping declared that he had wanted them 'to congregate . . . into the Church of England'. Asked by one of the elders, John Denne, why they wished to introduce their children into a church which they were prepared to admit was false, the Eppings could make no reply.[39] They were clearly no match for the Baptist church leaders in theological debate, but their loyalty to baptism, which they themselves were either unable or unwilling to explain, would appear to be clear testimony to the popularity of the established rites of passage and the resilience of traditional culture.

There is also little doubt that, like attempts to marry in church, the securing of an Anglican baptism for their children assumed great symbolic importance for those opposed to the governments of the 1640s and 1650s. The Puritan regimes of these years certainly seem to have regarded the defiant adherence of many to the traditional rites of passage as a serious threat; in April 1645, three months after the publication of

[37] *Verney Memoirs*, vol. 1, p. 355.
[38] Macfarlane (ed.), *Josselin Diary*, p. 382.
[39] Underhill (ed.), *Fenstanton Records*, pp. 26–7, 32, 59.

the *Directory*, Thomas Morton, the eighty-year-old Bishop of Durham, was questioned by the House of Commons and subsequently imprisoned for six months in the Tower of London for officiating at the Anglican baptism of the daughter of John Manners, the Parliamentarian earl of Rutland.[40] Elaborate christenings according to the old rite were also a conspicuous feature of life at the court of the exiled Charles II and, within weeks of his Restoration in 1660, Charles was acting as godparent at the christenings of his servants' children; one such christening in August 1660, for the daughter of the governor of the Tower of London, was followed by 'great feasting and banquetting'.[41] With the return of the established Anglican church, the old Anglican rite of baptism, including the sign of the cross and the use of godparents and the font, was officially restored. At Earls Colne, Ralph Josselin performed his first baptism for twelve months in January 1662, and the following November he began to baptize using the *Book of Common Prayer*. This action seems to have met with the approval of his parishioners, for he noted in his diary 'the whole congregation in a manner staying'.[42]

Another important rite associated with childbirth which also continued to be performed during these years despite official disapproval, was the churching of women. This service, a christianized version of the Jewish rite of Purification, marked the official readmittance to the church of women who had recently given birth. Often held around the time of the new child's baptism, it involved the recital of a number of set prayers over the mother. Puritans had long been opposed to the ceremony, and objected strongly to the stipulation that the new mother should wear a veil during the service and recite the 121st Psalm, which contained a number of obscure references, such as 'the sun shall not smite thee by day, nor the moon by night.' John Milton, in particular, made no secret of his contempt for the ceremony, claiming in 1642 that thanking God for the mother's protection from 'sunburning and moonblasting' gave the impression that 'she had been travailing not in her bed, but in the deserts of Arabia.'[43]

In 1641, a Long Parliament committee which was considering alterations to the *Book of Common Prayer* suggested that the churching service should be modified to include a new thanksgiving prayer

---

[40] *DNB*, Thomas Morton (1564–1659); and *Commons Journal*, vol 4, p. 104.
[41] Bray (ed.), *Diary and Correspondence of John Evelyn*, p. 836; HMC *Appendix to Fifth Report*, p. 174.
[42] Macfarlane (ed.), *Josselin Diary*, pp. 485, 493.
[43] John Milton, *An Apology Against a Pamphlet Called a Modest Confutation*, in Wolfe (ed.), *Complete Prose Works of Milton*, vol. 1, p. 939. See also Keith Thomas, *Religion and the Decline of Magic* (London, 1971), pp. 68–9.

compiled from suitable verses taken from a number of different psalms.[44] Several years later, the members of the Westminster Assembly Of Divines also took the ceremony into consideration, but eventually decided not to include it in their Presbyterian *Directory*, published in 1645.[45] During the following fifteen years, few incumbent clergymen appear to have regularly performed the ceremony, but within some families there is once again evidence of a continuing desire to give thanks for the safe delivery of mothers from childbirth. As John Evelyn's local parish minister was either afraid or unwilling to church the diarist's wife after her deliveries in the mid-1650s, private churching ceremonies were conducted at Evelyn's house by the same Royalist clergyman who christened several of their children.[46] At Kidderminster in the 1650s, an entirely new thanksgiving service was introduced by the minister, Richard Baxter. A staunch Presbyterian, Baxter fully shared the widespread Puritan misgivings about the Anglican churching ceremony with its 'feastings and gossippings', but his parishioners' attachment to some form of ceremony marking a woman's safe delivery from childbirth prompted him to establish the new ceremony, and he later described in his autobiography how, during the 1650s: 'Every religious woman, that was safely delivered ... if they were able, did keep a Day of Thanksgiving with some of their neighbours with them, praising God and singing psalms, and soberly feasting together.'[47] At the Restoration in 1660, the Anglican ceremony of churching duly returned along with the old form of baptism, although the 121st Psalm – the victim of Milton's biting sarcasm – was replaced by new prayers.[48] Clearly, some men and women in revolutionary England continued to regard both baptism and churching as important aspects of family life, and were thus opposed to, and prepared to resist, any official pressure to abolish or reduce the significance of these traditional rituals of childbirth.

During the first months of a new infant's life its chief requirement was of course food. An obvious and normally sufficient supply of this was provided by the mother's own milk, but many mothers in early-modern England, particularly those of a high social rank, declined to breast-feed their own children and instead employed a wet-nurse to carry out the task for them. Their reluctance to breast-feed their children arose not

---

[44] F. Proctor and W. H. Frere, *A New History of the Book of Common Prayer* (London, 1951 edn), pp. 151–4, 198.
[45] William A. Shaw, *A History of the English Church During the Civil War and Under the Commonwealth* (2 vols, London, 1900), vol. 1, p. 350.
[46] De Beer (ed.), *Diary of John Evelyn*, vol. 3, pp. 76, 90, 147, 195.
[47] *Reliquiae Baxterianae*, p. 83.
[48] Thomas, *Religion and Decline of Magic*, pp. 69–70.

only from a desire to avoid inconvenience and broken sleep, but also from the widespread belief that the child's attentions might adversely affect their looks or health. In addition, as it was widely believed that women should refrain from sexual relations while they were feeding their children, some husbands may also have discouraged their wives from breast-feeding. A number of late-sixteenth- and early-seventeenth-century moralists and theologians, however, had condemned the practice of wet-nursing, on the grounds that children were often exposed to danger by negligent nurses and that the undesirable temperament of such nurses might be passed to the highly impressionable child through the milk. Puritan authors of manuals of domestic conduct, such as William Gouge, William Perkins, Richard Cleaver and John Dod, has been particularly critical of wet-nursing and, as a result, mothers in Puritan households may have been more willing to breast-feed their own children.[49]

It is, however, unlikely that the acquisition of power by Puritan regimes in England after 1642 had any marked effect upon general attitudes towards breast-feeding. Some women with strong attachments to the parliamentary cause were firm supporters of the practice; the second wife of the parliamentary general, the Earl of Manchester, for example, breast-fed seven of her eight children, and later had the fact recorded upon her tombstone as a matter of pride.[50] There is, however, no evidence of any concerted attempt on the part of either the secular or the ecclesiastical authorities to encourage the practice, and probably only a very small number of women dispensed with the wet-nurse during the 1640s and 1650s because they had been persuaded that their own milk was better for their children. None the less, a greater number of women than normal were obliged to feed their own children during the 1640s, if only because the wartime conditions made it more difficult for them to obtain the services of nurses. Throughout the sixteenth and early seventeenth centuries, many hundreds of infants from London had been sent out to wet-nurses in the surrounding rural shires.[51] After the outbreak of war in 1642, however, travel and communication in the south-east of the country were seriously disrupted and counties such as Berkshire began to suffer greatly from the depredations of the rival armies. As a result, the numbers entrusted to rural wet-nurses declined markedly, and, with the supply of wet-nurses in the capital insufficient to

---

[49] Stone, *Family, Sex and Marriage*, pp. 426–32; and Houlbrooke, *The English Family*, pp. 132–4.
[50] Stone, *Family, Sex and Marriage*, p. 428.
[51] I owe this point to Gillian Clark, who is engaged in a study of London 'nurse children' in the early-modern period.

cope with the resultant increase in demand, London mothers were forced into feeding their own children. Writing to his wife Mary about arrangements for her lying in in London in 1647, Sir Ralph Verney advised her to 'look out a careful, rather than a fine nursekeeper, for 'twill be impossible for you to be without one', adding 'if you need two, take them; spare no charge wherein your health is concerned.' Mary, however, appears to have had considerable trouble finding even one wet-nurse, and after she had reluctantly decided to employ a woman whom she clearly considered somewhat unsatisfactory, she wrote to Sir Ralph that

> ... she looks like a slattern, but she sayeth, if she takes the child, she will have a mighty care of it ... Nurse will be paid 14 shillings a week and two loads of wood; truly, 'tis as little as we can offer her ... for nurses are much dearer than ever they were ... poor child, I pray God bless him and make him a happy man, for he hath but a troublesome beginning.[52]

Wet-nurses were probably also in short supply in Oxford, where the population was swollen by the personnel attached to the royal court and administration, and those wives like Anne Fanshawe, who travelled extensively with their husbands after 1646 also had sometimes to forgo the services of wet-nurses. The Civil War may well, therefore, have brought about an increase in the number of mothers breast-feeding their own children, not because of any widespread change of attitude on the part of women, but rather because, as the services of wet-nurses became more difficult to obtain, some new mothers were left with little alternative.

Another important aspect of child-rearing which had been consistently stressed by pre-1640 Puritan moralists was education. For the more committed Protestants, education was an important means of repairing the damage inflicted upon human nature by the Fall and thus a major weapon in the struggle against the forces of the devil. In addition, with the early decades of the seventeenth century witnessing an increase in millenarian speculation about the imminence of the end of the world, education assumed an even greater importance as the mechanism by which men and women could be prepared for the last days. When the outbreak of civil war gave Puritans an opportunity to wield real power, educational reform became a central political issue, and, as Charles Webster has noted, 'the onset of the Puritan revolution was marked by a

---

[52] *Verney Memoirs*, vol. 1, p. 380.

substantial increase in pressure for universal education.'[53] Many of the English Revolution's most fervent supporters shared a desire to see radical changes in education; the long list of committed Parliamentarians who supported both a substantial extension of educational opportunities and a liberalization of the narrow, scholastic curriculum included John Milton, Richard Overton, William Walwyn, Gerrard Winstanley, Samuel Hartlib, John Dury, James Harrington, William Dell and John Webster. In his *Vox Populi*, published in 1642, Samuel Harmer advocated the appointment of a schoolmaster for every English parish, their salaries to be paid by the state. Later in the 1640s, the Levellers called for the establishment of enough schools to assure universal literacy, and Gerrard Winstanley argued that free education for both sexes should continue until the age of forty. Proposals for an expansion of higher education included plans to establish a university in London.

Some initiatives for educational reform were set in motion. In June 1641, the Long Parliament decided to abolish deans and chapters and to allocate their lands to a scheme for the 'advancement of learning and piety'. Shortly afterwards, a parliamentary committee was given the responsibility of examining the state of the country's free schools and universities. In November 1641, the MPs who drew up the Grand Remonstrance urged Parliament to purge the two universities, 'that the streams flowing from thence may be clean and pure'; and the same winter, the radical Czech educational reformer Comenius visited England for a short time to discuss reform proposals with Samuel Hartlib. Comenius had advocated the implementation of a more liberal curriculum in schools, which would have reduced the dominance of Latin and grammar and put more emphasis on the study of the natural environment and economics. Little further progress was made during the war years, but in 1647 Hartlib was appointed as a parliamentary agent for the advancement of learning, and over the next few years he and his associates published about fifty tracts on educational topics. By the late 1640s, Oxford and Cambridge universities had been purged of Royalist influences and encouraged to introduce more modern curricula, and in 1657 a new university college for the north of England was established at Durham. In addition, during the early 1650s, several parliamentary committees, including the Committee for Charitable Uses and the Committee for the Propagation of the Gospel in Wales, helped to organize the founding of a number of new schools. In 1653, one of the proposals of Barebone's Parliament's Committee for the Advancement of

[53] Charles Webster, *The Great Instauration: Science, Medicine and Reform 1626–1660* (London, 1975), p. 207. The remainder of the discussion on education is based on Webster, pp. 100–245.

Learning, was that mechanical schools for the lower orders should be established throughout the country.

However, despite these initiatives, very few concrete reforms were actually achieved; the provision of basic elementary education remained extremely patchy and only fairly modest changes occurred at the universities. The aspirations of the reformers remained largely unfulfilled and much of the small amount of reform which had been achieved was later overturned at the Restoration. The English Revolution had, in fact, only a very minor impact upon the practical education of children; none the less, some conservatives remained profoundly disturbed by the proposed educational reforms, believing that the freer intellectual environment of revolutionary England was potentially damaging to children. Dissatisfied with the instruction on offer from the parish clergy during the 1650s, John Evelyn personally supervised his children's religious education, and in October 1655 he remarked in his diary:

> In the afternoons I frequently stayed at home to Catechize and Instruct my Family, those exercises universally ceasing in the parish churches, so as people had no Principles and grew very ignorant of even the common points of Christianity, all devotion being now placed in hearing sermons and discourses of speculative and notional things.[54]

Turning to the question of how the divisions and upheavals of the civil-war period affected relationships between parents and young children, one finds clear evidence within some families of the distortion of relationships and the weakening of emotional bonds. Children sometimes suffered as a result of political divisions between their parents. When the Royalist colonel, John Bodvile of Anglesey quarrelled with his wife Anne during the Civil War, he took their three daughters away from her and placed them in the care of his mother. Anne later requested Parliament that they be returned to her, complaining that her mother-in-law was educating them in 'opinions of averseness to the Parliament and irreligious courses', and the House of Lords subsequently ordered that the girls be taken away from their father and grandmother and put under the control of their maternal grandfather, Sir William Russell.[55]

Even when both parents shared the same political and religious standpoint and were united in facing the problems caused by war and revolution, their children's development could still be adversely affected

---

[54] De Beer (ed.), *Diary of John Evelyn*, vol. 3, p. 160.
[55] *Lords Journal*, vol. 8, pp. 565, 568, 571, 575, 585, 599; and *Cal. Com. Comp.*, vol. 2, pp. 1599–1602.

either by the serious financial problems which were suffered by many families, or by the premature death or long absence of a father or mother. In 1647, Thomas Fuller commented in his *Good Thoughts in Worse Times*: 'Many parents (which otherwise would have been loving pelicans) are by these unnatural wars forced to be ostriches to their own children, leaving them to the Narrow mercy of the wide world.'[56] The records of the parliamentary committees which negotiated with the defeated Royalists in the late 1640s and early 1650s contain many appeals for relief from parents who claimed that, as a result of heavy taxation, imprisonment or the confiscation of their estates, their children had been deprived of adequate food or shelter.[57] Anthony Farindon, the Royalist minister of Bray in Berkshire who was ejected from his living and had his lands sequestered during the Civil War, later accused his successor, Ezekial Woodward, of bringing his wife and children to the point of starvation by keeping from them the fifth of the confiscated estate which was allowed for their maintenance.[58] In June 1650, Margaret Trowt of Faversham in Kent petitioned the Committee for Compounding for 'an act of mercy', claiming that as a result of the sequestration of her husband's estate and his subsequent desertion, she and her seven small children were near destitute and had become 'a sad spectacle of misery to her neighbours'.[59] Two years later, Nicholas Borlace of Newlyn in Cornwall complained that the local Cornish parliamentary committee had confiscated his whole estate and, 'not suffering him with eight children to have bread to eat of their own corn', had forced them ' to live on the mere charity of their neighbours'.[60] During the early 1650s, Sir David Husterville was forced into exile and later imprisoned because of the debts he had amassed during the 1640s; in 1650, his wife informed the Committee for Advance of Money that she was in 'a sad condition with a charge of 10 children', and in 1652 Sir David petitioned the committee for his release from the Fleet prison, on the grounds that his confinement was destroying his family and that he had already lost three children 'through want'.[61] In 1656, Francis Purcell, a Catholic recusant from Yealfields in Staffordshire, claimed that he had been so badly affected by the various confiscations and exactions he had suffered that, unless he were allowed to compound,

---

[56] Thomas Fuller, *Good Thoughts in Worse Times* (London, 1647), p. 106 (TT).
[57] For examples see *Cal. Com. Comp.*, vol. 2, pp. 833, 937, 963, 970, 1024, 1078, 1105, 1477–8.
[58] *DNB*, Anthony Farindon (1598–1658).
[59] *Cal. Com. Comp.*, vol. 2, pp. 1422–3.
[60] Ibid., vol. 3, p. 2002.
[61] *Cal. Com. Advance Money*, vol. 2, pp. 959–60.

he would be forced to 'desert his wife and children, or end his days in a loathsome prison'.[62]

The Civil War was also responsible for making large numbers of children orphans, and for temporarily depriving many others of their parents. Many hundreds of fathers perished in the battles of the Civil War, and after the fighting had ceased in 1646, execution, exile and imprisonment produced further separations. In many cases, children who had been deprived of their parents were cared for by relatives or friends. Requesting his release from prison in April 1643, John Montfort of London informed the Committee for Advance of Money that he was responsible for the well-being not only of his own family, but also of 'diverse other fatherless children', who had been committed to his charge by their deceased parents.[63] In letters written on his death-bed in Ireland in 1644, Sir Abraham Shipman informed his brother and another kinsman of his impending demise, and asked their 'favour to three fatherless and motherless infants . . . that you would not any way slacken your affection towards them by my death.'[64] In 1652, Charles, Lord Strange, whose father, the Earl of Derby, had been executed by Parliament the previous year, claimed that his family were living in utter poverty. Similarly, in December 1656, the children of Sir John Penruddock, who had been executed for planning the Royalist rising in Wiltshire in 1655, petitioned Oliver Cromwell to be allowed some subsistence from their father's confiscated property, explaining that they were 'laden with debts' and obliged to depend upon the 'charity of a distressed mother or of an encumbered infant brother'.[65]

But even in those cases where relatives were prepared to look after the children of those who had been killed, imprisoned or driven into exile, normal family relations were still distorted by the absence of the real parents. The sort of problems which could arise can be seen within the Buckinghamshire Verney family. For much of the civil-war period, Sir Ralph Verney and his wife Mary were in exile in France and were separated from their young son John who had remained with other members of the family at their home at Claydon in Buckinghamshire. When Mary Verney returned to England after the end of the war and was reunited with the seven-year-old John, whom she had not seen for four years, she was far from happy with the child's physical condition and educational progress. In a letter to Sir Ralph, she informed him that John

---

[62] *Cal. Com. Comp.*, vol. 5, p. 3184.
[63] *Cal. Com. Advance Money*, vol. 1, p. 138.
[64] HMC *Appendix to Fourth Report*, pp. 271–2.
[65] *Cal. Com. Comp.*, vol. 2, p. 1101; *CSPD 1656–7*, p. 201.

had been spoilt in their absence and suggested he should join them in France, declaring:

> . . . and, truly, I think [it] would be much finer if we had him in ordering, for they let him eat everything that he hath a mind to, and he keeps a very ill diet; he hath an Imperfection in his speech and, of all things, he hates his book, truly 'tis time you had him with you, for he learns nothing here.[66]

Another family within which the children were deprived of their parents was the royal family. During the Civil War, two of Charles I's younger children, the Princess Elizabeth and Henry, Duke of Gloucester, were held in custody by Parliament at St James's Palace in London. After a separation lasting five years, they were reunited with their father in July 1647, when Charles's army captors allowed a meeting to take place at Maidenhead. When the seven-year-old Prince Henry, who had been parted from his father when he was only two, failed to recognize Charles, the king was reported to have told him 'I am your father, child, and it is not the least of my misfortunes that I have brought you and your brothers and sisters into the world to share my miseries.'[67] During the following eighteen months, the army allowed Charles a number of regular meetings with his children at Hampton Court and Syon House, and, on the day before his execution in January 1649, Elizabeth and Henry were allowed to visit their father for the last time. Charles told them not to mourn for him, gave them instructions about their education and made Henry promise not to allow Parliament to make him king while his elder brothers were still alive. Exposure to such traumatic events at a young age may well had damaging psychological effects upon the children, and was probably a contributory factor in Elizabeth's premature death the following year. The thirteen-year-old princess had been inconsolable at the time of the execution and never fully recovered from her grief and shock at the loss of her father; Sir Theodore Mayerne, the royal physician, commented at the time that 'the Princess Elizabeth, who was aforetime sad and somewhat liable to complain of the spleen, and suffered a little from scurvy, from the death of her father . . . fell into a great sorrow, whereby all the other ailments from which she suffered were increased.' Shortly after her father's execution, she developed a stomach tumour and she died at Carisbrooke Castle on the Isle of Wight in September 1650.[68]

[66] *Verney Memoirs*, vol. 1, p. 379.
[67] Morrah, *A Royal Family*, p. 98.
[68] Ibid., pp. 114–19.

With regard to relationships between parents and older children, conservative moralists had long feared that the patriarchal structure of the family would be a casualty of internecine violence in the state, and that a decline in the respect shown to parents would be the inevitable result of civil conflict. Such commentators, who supported traditional authority in both state and family and believed that monarchical and familial absolutism were interdependent, also feared that if one collapsed the other would quickly follow. William Shakespeare, for example, had warned some years earlier in *Troilus and Cressida* that, if civil disorder broke out, 'the rude son should strike his father dead.'[69] When, in 1643, the Parliamentarian minister Herbert Palmer preached the sermon *Scripture and Reason pleaded for Defensive Arms*, in which he justified resistance to the king on the grounds that the power of fathers was conditional, the fears of these conservatives appeared to be being realized.[70]

Several witnesses to the events in England between 1640 and 1660 claimed both that the civil war had its origins in disputes within families and that it had resulted in a decline in parental respect and authority. Reviewing the recent disturbances in both England and her American colonies in his *Fruitful Discourse Touching the Honour due from Children to Parents and the Duty of Parents to Children*, published in London in 1656, the New England minister, Thomas Cobbet, argued that if the backgrounds of those who had provoked the recent political troubles were investigated, 'they would be found to be persons who have been and are unnatural to their Parents.' He also argued that children had recently grown much more disrespectful towards their parents, and that there were too many who 'carry it proudly, disdainfully and scornfully towards parents, and it's well if their very parents escape their flouts.'[71] Edward Hyde, the Earl of Clarendon, also suggested in his autobiography that during the revolutionary years 'Children asked not blessing of their Parents . . . young Women conversed without any circumspection or modesty . . . Parents had no Manner of Authority over their Children, nor Children any Obedience or Submission to their Parents; but every one did that which was good in his own Eyes.'[72]

Such conservatives believed, therefore, that the political problems of

---

[69] William Shakespeare, *Troilus and Cressida*, 1. iii. 115.
[70] Herbert Palmer, *Scripture and Reason Pleaded for Defensive Arms* (London, 1643), *passim*.
[71] Cobbet, *Fruitful Discourse*, pp. 84, 93–5.
[72] Edward Hyde, Earl of Clarendon, *The Life of Edward Hyde, Earl of Clarendon* (Oxford, 1827 edn), pp. 358–9; quoted by Thomas in 'Women and the Civil War Sects', p. 57.

the 1640s and 1650s could only be solved by the placing of greater emphasis upon the need for obedience in the family. They held that the fifth commandment, 'Honour thy Father and thy Mother', gave divine sanction to the power of both kings and heads of families, and frequently cited it against those who wished to overturn the status quo. During the debates in the General Council of the Army at Putney in the autumn of 1647, the socially conservative landowner Henry Ireton had reminded the radical Levellers of their duty to obey this commandment, and in 1649, the Royalist Lord Arthur Capel claimed on the scaffold that his support for the fifth commandment had cost him his life.[73] Before his execution in the late 1650s, the Royalist Sir Henry Slingsby wrote the short book, *A Father's Legacy to his Sons*, in which he gave his sons detailed advice about how they should conduct themselves after his death. He laid particular stress in the work upon the importance of obedience to authority, declaring: 'Subjection to Superiors is a precept of high consequence ... For you, my sons, be it your especial care to submit yourselves to your Superiors in all lawful things. It is an indispensible injunction: and ought by persons of each distinct quality, when they are conscientiously thereto obliged, to be religiously observed.'[74]

There is some evidence to suggest that such contemporary anxieties and preoccupations may to some extent have been justified, and that the disruptions of the years 1640–60 may indeed have had an adverse effect upon the behaviour of adolescents. When Mary Verney returned to Claydon in 1647, she found not only that her own son's development had been adversely affected by separation from his parents, but also that, in the absence of any restraining influence from their father, Sir Edmund, who had been killed at the battle of Edgehill, or from their elder brother, Sir Ralph, who was in France, her sisters-in-law had become insolent and unruly. In one letter she told Sir Ralph that she was afraid that they might actually sell off some of Claydon's more valuable contents, exclaiming in frustration: 'I did never in my life see or hear of so much indiscretion as is amongst them; truly, there is not one of them that hath any discretion.'[75]

What is known of the family backgrounds of some of the most active revolutionaries would also seem to lend some credence to the widespread contemporary belief that the troubles of the 1640s had originated within families. Several of the most prominent supporters of the English

---

[73] C. H. Firth (ed.), *The Clarke Papers*, Volume 1, Camden Soc. Publs, NS 49 (1891), 390; HMC *Beaufort MSS*, p. 34; quoted by S. D. Amussen in 'Gender, Family and the Social Order, 1560–1725', in A. Fletcher and J. Stevenson (eds), *Order and Disorder in Early Modern England* (Cambridge, 1985), pp. 197–8.

[74] Sir Henry Slingsby, *A Father's Legacy to His Sons* (London, 1658), pp. 24–5.

[75] *Verney Memoirs*, vol. 1, p. 429.

Revolution appear to have had unsatisfactory relationships with their parents. The Ranter Lawrence Clarkson had quarrelled with his father in the 1630s and had refused to attend family prayers because the *Book of Common Prayer* was used.[76] Relations between the Leveller leader, John Lilburne, and his father Richard were also strained, and in 1638 the father warned another son, Henry, not to emulate John, whom he claimed had caused him 'the greatest grief'.[77] Another radical, the republican Algernon Sidney, also seems to have been on poor terms with his father, the Earl of Leicester. In a letter to his son shortly after the Restoration, Leicester accused Algernon of neglecting him and leaving him 'sick, solitary and sad at Penshurst'. He added that he had ignored all the advise he had given him in the past, asserting:

> . . . how little weight my opinions and counsel have been with you, and how unkindly and unfriendly you have rejected the exhortations and admonitions, which, in much affection and kindness, I have given you on many occasions, and in almost every thing from the highest to the lowest that have concerned you.[78]

Some revolutionaries then clearly quarrelled with their parents, but in the absence of more corroborative evidence it is impossible to state whether such generational conflict was a common feature of the backgrounds of seventeenth-century radicals.

What is clear, however, is that during the 1640s and 1650s many children found themselves at odds with their parents as a result of conflicting ideological standpoints. The breaches and ill feeling which resulted when fathers and sons fought on opposite sides during the Civil War have been discussed above.[79] In addition, religious divisions could also prove extremely damaging to relations between parents and children. Familial conflict over religious belief did not, of course, begin in the 1640s; in 1633, a farmer's son from Shropshire had murdered both his mother and brother after a quarrel over whether communion should be received kneeling.[80] However, in the atmosphere of intense religious controversy which existed between 1640 and 1660, the potential for disagreement was enhanced. John Rogers, who later became a prominent Fifth Monarchist, claimed that he was thrown out of his father's house in

---

[76] Stone, *Family, Sex and Marriage*, p. 245.
[77] Gregg, *Free-Born John*, p. 73.
[78] Blencowe (ed.), *Sydney Papers*, pp. 208. See also pp. 205, 212, 214–27.
[79] See ch. 3 above.
[80] Thomas, *Religion and Decline of Magic*, p. 176.

1642 because of his Puritan beliefs; describing later the alienation he had experienced as a young man, he declared that:

> near relations cast me off and I was looked upon as disobedient for keeping company with such as were godly puritans and accounted then Roundheads, and for praying and holding communion with them (though commanded to the contrary). At length I found so little love and so much malice from some that I was turned out of doors.[81]

During the 1650s, a number of individuals complained to Parliamentary committees that they had been persecuted by their parents because they differed from them in religious outlook. In July 1651, William Bottle of Thornton in Lancashire claimed that he had been turned out of the family home by his recusant parents after he refused to accept their Catholicism; the same year, Robert Knevitt of Drury Lane in London asserted that his recusant father, Sir Philip Knevitt of Buckenham Castle in Norfolk, who had not wanted him to inherit the family estates because he was a Protestant, had pretended that he had sold them to an Inner Temple lawyer.[82] A serious quarrel also arose within the Cosin family in the early 1650s when John, the son of the conservative Anglican divine, John Cosin, became a Roman Catholic. Writing to John Evelyn from Paris in December 1651, the younger John admitted that his absence from his father had made it easier for him to go against his wishes, and he defended the Catholic priests who had received him into the Roman Church from critics who had declared: 'What a barbarous and unconscionable thing it is to separate a son from his father, and to encourage him in this act of disobedience against him.'[83]

More frequently, however, it was the radical religious sects that were accused of setting children against their parents and of undermining parental authority. One of the earliest accusations from the revolutionary period concerned the activities of the Family of Love. In 1641, the pamphlet *A Description of the Sect called the Family of Love* reported how, after she had spent some days with a group of Familists near Bagshot in Surrey, one Susan Snow had become unruly and rebellious and a cause of great worry to her parents.[84] Thomas Edwards later

---

[81] Rogers, *Life and Opinions of a Fifth Monarchy Man*, p. 18. See also *DNB*, John Rogers (1627–65).

[82] *Cal. Com. Comp.*, vol. 4, p. 2844; *Cal. Com. Advance Money*, vol. 2, p. 970.

[83] Bray (ed.), *Diary and Correspondence of John Evelyn*, pp. 561–3. See also *DNB*, John Cosin (1594–1672).

[84] *A Description of the Sect called the Family of Love* (London, 1641), *passim* (TT).

accused the religious radicals of arguing that 'Parents are not to catechize their little children nor to set them to read the Scripture or to teach them to pray, but must let them alone for God to teach.' He also warned that if religious toleration were allowed fathers 'should never have peace in their families more, or ever after have command of wives, children, servants.'[85] In 1656, his fellow Presbyterian, Richard Baxter, also accused the Quakers and the other radical religious groups of conspiring to 'turn the hearts of the children from their fathers',[86] and in the same year Thomas Cobbet remarked:

> ... I fear there are too many other petty Antichristian spirits in these days, who by other erroneous tenents ... leaven their disciples, and such as they can subtlely draw after them, with a Spirit of Alienation, even from their own good Parents, if they will not be of their corrupt Judgements and opinions.[87]

Such statements were the product of conservative alarm and as a result were frequently overstated. None the less, they may not have been entirely without foundation. Many of those who joined the new Quaker movement in the 1650s, for example, were subsequently unwilling to acknowledge the traditional hierarchies of the state or the family, or to accept that they were subservient to any of their 'fellow creatures'. As a result, young Quaker men and women often found themselves at odds with their parents, particularly when they refused to show them the customary marks of deference, such as standing bare-headed before them. One young convert to Quakerism who became involved in a serious and violent dispute with his father was Thomas Ellwood of Crowell in Oxfordshire. Soon after he became a Quaker at the end of 1659, Thomas decided that he must stop using 'flattering titles' towards his fellow men, but initially he found himself quite unable to abandon his previous deferential carriage towards his father. Later, however, after he had attended several Quaker meetings at the house of the Penington family at nearby Chalfont St Peter, he became convinced that 'the honour due to parents did not consist in uncovering the head and bowing the body to them.' Accordingly, the following day he appeared before his father, the Oxfordshire JP, Walter Ellwood, wearing his hat. This act of defiance sent his father into an uncontrollable rage and he immediately physically attacked Thomas and threw the hat to the ground. Thomas afterwards left the house and journeyed on foot to Chalfont. Deeply

---

[85] Edwards, *Gangraena*, part 1, pp. 34, 156.
[86] Richard Baxter, *Gildas Salvianus, The Reformed Pastor* (London, 1656), preface.
[87] Cobbet, *Fruitful Discourse*, p. 45.

disturbed at his father's reaction, he reflected upon the nature of parental power as he walked, reassuring himself that it '. . . was not wholly arbitrary and unlimited, but had bounds set unto it: so that in civil matters it was restrained to things lawful, so in spiritual and religious cases it had not a compulsory power over conscience, which ought to be subject to the Heavenly Father.'

The dispute continued over the next few months, during which time the initial scene was re-enacted a number of times. Thomas was subjected to several serious assaults and remained a virtual prisoner in his father's house during the winter of 1659 to 1660. The conflict within the household intensified when both his sister and the family servants attempted to support Thomas and also fell foul of the father. The impasse was only eventually resolved through the intervention of the Quaker, Isaac Penington the elder. After visiting Crowell and telling Walter Ellwood that he had initially reacted in a similar fashion when his son Isaac had become a Quaker, he persuaded him to allow Thomas to live with the Peningtons at Chalfont. Thomas later made several trips home, but the differences between him and his father continued. After a short period in gaol at Oxford, he was once more held against his will at Crowell, but managed to escape. When Walter Ellwood moved to London with his daughter in the early 1660s, Thomas moved back to Crowell and lived there alone. In 1669, the father refused to acknowledge Thomas's Quaker marriage because it had not been solemnized in church. The rift between father and son was never healed, and the Ellwood family remained permanently divided by its religious differences.[88]

On the eve of the Civil War, the political and religious radical, Sir Henry Vane the younger, experienced a similar particularly acute conflict between his loyalty to his father and to the Parliamentarian cause which he fervently supported. In late 1640, Sir Henry Vane the elder, who was secretary to the Privy Council, gave his son permission to look amongst his private papers for a document relevant to his marriage settlement. In the course of his search, the younger Vane found some rough notes that his father had made during a Council meeting some months before, which indicated that Thomas Wentworth, the Earl of Strafford, had suggested to Charles I that he could bring over an army from Ireland to deal with any trouble from an English Parliament. Vane immediately realized that the highly incriminating document would be invaluable to those in Parliament who were seeking Strafford's impeachment, but also that to make known its existence would be a serious breach of his father's trust.

---

[88] Thomas Ellwood, 'Life of Thomas Ellwood', in *Autobiography* 11 (1827), 23–77, 93, 158.

Faced with a choice between his loyalty to his father and to the political cause which he fervently espoused, Sir Henry put his political affiliations first. After hesitating for several days, he told John Pym of his discovery, and, several months later, Pym alluded to the existence of the document in a speech to the House of Commons during the proceedings against Strafford. According to the Earl of Clarendon, the younger Vane then explained to the House what had happened, commenting that

> he knew this discovery would prove little less than his ruin in the good opinion of his father; but having been provoked by the tenderness of his conscience toward his common Parent, his country, to trespass against his natural father, he hoped he should find compassion from that House, though he had little hope of pardon elsewhere.[89]

The elder Vane afterwards confirmed that the story was true and, thankful for the new evidence against Strafford, the Commons subsequently passed a motion that the two Vanes should remain on good terms. The Earl of Clarendon, however, remained suspicious that the elder Sir Henry might have been far more implicated in the attack upon Strafford than the story suggested.[90]

The troubled political and religious climate of 1640s and 1650s clearly, then, did create some additional generational tension and cause some serious conflicts between some parents and their children. It is important, however, not to exaggerate the scale of any such discord. For, within many other families during these years, relations between parents and children were largely unaffected by wartime dislocation and political and religious discord, the mutual obligations and emotional attachments of parents and children remaining of far greater importance than any considerations of an ideological nature. At the beginning of 1641, John Evelyn was much more upset by the last illness and death of his father than by the disturbing political events unfolding at Westminster, and he later remarked in his diary: '. . . thus we were bereft of both our Parents in a period when we most of all stood in need of their counsel and assistance.'[91] Despite all the political frustrations and disillusionments he had suffered during the 1650s, it was the death of his daughter, Elizabeth, from cancer in 1658 that did most to weaken Oliver Cromwell's political resolve and sense of purpose, and to hasten his own death a few months later; on hearing the news of her demise, he was

---

[89] Clarendon, *History of Rebellion*, vol. 1, p. 304.
[90] Ibid., pp. 301–6.
[91] De Beer (ed.), *Diary of John Evelyn*, vol. 2, p. 26.

reported to have called for his Bible and turned to the same text which he claimed had saved his life after the death of his son Robert in 1639, an incident he described as 'a dagger to my heart'.[92]

We have seen in chapter 3 how some of those parents and children who were divided by civil-war allegiance were anxious to prevent their differences causing permanent rifts between them. In addition, when similar conflicts of loyalty between family and church developed during this period, family ties often proved a stronger force than denominational allegiance. This was true even within the ranks of some of the most highly committed religious radicals. When the serving-girl Elizabeth Noble was denounced before the Fenstanton Baptists in 1654 for disobedience and negligence, her father John, who was also a member of the congregation, became extremely angry and launched a bitter attack upon her accuser, one of the church leaders, John Denne.[93] Three years later, the officers of the neighbouring Baptist church at Warboys denounced John Dunn, the son of one of their elders, William Dunn, for deserting a girl from London whom he had been planning to marry, ordering him to return to the capital and proceed with the match. Again, the father took the son's side and both were subsequently excommunicated.[94] The Presbyterian Richard Baxter not only acknowledged the great strength of the bond between parents and children, but also made specific use of it in his attempts to spread new religious practices. At Kidderminster in the 1650s, he found that one of the best ways to advance the religious reforms he was struggling to introduce was to win over the town's children and allow them to persuade their parents to adopt them; he later commented in his memoirs that 'They that would not hear me, would hear their own children . . . Many that would not be brought to it themselves, were proud that they had understanding, religious children.'[95]

Nor was the irreparable family break-up experienced by the Ellwoods the inevitable result of ideological division. When Richard Davies of Welshpool became a Quaker in the late 1650s, his parents were at first extremely upset and angry. His father threatened to disinherit him and, according to Richard, told his other relatives '. . . that they thought to have had comfort of me, but now they expected none, but that I would go up and down the country crying Repent!, Repent!' On this occasion, however, a serious breach was prevented by Davies's mother who, as he later wrote:

[92] Abbott (ed.), *Writings and Speeches of Cromwell*, vol. 4, pp. 864–7.
[93] Underhill (ed.), *Fenstanton Records*, pp. 110–1.
[94] Ibid., pp. 274–5.
[95] *Reliquiae Baxterianae*, p. 89.

came tenderly to me and took a view of me, looking on my face, and she saw that I was not, as they said, bewitched or transformed into some other likeness ... And, when I discoursed with her out of the scriptures, her heart was much tendered and affected with the goodness of God towards me; she went to see my father and said unto him, 'Be of good comfort, our son is not as was reported of him, we hope to have comfort of him yet.[96]

In addition, within some families, rather than causing division and enmity between parents and children, the domestic trials and misfortunes which came in the wake of political and religious conflict fostered instead a deeper mutual appreciation. On the outbreak of civil war in 1642, many parents were extremely unhappy about their sons enlisting in the rival armies, and some were later to experience great pain and heartache when they failed to return. When the Yorkshireman Samuel Priestley told his mother at the start of the war that he was joining the parliamentary forces, she attempted to keep him at home through 'entreaty and persuasions', and later followed him in tears as he departed.[97] In February 1643, the pamphlet *The Widows' Lamentation*, which purported to express the views of mothers in the capital, declared:

> ... what can be more doleful and of greater terror to the weakness of our sex, than to hear that those sons of our blessings, the lively images of our husbands, should be taken from us by violent deaths, we having not the privilege to express the last testimony of our loves, as to close their eyes or follow their corpses to the grave.[98]

Lady Brilliana Harley's letters to her son, Edward, during the early stages of the war reveal her intense concern for his safety; in one letter she wrote: 'I hope the Lord will in mercy give you to me again, for you are both a Joseph and a Benjamin to me.'[99] The republican, Edmund Ludlow, believed that his father's death during the war had been partly caused by the grief he had suffered after the death in Royalist custody of his other son, Robert; and Margaret Cavendish, Duchess of Newcastle, remarked of her mother, who had lost two sons in the civil-war fighting, that she

---

[96] John Barclay (ed.), *Select Anecdotes and Instructive Incidents taken from the Publications of Several Members of the Society of Friends* (London, 1822), pp. 36–7.
[97] C. Jackson (ed.), *Yorkshire Diaries and Autobiographies in the Seventeenth and Eighteenth Centuries*, Surtees Soc. Publs, 77 (1886), 26–7.
[98] *The Widows' Lamentation*, p. 3.
[99] Lewis (ed.), *Letters of Lady Brilliana Harley*, pp. 203–5.

had 'lived to see the ruin of her children, in which was her own ruin.'[100] In the short term, such experiences caused only pain and regret, but in the longer perspective they were often responsible for deepening the feelings of love and affection that such parents felt for their offspring.

An increase in fondness was also a frequent result of the enforced separations of parents and children which the war occasioned. In January 1642, when Charles I left London following his unsuccessful attempt to arrest five members of the House of Commons, his courtier Endymion Porter accompanied him. Unlike the king, Porter left his family behind and several weeks later he wrote to his wife to tell her how much he was missing her and his children, declaring: 'I wish sweet Tom with me, for the King and Queen are forced to lie with their children now and I envy them their happiness.'[101] As we have seen, Charles was himself subsequently parted for some years from his younger children; when he was reunited with them in the period before his execution, his delight in their company and the solace they brought to him in the midst of his political trials was evident to many of those who witnessed them together. After one meeting at Hampton Court in late 1647, the newsbook *Perfect Occurrences* commented: 'The Duke of York sat on his majesty's right hand; his majesty is very fond of him and loving to all the children; he bears the young lady often in his arms.'[102]

At the other end of the political spectrum, the king's implaccable republican enemy, Henry Marten, also showed a similar deep affection for his three young children while facing extreme personal difficulties. During the time he was held in the Tower of London awaiting trial as a regicide after the Restoration, Marten wrote a number of letters to his mistress, Mary Ward, who was caring for some of his children. He referred constantly to the children in the letters, calling them his 'pretty brats' and 'thy three arm-loads of treasure', and appearing far more concerned for their welfare than about his own predicament. On one occasion he wrote: 'my little baby does not lie upon my lap but she lies almost as heavy as if she did, till I hear how she is.' Although he was one of the most committed of all seventeenth-century radical politicians, Marten declared in another letter that, as long as God kept his children well, he cared 'not a fig for all the Kites and Jackdaws in breeches or long-coats'.[103]

---

[100] Firth (ed.), *Memoirs of Edmund Ludlow*, vol. 1, p. 65; and Cavendish, *Life of William Cavendish*, p. 294.

[101] D. Townshend, *The Life and Letters of Mr Endymion Porter* (London, 1897), pp. 199-200.

[102] Quoted by Morrah in *A Royal Family*, p. 99.

[103] E. Gayton (ed.), *Col. Henry Marten's Familiar Letters to his Lady of Delight* (London, 1662), pp. 8, 11-12, 36-8, 57-9, 63-4, 66, 69, 78.

Several individuals who lived through the revolutionary events in England between 1640 and 1660 testified specifically to the way their children had been a source of joy and comfort in the face of the increased external uncertainties. In letters sent to his wife during the early part of the Civil War, the imprisoned Norfolk gentleman, Thomas Knyvett, revealed his constant concern over the health and well-being of his family; after receiving a letter from his young daughter, he wrote back: 'I must not forget to thank my dear Buss for her rare composure of her crumbs of comfort to her poor father; it made me almost cry like Pig'hogg, God bless her sweet face. When my cousin, Anthony, comes, Jack may come too for a night or two, for I shall joy to see him.'[104] When his daughter was ill with suspected rickets in 1647, Ralph Josselin asked God to bring about her recovery, describing her as 'a comfort unto me' in 'a dark time for fears, murmurings, discontents'.[105] In the early 1650s, the exiled Royalist Sir George Strode translated into English, Christoval de Fonseca's treatise on familial love, entitled *A Discourse of Holy Love*. Dedicating the work to his children, he explained that he had undertaken it 'to alienate the weight of my pressing afflictions', and declared:

> When I had finished and considered that the general subject of the whole work was love and the several parts thereof might tend to the better ordering of a Godly moral and civil life, I knew not unto whom more fitly to recommend it, as the legacy of a dying man, than to you, my dear children, the living Scions of my corporal stock, and the comfortable cares of my drooping age.[106]

What is probably, however, the most explicit testimony to the consolation that children offered their parents during this period is found in the doggerel verse autobiography of Sir John Gibson of Welburn in Yorkshire, which includes the lines:

> When uncivil civil wars withall
> Did bloodshed bring and strife,
> Twelve sons my wife Penelope
> And three fair daughters had,
> Which then a comfort was to me
> And made my heart full glad.[107]

---

[104] Schofield (ed.), *Knyvett Letters*, p. 113.
[105] Macfarlane (ed.), *Josselin Diary*, p. 94.
[106] Sir George Strode, *A Discourse of Holy Love* (London, 1652), dedicatory epistle (TT).
[107] J. C. Hodgson (ed.), *North Country Diaries*, Surtees Soc. Publs, 124 (1914), 52.

As was the case with relationships between wives and husbands, there was, therefore, no homogeneity of response from parents and children to the disturbing realities of war and revolution. Some parents found that, as a result of abnormal revolutionary pressures, they became both more physically and more emotionally estranged from their children, and ideological differences were also responsible for weakening and even destroying some families. None the less, only a small minority seem to have been prepared to follow the example of Sir Henry Vane the younger and put their duty to their 'common Parent' before their loyalty to their natural parents, and thus the familial structure of society was never seriously threatened during these years by widespread generational conflict. Indeed, within many families, parents and children drew closer together in the face of the increased external dangers, and, as a result, came to regard each other with a greater mutual respect. Within such families, the bond between the generations not only survived the crisis of the English Revolution, but emerged from it with its importance enhanced.

7
The Family and Illicit Sexual Relations

During the seventeenth century, as now, the powerful emotional drives of love and sexual attraction were two of the most fundamental influences upon the creation and operation of the family. New families were normally initiated during the period of courtship and romance which preceded marriage, and the subsequent success of a marriage was largely dependent upon the durability of the mutual love between husband and wife. Sexual relations within marriage were an important aspect of the intimacy between spouses, and, of course, essential for the creation of succeeding generations. Love and sexual attraction, however, were emotional forces which were also very common outside the family context. Single men and women frequently fell in love with, and sometimes indulged in sexual intercourse with, other single people whom they were subsequently either unable or unwilling to marry. Similarly, husbands and wives sometimes became infatuated by, and developed adulterous relationships with, third parties, often with disastrous consequences for their families. In these respects, the powerful drives of love and sexual attraction were serious potential threats to, as well as important ingredients of a stable family life.

It is important to stress at the outset that these two impulses figured large in the consciousness of a great many men and women in the seventeenth century, and that even during the revolutionary period from 1640 to 1660, thousands of individuals living in England were far more preoccupied by their expectations of romantic attachment or sexual fulfilment than they were by the momentous political events they were witnessing. This fact is clearly evident in several collections of love letters which survive from the period, such as those from Sir Thomas Hervey to Isabella May and those from Dorothy Osborne to William Temple. Sir Thomas Hervey's secret love for Isabella May occupied all his waking

The Family and Illicit Sexual Relations

thoughts during the early 1650s, and the obstacles that prevented their marriage caused him extreme distress. On one occasion he wrote to her: 'At night I lie down to heaviness and in the morning rise again to sorrow.'[1] Dorothy Osborne's infatuation with William Temple during the same period similarly dominated her existence, and the political differences between her own Royalist family and the Parliamentarian Temples were of no relevance whatsoever to her.[2]

Even some of those most directly exposed to the new political and religious ideas which emerged during the 1640s and 1650s found them less forceful and appealing than the traditional attractions of romance and sex. John Milton's nephew, Edward Philips, was brought up in his uncle's serious and austere London household, where the progress of the English Revolution was the central concern of the head of the family. However, in embarking upon a literary career of his own in the 1650s, he rejected Milton's preoccupation with weighty ideological questions and compiled instead a light-hearted handbook for lovers. His popular *The Mysteries of Love and Eloquence or the Arts of Wooing and Complimenting*, published in 1658, contained a wealth of practical advice for the aspiring lover, including model conversations, a dictionary of rhymes and epithets, and reprints of romantic poems and songs.[3] Similarly, when in 1655 a Quaker woman from Chichester 'fell into love with one of the world', she put her feelings of love before her religious loyalties and severed her links with the Quaker movement in order to marry the man. Even the persuasive talents of the movement's leader, George Fox, could not prevail upon her to change her mind; after he had later talked and prayed with her for some time, Fox was forced to admit that 'a light thing got up in her and she slighted it.' The woman's marriage subsequently proved a disaster, but only after some considerable time was she prepared to return to Quakerism.[4]

However, if many remained more interested in their chances of finding love and sexual fulfilment than in the dramatic political and religious changes of their day, some of these changes did, none the less, have a noticeable impact upon their prospects in this sphere. The existence of the rival civil-war armies provided unaccustomed opportunities for romance and sexual adventure, both for the soldiers themselves and for the womenfolk of the communities upon which they were quartered. The

---

[1] S. H. A. Hervey (ed.), *The Letter Books of John Hervey, 1st Earl of Bristol* (3 vols, Wells, 1894), vol. 1, pp. 1–32, esp. pp. 6–7.
[2] Hart (ed.), *Letters of Dorothy Osborne, passim*.
[3] Edward Philips, *The Mysteries of Love and Eloquence, or the Arts of Wooing and Complimenting* (London, 1658), *passim* (TT); and *DNB*, Edward Philips (1630–96?).
[4] Nickalls (ed.), *Journal of George Fox*, p. 230.

coming of civil war also brought about the breakdown of the church courts, which for centuries before 1640 had been responsible for the punishment of offences against traditional morality. As a result of the disappearance of these courts, the 1640s witnessed a temporary relaxation of the laws against sexual transgression, and this in turn may have been one reason for the emergence in the late 1640s of groups of radical antinomians, such as the Ranters, who challenged the whole of the contemporary moral and sexual code. The response of the rulers of the new English republic to the threat from these antinomians was the passing in 1650 of new draconian legislation against sexual offenders, by which fornication became punishable with imprisonment and adultery with death.

The overall effect of these developments has been the subject of considerable historical debate. Some historians have suggested that something approaching a sexual revolution occurred in mid-seventeenth-century England. Christopher Hill has argued that the breakdown of the church courts lessened the intrusion by the authorities into the sexual activities of the lower orders, and thus had a widespread 'liberating effect',[5] and in *The Popular Movement for Law Reform*, D. Veall claimed that English men and women were much freer from moral censure during the 1640s and 1650s than they had been before 1640 or would be again after 1660.[6] If there was in fact greater freedom in the sphere of sexual relations in Interregnum England, this would have come as no surprise to a later revolutionary theorist, Friedrich Engels, who remarked in the nineteenth century that

> It is a curious fact that, with every great revolutionary movement, the question of free love comes into the foreground. With one set of people, as a revolutionary progress, as a shaking off of old traditional fetters no longer necessary; with others as a welcome doctrine, comfortably covering all sorts of free and easy practices between man and woman.[7]

Others, however, have argued that the indices of illicit sexual behaviour which exist for the period 1640–60, such as the recorded bastardy rates, do not appear to confirm a picture of a sexually liberated society, and the recent work of Colin Davis has also raised important questions about the

---

[5] Hill, *World Turned Upside Down*, pp. 253–9.
[6] D. Veall, *The Popular Movement for Law Reform* (Oxford, 1970), *passim*, esp. pp. 139, 141.
[7] Quoted by Hill in *World Turned Upside Down*, p. 247.

The Family and Illicit Sexual Relations 145

scale and significance of the Ranter phenomenon. In this chapter we shall investigate the impact of the developments outlined above, and attempt to assess how great a threat they posed to the traditional familial structure of seventeenth-century English society.

The coming of war in 1642 undoubtedly brought many young men and women enhanced possibilities for romantic attachment and sexual adventure, either as a result of the interruption of normal familial controls or through their service in, or exposure to, the armies of the rival warring factions. In 1647, Mary Verney wrote from Buckinghamshire to her husband, Sir Ralph, informing him that his sister Elizabeth, who was living at Claydon House, had taken advantage of his absence to embark upon a relationship with a local servant and that 'they have often found her sitting on his lap.'[8] The attraction of soldiers for young girls was, of course, well known, and a cliché of the popular literature and ballads of the day, and many girls became romantically involved with the young men who were billeted upon their communities. The strength of the romantic attachment which could develop within a short space of time is vividly illustrated by an extraordinary incident which occurred in Buckinghamshire in the middle of the war. In the summer of 1644, a group of parliamentary soldiers laid siege to and subsequently burnt to the ground, Hillesden House, the home of the Royalist Sir Alexander Denton. During the final sack of the house, Sir Alexander's sister, Susan Denton, fell in love with Jeremiah Abercromby, one of the troopers who was engaged in the destruction of her family home. After a courtship which took place during the few hours before the women of the house were evacuated to Claydon House several miles away, the pair decided to marry. One of the woman's relatives later commented, probably with some under-statement, that 'I think few of her friends like it, but if she hath not him she will never have any, it is gone so far.' The couple were duly married several days later, but Jeremiah, who continued to fight for Parliament, was killed the following year.[9] That Susan Denton could have become so fondly attached to a total stranger whom she had initially met as an enemy and the destroyer of her home, would seem to be striking testimony to the power of love and its ability to make nonsense of divisions based upon less enduring sentiments.

Some wartime liaisons proved reasonably long-lasting and resulted in marriage, but, as the troops were frequently on the move and as many of them had left wives and children at home, they more frequently ended in disappointment and betrayal. In his history of the parish of Myddle in

[8] Slater, *Family Life*, pp. 79–80.
[9] *Verney Memoirs*, vol. 1, pp. 318–9.

Shropshire in the seventeenth century, Richard Gough related the story of one married woman from the parish who had become involved with a soldier during the 1640s. According to Gough, the 'lovely handsome woman' had married a local gentleman 'more to please her father than herself' and had later given birth to his son. Subsequently, however, she deserted her husband and child, and ran away with an army captain. The officer had promised to take her with him to Ireland, but he abandoned her shortly afterwards in Chester. After Gough's grandfather had stepped in to mediate on the woman's behalf, her husband agreed to accept her back on the payment of a second marriage portion; she died, however, a short time after. As a comment on the story, Gough quoted the Latin epigram 'Nulla fides pietasque viris qui castra sequuntur' (There is no faith or reverence in those who follow wars).[10]

Many liaisons between women and civil-war soldiers amounted to little more than opportunities for short-term sexual gratification. From his study of sexual attitudes and practices in seventeenth-century Somerset, G.R. Quaife discovered that the soldiers billeted on communities in this part of the west country during the war often became involved in sexual relationships with local women; in his view, the soldiers frequently enjoyed female company and had 'considerable sexual opportunities'. Quaife also found that many of the neighbours of women who fraternized with the soldiers assumed that they would indulge in illicit sex and feared that the outcome would be a spate of bastard children whom the community would be forced to support, but that large numbers of west country women nevertheless continued to consort with the soldiery even in the face of this widespread hostility from other villagers. He cites one incident in which, on finding a village girl sitting under a hedge with a soldier, one of her neighbours had immediately attacked her with a sword.[11] Large numbers of prostitutes also travelled with the armies and, despite a number of initiatives, such as Charles I's proclamation of 13th July 1643, which attempted to dissuade the soldiers from resorting to them, they appear to have found a ready supply of customers.[12]

While some young women involved themselves with the soldiers voluntarily, others found themselves the focus of their attentions against their wills. The author of *The Scourge of Civil Warre, The Blessing of Peace*, published in 1645, warned readers that war 'enforceth the Mother to behold the Ravishment of her own Daughter', whereas peace in

---

[10] R. Gough, *The History of Myddle*, ed. D. Hey (Harmondsworth, 1981) p. 159.
[11] Quaife, *Wanton Wenches*, pp. 46, 49.
[12] Fraser, *Weaker Vessel*, p. 196.

contrast 'Shields the Wife from Soldiers' force, keeps virgins undefiled.'[13] Many stories of the abusing of women by soldiers exist from the civil-war years, such harassment normally taking the form of verbal or physical attacks, the stripping off of clothing and the offering of persistent unwanted sexual advances. In December 1642, Edward Read stated in a letter to Sir John Coke that 'our soldiers are not so modest with ladies in their plundering, neither of the king's side nor the Parliament's, when they are once at work'; and according to the Berkshire gentleman, William Trumbull, some of the soldiers quartered at his house at Easthampstead during the war pulled one of his serving girls from her bed and assaulted her.[14] In 1645, Sir Ralph Verney was informed by his brother Thomas that their sisters who were living at Claydon House were 'subject to the affrights of rude soldiers, rushing in at all hours both by day and night.'[15] Lord Goring's Royalist troops possessed a particularly bad reputation and were notorious for the numerous robberies and rapes they had allegedly committed in the west country.[16] In addition, some women appear to have been the victims of their communities' need to placate the unruly soldiery; when a number of Royalist cavalry descended upon the village of Doulting in Somerset in 1645, abusing and assaulting the inhabitants and demanding a woman to entertain them, the village forced one Joan Eaton to attend them, and she spent the whole night with the soldiers. She was afterwards ostracized by the rest of the village and, as a consequence, forced to continue to sell herself to the soldiers of both sides.[17]

Many of the soldiers who were offered increased opportunities for romance and sexual adventure as they travelled across England in the rival civil-war armies had left at home wives and lovers who were correspondingly deprived of the normal focus for their amorous and sexual pursuits. There is evidence to suggest that some of these abandoned women may have been courted by other civilian males and that a number may have acquired temporary replacements for their absent menfolk. The early months of the Civil War saw the publication in London of a number of satirical pamphlets which took as their subject the sexual frustrations of the capital's womenfolk. *The Resolution of the Women of London to Parliament*, which appeared in August 1642, stated that some of the wives whose husbands were away had decided to

[13] *Scourge of Civil Warre*, unpag.
[14] HMC *Cowper MSS*, vol. 2, p. 327; Durston, 'Berkshire', vol. 1, p. 206.
[15] Slater, *Family Life*, p. 80.
[16] D. Underdown, *Somerset in the Civil War and Interregnum* (Newton Abbott, 1973), p. 87.
[17] Quaife, *Wanton Wenches*, p. 50.

'maintain a friend, that upon occasions may do us pleasure', and went on to claim that, as the large numbers of unmarried women in the capital were finding it more difficult to find potential marriage partners: 'some maids are fully resolved to expose themselves and their commodities to trading, not doubting but to have three for one for every adventure, and afterwards make very good wives for hungry soldiers at their return from the wars.'[18] At the beginning of 1643, a petition claiming to represent the views of some of London's midwives argued that many wives in the capital, deprived by the war of their normal sexual partners, had been tempted to 'yield up the the Fort to the flattering enemy of their long preserved chastity.'[19] Several weeks later, *The Humble Petititon of Many Thousands Wives and Matrons of the City of London and Other Parts of the Kingdom* also suggested that, with their husbands away fighting, some wives in the city had been forced to 'steal or borrow [sex] from neighbours'.[20]

Some of these stories may not have been entirely without foundation. The long absences of husbands which the war occasioned certainly gave wives the opportunity to indulge in extramarital sexual relations, and some men would have been very willing to tempt them to commit adultery. Quaife cites the example of a woman from Clutton in Somerset, who was propositioned while her husband was serving as a soldier in Ireland, and told by her would-be lover that her husband 'used the company and lay with women in Ireland and had carnal knowledge of their bodies, and he would wish her to do the like with men here in England.' Quaife in fact suggests that large numbers of the civil-war soldiers returned home to find that their wives had been unfaithful in their absence, and some discovered that, presuming them to be dead, their wives had become involved in long-standing adulterous relationships with other men.[21]

Another development which may have encouraged a temporary increase in illicit sexual activity during the 1640s was the collapse of the church courts. For centuries before 1640, these courts had supervised the implementation of the contemporary moral code and, in particular, had meeted out humiliating punishments to convicted fornicators and adulterers. During the 1630s, when the established church had been under the control of the conservative archbishop of Canterbury, William

---

[18] *The Resolution of the Women of London to Parliament* (London, 1642), unpag. (TT).
[19] *The Midwives' Just Petition*, unpag.
[20] *The Humble Petition of Many Thousands Wives and Matrons of the City of London and Other Parts of the Kingdom* (London, 1643), p. 6 (TT).
[21] Quaife, *Wanton Wenches*, p. 126.

Laud, the ecclesiastical courts had carried out their work extremely conscientiously and had vigorously prosecuted moral offenders from all social ranks. In 1641, however, the Long Parliament abolished the most important ecclesiastical court, High Commission, and soon afterwards the church courts also began to disappear from the provinces. According to some contemporaries, the next few years saw a significant increase in promiscuous behaviour. In the satirical pamphlet *The Spiritual Courts Epitomized*, published in 1641, two lawyers lamented the loss of their lucrative ecclesiastical business; one admitted that 'No more can we send our Messengers into the Country, that pry into People's actions there', and the other declared that 'your whores that would have hanged themselves before to please us, now call us civil villains.'[22] In 1647, the conservative clergyman, Thomas Fuller, declared in his *Good Thoughts in Worse Times* that 'Vice these late years hath kept open house in England . . . No penance for the adulterer, stocks for the Drunkard . . .'; and in his memoirs written in the 1670s, Sir Philip Warwick described the Court of High Commission as 'the terror of such scandalous sinners', and claimed that after its demise adultery and fornication had been committed 'barefacedly'.[23]

Among the groups and individuals accused of taking advantage of this freer environment were some of those most closely associated with the dramatic political and religious changes taking place in England during these years. Those seeking evidence of a connection between political radicalism and sexual liberation could begin their investigations with the activities of Henry Marten. Arguably the most radical of all Charles I's parliamentary opponents, Marten advocated a republican solution to England's political crisis from an early stage, and as a result of his virulently anti-monarchical stance, he was ejected from the House of Commons by his fellow MPs in 1643. In the late 1640s, he was associated with the Levellers' demand for sweeping reforms in a democratic direction, and in the 1650s he became increasingly opposed to Oliver Cromwell's unrepresentative military rule. Marten was also equally notorious for his fascination with women, and was thoroughly disapproved of by many of his contemporaries on account of his alleged promiscuity. John Aubrey claimed that on the eve of the Civil War Charles I had called Marten an 'ugly rascal' and 'whoremaster', and that he was subjected to frequent attacks upon his personal morality from other Long Parliament MPs.[24]

[22] *The Spiritual Courts Epitomized* (London, 1641), p. 5 (TT).
[23] Fuller, *Good Thoughts in Worse Times*, p. 140; Warwick, *Memoirs of the Reign of King Charles I*, p. 175.
[24] Durston, 'Berkshire', vol. 2, pp. 100–9; and *DNB*, Henry Marten (1602–80).

What seems to have particularly outraged contemporary opinion was the fact that Marten had separated from his wife and was living openly during the 1650s with his long-term mistress, Mary Ward.[25] After Marten's arrest as a regicide at the Restoration, Edmund Gayton published a collection of some of his letters to Mary Ward, under the title *Col. Henry Marten's Familiar Letters to his Lady of Delight*. Gayton's main intention was to discredit Marten's political beliefs, and he drew a close connection between his political and his sexual radicalism; in the preface which was addressed to the regicide, he declared: '... let these letters stand a charge for ever against you, and testify what a Reformer you and your fellow-Governors of this nation were like to be, who, if they were all deciphered, I believe we should find them as true as yourself to the Smock, or your Page, Dick Pettingall.'[26] Another member of the Rump Parliament, Gregory Clement, was also denounced as an adulterer, and as a result was forced to give up his seat in Parliament in the early 1650s.[27]

Close connections were also drawn between sexual promiscuity and religious radicalism. One of the earliest accusations of indulgence in illicit sexual activity by religious radicals was made against the Familists, or Family of Love. This group had been introduced into England by its founder, Henry Niclaes, in the mid-sixteenth century, and thereafter had been periodically accused of promoting sexual licence; in 1641, the author of the pamphlet *A Description of the Sect called the Family of Love* accused a Familist group based at Bagshot in Surrey of celebrating the feast of the Greek god of fertility, Priapus, and of honouring the Roman poet Ovid, who had written the *Art of Loving*. The writer also claimed that the Familists' leader had seduced a young girl, who had been persuaded to attend their meetings.[28] As the influence of the radical sects spread during the civil-war years which followed, some observers believed that there was a consequent increase in promiscuous behaviour; in March 1645, Sir Samuel Luke, the parliamentary governor of Newport Pagnell, wrote to Cornelius Holland to inform him about the influence of sectarian preachers in that town, claiming:

> impiety is grown to such a height in this town that my eyes can no longer endure the sight of it, nor my ears the hearing ... If I stay here, I must have liberty to free the town of them, lest God in his

---

[25] HMC *Appendix to Fifth Report*, p. 192.
[26] Gayton (ed.), *Henry Marten's Familiar Letters*, preface.
[27] A. B. Worden, *The Rump Parliament* (London, 1974), p. 284.
[28] *A Description of the Sect Called the Family of Love*, passim.

wrath deal with us as he did with Sodom and Gomorrah, for here women can be delivered of children without knowing men (if they belie not themselves) and men and women can take one another's words and lie together and insist it not to be adultery.[29]

By the later 1640s, however, the bulk of the contemporary criticism was directed against the activities of the Ranters. As was seen in chapter 2, some of the most prominent theorists of this group, such as Lawrence Clarkson and Abiezer Coppe, advocated indulgence in casual, multi-partner sexual relations, and, according to a number of hostile accounts which were published in the early 1650s, such promiscuous activity was common at Ranter meetings. John Reading claimed in *The Ranters Ranting* that at their meetings 'each brother takes his she other upon his knee and the word (spoken in derision of sacred wit) being given, viz. Increase and Multiply, they fall to their lascivious embraces.'[30] It was also reported that women frequently took the initiative in these encounters; *The Ranters' Last Sermon* described how at one meeting a woman had approached a man offering to unbutton his codpiece, and the author of *The Routing of the Ranters* claimed that 'in this kind of coupling together (or making a conjunction copulative) the woman doth commonly make choice of the man she will dwell with.'[31]

Such Ranter principles were, of course, entirely incompatible with the normal operation of family life, and their adoption led some individuals to abandon their existing familial commitments and embark upon less conventional relationships. One man who, under the influence of Ranter ideas, openly carried on adulterous relationships was the minister of Langley Burrell in Wiltshire, Thomas Webbe. According to *The Wiltshire Rant*, written by the Wiltshire JP Edward Stokes, in 1650 Webbe moved his mistress into his house at Langley Burrell, and when his wife complained he tried to convince her that she too should take a lover. Webbe then allegedly arranged for a young man to have sexual intercourse with her while he himself was conducting a service in the church, and afterwards visited the couple in bed to congratulate them. Webbe's activities and the continuing *ménage à trois* subsequently came to the attention of Stokes and the other Wiltshire justices, who heard evidence that he had attempted to seduce women and had on one occasion shared a bed with a woman and another man. According to

---

[29] H. G. Tibbutt (ed.), *The Letter Books of Sir Samuel Luke 1644–5*, Bedfordshire Historical Soc. Publs, 42 (1963), 197.
[30] Quoted by Smith in *Ranter Writings*, p. 19.
[31] Ibid.; and *The Routing of the Ranters* (London, 1650), p. 6 (TT).

Stokes, Webbe continued to boast openly of his sexual relations with his 'fellow creatures', even after his arrest and subsequent release by an assize judge.[32]

Two other religious radicals, William Francklin and Mary Gadbury, believed that they had received a divine call to repudiate their families and live together as husband and wife. According to the hostile testimony of Humphrey Ellis, Francklin, a rope-maker from Stepney, had become convinced during the 1640s that he was another Christ and, as a result, had abandoned his wife and begun to associate with other women. When he met Mary Gadbury, a married woman from London whose husband had deserted her and was living in Holland, he was said to have told her that God had commanded him to separate from his family and that he had not had sexual relations with his wife for three years. He also told Gadbury that she was the woman that God had set aside for him. Towards the end of 1649, the pair travelled to Andover in Hampshire to proclaim Francklin as the new Messiah. Their activities later led to their arrest, and during the subsequent proceedings against them at the Hampshire quarter sessions, several witnesses claimed to have seen them in bed together. Gadbury, however, denied that they had ever had sexual relations and insisted that they had lain together 'without pollution or defilement'.[33]

Measures to deal with sexual offenders like Gadbury, Francklin and Webbe had been requested from within a few weeks of the meeting of the Long Parliament. In November 1640, the Commons Committee on Religion had received a petition from the clergy of Lincoln asking for stricter laws against fornication and adultery.[34] It was another four years, however, before the House of Commons took into consideration, in December 1644, a bill to deal with 'Incest, Adultery, Whoredom, Drunkenness, Swearing and Blaspheming the Name of God, and other enormous vices'. Despite an order that the bill should be 'put in due and lively execution', legislation failed to materialize at this stage.[35] Proposals were not seriously discussed again until February 1650, when further calls for reform prompted the MPs of the Rump into taking some action. The topic was debated on several occasions during the following three months, and in early May 1650 the Rump eventually passed its notorious and severe Act 'for suppressing the detestable sins of Incest,

---

[32] Stokes, *Wiltshire Rant*, passim.
[33] Ellis, *Pseudochristus*, passim.
[34] Keith Thomas, 'The Puritans and Adultery: The Act of 1650 Reconsidered', in D. H. Pennington and K. V. Thomas (eds), *Puritans and Revolutionaries* (Oxford, 1978), pp. 275–6.
[35] *Commons Journal*, vol. 3, pp. 721, 724; vol. 4, p. 35.

Adultery and Fornication'. The new legislation imposed the capital sentence without benefit of clergy upon all those found guilty of committing adultery. This was defined as sexual intercourse between a man and a married woman, intercourse between a married man and a single woman being only considered as fornication. For convicted fornicators the penalty of three months' imprisonment was prescribed, and those found guilty of prostitution were to be branded and whipped for a first offence and sentenced to death for any subsequent offence. In the case of adultery, however, the severity of the law was mitigated by several important provisos: the capital sentence would not be carried out upon any woman whose husband had been absent from home for three years or was 'by common fame reputed to be dead', or upon any man who was unaware that his sexual partner was married.[36] These qualifications made most cases of suspected adultery extremely difficult to prove.

Even after the passing of this draconian legislation, some contemporaries remained disturbed by what they saw as the continuing high level of illicit and immoral behaviour in the 1650s. Following the establishment of the Protectorate in 1653, Oliver Cromwell considered the improvement of the morals of the nation to be one of his most important duties as head of state. In August 1655, he issued a proclamation in which he complained that the 'good and wholesome laws' against moral offences were not being rigorously enforced, and that as a result 'ill-disposed persons have been hardened in their evil ways.'[37] When, in the same year, he appointed major-generals to control the English localities, he considered the eradication of immorality to be one of their most important tasks, and several of the major-generals took this aspect of their work extremely seriously and made strenuous efforts to close down illegal alehouses and brothels.[38]

Sexual promiscuity was also denounced in a number of literary works which appeared during the Interregnum. Several pamphlets which appeared in mid 1650s condemned the promiscuous activities which traditionally took place in Hyde Park on May Day. In 1656, one W.B. inveighed against the widespread immorality of his contemporaries in both *The Yellow Book* and *The Trial of the Ladies*, and claimed that 'the

---

[36] Firth and Rait (eds), *Acts and Ordinances*, vol. 2, pp. 387–9; and see Thomas, 'The Puritans and Adultery', pp. 258–80.
[37] *A Proclamation Commanding Speedy and Due Execution of the Laws against Drunkenness, Adultery and Fornication* (London, 1655), unpag. (TT).
[38] For details see Anthony Fletcher, *Reform in the Provinces: The Government of Stuart England* (London. 1986), pp. 252–62.

Devil's children are much in fashion, almost as ever I saw.'[39] Some contemporaries also believed that infanticide was common in London during the 1650s. On 11 February 1655, a proclamation dating from the reign of James I which condemned the murder of bastard children by their mothers, was read from the pulpit of all the London churches; reporting the incident, the newsbook *Several Proceedings of State Affairs* referred to infanticide as 'that great and now frequent sin', and pointed to the large number of prosecutions for the offence at the recent quarter sessions in the city.[40] In 1658, the author of *A Remedy for Uncleanness* also claimed that infanticide was rife, and suggested that it might be reduced by the introduction of polygamy.[41]

In addition, charges of immorality and sexual deviancy continued to be levelled at the religious radicals of the 1650s and, in particular, at the Quakers. In 1656, Jonathan Clapham declared that many Quakers were guilty of 'filthiness of the flesh' as well as 'filthiness of spirit', and reported that one Quaker had resorted to prostitutes and attempted to seduce a young girl in Norfolk, and that another had been imprisoned in Yorkshire for committing incest.[42] One popular ballad of the day even associated Quakerism with bestiality.[43] The early Quaker leader, James Nayler, was particularly singled out for denunciation for his sexual exploits. At the beginning of the Civil War, Nayler enlisted as a soldier for Parliament, leaving his wife and children at home at Wakefield in Yorkshire. Although he returned to the Wakefield area after the war, he shortly afterwards left his family and was suspected of carrying on an adulterous relationship with a woman whose husband was away at sea. After joining the Quakers in the early 1650s, he formed a close relationship with a number of prominent women in the new movement, including Martha Simmonds, Dorcas Erbury and Hannah Stranger. These associations and his undoubted attractions for many women led to accusations that he frequently practised adultery. The parliamentary committee which investigated his blasphemous entry into Bristol in 1656 concluded that Nayler believed that he could have sexual relations 'with any woman that is of his own judgement';[44] and in December 1656 the

---

[39] W.B., *The Yellow Book* (London, 1656), *passim* (TT), and W.B., *The Trial of the Ladies* (London, 1656), p. 14 (TT). See also *A Serious Letter Sent by a Private Christian to the Lady Consideration* (London, 1655) (TT).
[40] *Several Proceedings of State Affairs*, 8–15 Feb. 1655 (TT).
[41] *A Remedy for Uncleanness*, dedicatory epistle.
[42] Jonathan Clapham, *A Full Discovery and Confutation of the . . . Quakers* (London, 1656), p. 51 (TT).
[43] Hill, *World Turned Upside Down*, p. 256.
[44] *DNB*, James Nayler (1617?–60).

pamphlet *Satan Enthroned in his Chair of Pestilence*, relating the details of a visit that one Alice Brooks had paid Nayler in Newgate gaol, claimed that the women had told him 'it was given to her to come to him for a covering.'[45]

A small number of Quakers and other religious radicals may have posed an additional, though entirely different, threat to the family through their advocacy of total sexual abstinence. John Pordage's call to his parishioners at Bradfield to avoid marriage and practise 'Christian Eunuchism' has already been noted in chapter 2. In addition, when the Quaker leader, George Fox, was asked shortly after his own marriage whether the purpose of marriage was procreation, he was said to have replied: 'I never thought of any such thing, but only in obedience to the power of the Lord, and I judged such things as below me.[46]

There is, then, a good deal of evidence to suggest that illicit sexual activity was comparatively common in England between 1640 and 1660. However, in order to assess whether it was substantially more prevalent during these years than in the more settled periods that came before and after, and whether it thus posed a serious threat to a traditional society based upon monogamy and the nuclear family, it is necessary to investigate more closely the widespread contemporary perception of a marked decline in traditional morality during the revolutionary years.

Some of the evidence cited above which indicates an apparent growth in sexual promiscuity may not be entirely trustworthy. The significance of reports of the sexual transgressions by the soldiery during the civil-war years is easily exaggerated. Clearly, some promiscuity and sexual harassment did take place, but the numbers under arms at any one time were never more than a very small proportion of the country's total male population. In addition, stories of civil-war outrages were frequently embroidered by rumour-mongers, for both sides quickly recognized the propaganda value of depicting their opponents as rapacious libertines, and thus tended to exaggerate any incidents which did occur. Parliamentarian reports of the outrages supposedly committed in the north of England by Sir Marmaduke Langdale's Royalist cavalry, for example, appear to have been largely without foundation.[47] During May 1647, when Ralph Josselin learnt that numbers of New Model Army foot soldiers were marching through Essex towards his village of Earls Colne, he was alarmed by the reports of their 'abusing of women' and asked God for protection from 'their violence and insolency'. When they actually arrived at Earls Colne, however, he found them to be 'very quiet

---

[45] *Satan Enthroned in his Chair of Pestilence* (London, 1656), p. 23–4 (TT).
[46] Nickalls (ed.), *Journal of George Fox*, p. 557.
[47] Fraser, *Weaker Vessel*, p. 196.

and orderly'. Six months later, when more troops were quartered in Josselin's village, he again found them 'very erroneous fellows, but otherwise indifferent civil', and he later recorded that, in the whole of the six weeks they had spent in the village, the community had not received any 'affronts' at their hands.[48] Some civilians also found it convenient to blame their own sexual misconduct upon the soldiery; in Essex in 1645, a man who had had sexual intercourse with a fourteen-year-old serving girl was accused of telling her that 'she might lay it to a soldier in the army.'[49]

Nor were the humorous and scurrilous accounts mentioned above, which related how the soldiers' abandoned wives and sweethearts had resorted to fornication and adultery, very reliable.[50] Salacious gossip has always been a profitable subject for unscrupulous publishers and has likewise invariably found a large and credulous audience. More significantly, given that the central message of such publications was that London's menfolk would be well advised to return from the parliamentary armies as soon as possible, they were probably the work of Royalist sympathizers, whose intention was to reduce the numbers and undermine the morale of their opponents' forces. Again, some of those who claimed they had witnessed an increase in promiscuity during the 1640s had a vested interest in the propagation of such a view. Both Thomas Fuller and Sir Philip Warwick were strong supporters of the Stuart monarchy, and drew attention to the supposed decline in respect for the traditional sexual code during the Interregnum as evidence of the moral bankruptcy of Charles I's opponents.

The threat to conventional morality represented by the radical religious groups is also easily overestimated. The total membership of all the various radical sects in England during the period 1640–60 was never more than a small percentage of the country's total population,[51] and even within the sectarian congregations, the great majority fully upheld the traditional Christian sexual code and had no wish to overthrow the traditional moral code or replace the familial structure of society. The charge of sexual promiscuity, however, is a piece of mud that has frequently been slung, often on the basis of very little evidence, at those in the past who have professed extreme, heterodox opinions.

---

[48] Macfarlane (ed.), *Josselin Diary*, pp. 94–5, 108–9.
[49] Sharpe, *Crime*, p. 59.
[50] *Resolution of the Women of London*, passim; *Midwives' Just Petition*, passim; and *Humble Petition of Many Thousands Wives and Matrons*, passim.
[51] John Morrill has estimated that the total membership of all the sects was probably only about 5 per cent of the adult population of the country in the 1640s, and perhaps a slightly higher figure after the emergence of the Quakers in the 1650s. See Morrill, 'The Church in England 1642–9', p. 90 and n. 4.

The Family and Illicit Sexual Relations   157

Defending himself in 1649 against accusations that he was in favour of polygamy, the prominent Leveller, William Walwyn, declared in *The Fountain of Slander Discovered*:

> Another new thing I am asperst with is that I hold Polygamy . . . and this scandal would intimate that I am addicted to loose women; but this is another venomed arrow drawn from the same political quiver, and shot without any regard to my inclinations; and shows the author to be empty of all goodness and filled with a most reckless malice, for this is such a slander as dogs me at the heels home to my house; seeking to torment me even with my wife and children and so to make my life a burden unto me.[52]

Although, as we have seen, Jonathan Clapham roundly denounced the Quakers for their sexual deviancy in his *A Full Discovery and Confutation of the . . . Quakers*, he admitted that he had little concrete evidence that they had committed sexual sins, asserting only that 'we have sufficient conviction that they may be guilty.'[53] In reality, many Quakers upheld more exacting moral standards than their more conventional contemporaries. When, in 1656, George Fox and a group of Quakers in Launceston prison asked their gaoler what cases were due to come before the next quarter sessions and received the reply that thirty people were to be indicted for the 'small matter' of bastardy, they 'thought it very strange that they that professed themselves Christians should make small matters of such things'.[54]

With regard to the Ranters, in an important recent study *Fear, Myth and History: The Ranters and the Historians*, Colin Davis has argued persuasively that, as a result of the combined efforts of hostile contemporaries and sympathetic historians, the movement's contemporary significance has been greatly exaggerated. Davis has shown how some contemporary observers deliberately played up the significance of the Ranter movement and portrayed the group as 'folk-devils', in order to provoke an outraged 'moral panic' which would help to shore up the widespread attachment to the traditional moral code. He has also pointed out how accusations of Ranterism came to be used as weapons in the power struggles within the early Quaker movement, and suggested how some later historians, fascinated by the unconventionality of the ideas of the Ranters, have subsequently accorded them an unjustified contemporary importance.[55] While his conclusion that the Ranters never

---

[52] William Walwyn, *The Fountain of Slander Discovered* (London, 1649), p. 7 (TT).
[53] Clapham, *Full Discovery and Confutation*, p. 51.
[54] Nickalls (ed.), *Journal of George Fox*, p. 264.
[55] Davis, *Fear, Myth and History*, passim.

really existed may be something of an over-reaction to the historiographical distortions he has exposed, Davis's study would seem to indicate that the Ranters never represented a serious threat either to the accepted sexual ethics or to the traditional familial structure of seventeenth-century English society.

As we have seen above, even after the break-up of the Ranter movement in the early 1650s, fear and concern about promiscuous behaviour continued to be voiced during the Interregnum, and successive Puritan governments conducted concerted campaigns aimed at reducing vice and improving the country's moral standards. Such campaigns, however, may have been occasioned less by the existence of especially poor moral standards in the nation during these years, than by the obsession with order and moral probity shared by many of the Puritan revolutionaries who now exercised power. Oliver Cromwell was just one of a number of leading Puritan politicans who were determined to improve the morality of what they saw as God's chosen nation, but who, under the influence of their own stringent Calvinist discipline, aspired to unrealistically high standards. Those who drew up the 1650 Adultery Act were clearly worried about the numbers of sexual offenders, but the following years failed to bring any great avalanche of convictions in the localities. Prosecutions for adultery were extremely rare and only three people appear to have been executed for the offence. In addition, in most counties magistrates imprisoned only a small number of convicted fornicators each year.[56] While this low level of prosecution can probably partially be explained by the unwillingness of juries to convict and of justices to impose the act's draconian penalties, it also suggests that, unlike those in power in London, few people in the localities believed they were witnessing a dramatic growth in illicit sexual activity.

Nor is any increase in such activity confirmed by the figures for the number of illegitimate children born in England in the 1650s. Despite the fact that justices in a number of English counties are known to have made a special effort to uncover cases of bastardy and establish paternity,[57] the

---

[56] Thomas, 'The Puritans and Adultery', p. 258; J. S. Morrill, *Cheshire 1630–1660: County Government and Society During the English Revolution* (London, 1974), p. 246; Sharpe, *Crime*, pp. 59–70; Inderwick, *The Interregnum*, pp. 33–9; Quaife, *Wanton Wenches*, p. 81; Aylmer, *The State's Servants*, pp. 306–7. For examples see Harbin (ed.), *Quarter Sessions Somerset*, pp. 225, 301, 335, 346, 361, 379; Atkinson (ed.), *Quarter Sessions Records*, pp. 77–252; Wake (ed.), *Quarter Sessions Northampton*, pp. 108–211; and Jeaffreson (ed.), *Middlesex Records*, pp. 202–96.

[57] P. Laslett, *Family Life and Illicit Love in Earlier Generations* (Cambridge, 1977), p. 125; and P. Laslett, K. Oosterveen and R. Smith (eds), *Bastardy and Its Comparative History* (London, 1980), p. 14.

figures compiled by demographic historians fail to reveal any increase in the rates of illegitimate births or pre-nuptial pregnancy. On the contrary, they seem to suggest that during the 1650s the rates were at a lower level than at any other time in the seventeenth century. Keith Wrightson has argued persuasively that this apparent decline in bastardy rates is in fact an illusion, caused not by the success of the Puritan campaign against immorality, but rather by the greater inadequacy of the registration system during these years.[58] However, if there is no real evidence of a marked decline in the numbers of bastards born during the 1650s, there is certainly no suggestion of any significant increase either, and it would appear, therefore, that the incidence of pre-nuptial pregnancy and illegitimacy in England during the revolutionary years between 1640 and 1660 remained broadly similar to what it had been before 1640 and would be after 1660.

War and revolution, therefore, did provide new opportunities for romance and sexual adventure for some English men and women. The large concentrations of itinerant, and sometimes undisciplined, young men in the civil-war armies undoubtedly represented a temporary threat to sexual sobriety, and the absence during the 1640s of any effective sanctions against illicit sexual activity may have encouraged some to advocate and practise freer sexual ethics. Most of the soldiers, however, disappeared relatively quickly after 1646, and any sexual latitude that continued to exist during the late 1640s also proved shortlived. Nor should we forget that all societies, revolutionary or otherwise, that are established on the foundation of the monogamous nuclear family, have contained their fair share of fornicators and adulterers. In addition, those who engaged in such activities in England during the 1640s were never more than a small minority, and were regarded with widespread distrust and suspicion by the more conventional majority. It is also clear that, following the establishment of the republic and the stabilization of the political situation in the early 1650s, central and local government re-established procedures for dealing with those who transgressed the conservative Christian moral code, denouncing them and punishing them in much the same way as they had for many years before 1640. In reality, therefore, the 'sexual revolution' of the period 1640–60 amounted to no more than a small-scale and temporary dabbling in sexual experimentation, and, as such, it was never able to pose any real threat either to the accepted moral and sexual code of seventeenth-century English society, or to its traditional familial structure.

[58] Keith Wrightson, 'The Nadir of English Illegitimacy in the Seventeenth Century', in Laslett, Oosterveen and Smith (eds), *Bastardy*, pp. 176–92.

8
Conclusion

On the eve of the Civil War in 1641, the Presbyterian, Thomas Edwards, warned his contemporaries that the mounting calls for the abolition of the state church and the establishment of religious toleration would have disastrous consequences for the family. In his *Reasons Against the Independent Government of Particular Congregations* he declared:

> O how will this overthrow all peace and quiet in families, filling husbands and wives with discontents, and setting at variance Father and children, each against other, weakening that fervent love in those relations! O how will this occasion disobedience, contempt, neglects of Governors from inferiors of the family, whilst the Governors be looked upon by them as not in a true church! O how will this toleration take away . . . that power, authority which God hath given to Husbands, fathers and masters, over wives, children, servants . . . .[1]

Rather more than a decade later, after England had experienced ten years of bitter ideological conflict, Thomas Cobbet suggested that some of Edwards's worst fears had indeed been realized. In his *Fruitful Discourse Touching the Honour due from Children to Parents and the Duty of Parents to Children,* written in 1654, he pointed to the 'corruptions in the family in these declining and degenerate days', and commented 'Something is no doubt amiss in parents, something in children . . .'[2] The evidence presented in the preceding chapters, however, suggests that these and other similarly alarmist contemporary assessments of the impact of the revolution upon family life are not to be entirely

---

[1] Edwards, *Reasons Against the Independent Government of Particular Congregations*, pp. 26–7.
[2] Cobbet, *Fruitful Discourse*, epistle to reader.

trusted. As we have seen, the period from 1640 to 1660 did see calls for the abolition or fundamental remodelling of the traditional structure of the family, and the added pressures of these years did in some instances produce more discord and detachment in family relationships. However, as has also been argued above, in many other cases these same pressures strengthened the bonds between near relations and led to a greater appreciation of the need for familial support. What then was the overall effect of the upheavals of these years upon family life? Was the traditional seventeenth-century family a casualty of the revolution, or was it sufficiently resilient to ward off the new threats? Is there, indeed, a case for arguing that, in rising to meet the challenge from unprecedented external attacks, the family may have emerged from the revolution a stronger and more healthy institution? Although the scarcity of evidence makes it difficult to make dogmatic pronouncements, some tentative answers can perhaps now be put forward.

Two distinct types of threat to traditional family life emerged during the English Revolution – the dislocation of normal familial relationships through the premature death, exile and imprisonment of relatives, and the challenge to its nexus of loyalties and affections presented by the rival demands of new ideologies. With regard to the first of these, many families were damaged by wartime fatalities for, like all wars, the English Civil War produced large numbers of widows and orphans. In an attempt to alleviate their plight, Parliament passed a series of ordinances for the levying of taxes for the relief of the dependents of killed or maimed parliamentary soldiers, but in the difficult administrative conditions of war their full implementation was never possible.[3] As only the victors could expect any such consideration, many of the families of Royalists killed in the civil-war fighting faced serious material deprivation without any such external support. In addition, in the aftermath of the fighting the execution, exile and imprisonment of the defeated Royalists led to further separations of wives from husbands, and parents from children. Many Royalists also suffered acute problems as a result of the confiscation of their lands by the Parliamentarians, and some of them claimed that the loss of the revenue from their estates had brought their wives and children to the brink of destitution. One family which was particularly badly hit was the Newport family of Shropshire: in his will, written in 1648, Richard, Baron Newport of High Ercall, claimed that 'By the malignity of the recent times my family is dissolved, my chief house High Ercall is ruined, my household stuff and stock sold from me for having assisted the King.'[4] Normal family relations on both sides of

[3] Firth and Rait (eds), *Acts and Ordinances*, vol. 1, pp. 36–7, 102–3, 328–30, 938–40.
[4] *DNB*, Richard Newport (1587–1651).

the political divide were further strained by the war-induced economic depression of the late 1640s.

If some families were adversely affected by separations and material deprivation, others were neglected for the sake of more pressing public concerns, or torn apart by internecine conflicts of allegiance. Faced with conflicts of interests between their loyalty to their families and their commitment to the political causes of the 1640s and 1650s, a number of English men and women decided to put their public duties first. According to his wife Margaret, William Cavendish, the Royalist Duke of Newcastle, had on several occasions declared that 'his love to his gracious master, King Charles the Second, was above the love he bore to his wife, children, and all his posterity.'[5] During the parliamentary siege of Colchester in 1648, the Royalist governor, Lord Arthur Capel, refused to surrender the town even when his sick son was brought to the besiegers' lines.[6] We have also seen above how in the highly charged climate of ideological conflict in mid-seventeenth-century England, differences of political outlook frequently led to tensions and estrangements within families. A number of fathers, sons and brothers faced each other across the civil-war battlefields from the rival encampments, and considerable numbers of the soldiers of both sides counted more distant relatives amongst the ranks of their enemies. Such divisions could hardly fail to create some animosities between husbands and wives, parents and children, siblings and other kin, and the problems that divergent political allegiance caused within the Feilding and Verney families, for example, have been discussed above.[7] In addition, as the legitimacy of power in both the state and the family rested upon a common foundation, another potential consequence of the Civil War and the Parliamentarians' violent frontal assault upon the traditional hierarchical state, was the weakening of the theoretical basis of patriarchy in the family, and within some families the absolute power of fathers did indeed come under attack from both wives and children during these years.

Another new and potentially divisive pressure upon family relations, was conflicting religious allegiance. In the environment of increased religious freedom which existed in England during the 1640s and 1650s, a number of radical alternatives to the state church emerged, and many of these groups insisted that their members' first loyalty lay not with their blood relatives, but with their new sectarian 'families'. In support of this view, sectaries such as Katherine Chidley were able to quote no less an authority than Jesus Christ himself, who had told his earliest disciples

---

[5] Cavendish, *Life of William Cavendish*, p. 245.
[6] HMC *Beaufort MSS*, pp. 45–6.
[7] See above, ch. 3.

Conclusion 163

that 'he that loveth father or mother more than me, is not worthy of me, and he that loveth son or daughter more than me, is not worthy of me', and that 'every one that hath forsaken houses, or brethren or sisters or father or mother or wife or children for my sake, shall receive a hundredfold and shall inherit everlasting life.' Christ had also prophesied that as his teaching spread 'the brother shall deliver up the brother to death, and the father the child: and the children shall rise up against their parents, and cause them to be put to death.'[8] In accordance with such statements, when some seventeenth-century religious radicals found themselves with a conflict of interests between their loyalties to their family and their church, they were prepared to renounce their familial responsibilities for the sake of their religious beliefs. After Elizabeth Hooton, one of the first women to embrace Quakerism, had joined the new movement, she deserted her family to become an itinerant preacher.[9] Similarly, once Thomas Ellwood's conversion to Quakerism had brought him into violent conflict with his father and made it virtually impossible for the two of them to live under the same roof, Thomas took refuge with an alternative, spiritual 'family', joining the Quaker household of the Penington family at Chalfont St Peter.[10] The anguish which could result from such repudiations of close relatives was particularly vividly portrayed by John Bunyan in *Pilgrim's Progress*; when the hero, Christian, sets out on his long journey to the Celestial City, 'his wife and children . . . cry after him to return . . . but he put his fingers in his ears and ran on, crying life! life! eternal life.'[11]

The radical religious sects further threatened the patriarchal structure of the seventeenth-century family by placing important limitations upon the power that fathers could wield over their wives and children, and counselling their members to resist the commands of husbands and fathers when they believed them to be in conflict with divine injunctions. The fact that he had been forced to disobey his father in order to follow his Quaker beliefs was a cause of great sorrow and anxiety to Thomas Ellwood, but, having convinced himself that his father possessed no authority over him in spiritual matters, Thomas remained defiant even in the face of a series of physical beatings at his hands, and rather than compromise his new creed, he chose instead to accept permanent estrangement from his family.[12] As was seen in chapter 5, when the

---

[8] Matthew 10: 37; 19: 29. See also Chidley, *The Justification of the Independant Churches of Christ*, pp. 25–6.
[9] Fraser, *Weaker Vessel*, p. 358.
[10] 'Life of Thomas Ellwood', pp. 23–77, 93, 158. See also ch. 6 above.
[11] Quoted by M. Walzer in *The Revolution of the Saints* (Cambridge Mass., 1965), p. 198.
[12] 'Life of Thomas Ellwood', pp. 23–77, 93, 158.

itinerant Quaker, Jane Holmes, started to hold open-air religious meetings at Malton in Yorkshire in 1652, several men complained that their families had begun to disobey them: Major Baildon told the Yorkshire justices that Holmes had 'by delusion drawn the affection of his wife from him, so as he cannot keep her at home', and Thomas Dowsley claimed that Holmes was an 'instrument of drawing his wife and son from him', adding that his son 'doth deny him his true obedience unto him, and denies that he is any more to him than any other man.'[13]

Again, as was seen in chapter 7, the Ranters and some of the other extreme religious radicals advocated a completely new set of sexual ethics, totally at variance with the Christian ones upon which the traditional family had for centuries been founded. Some of those who came under the influence of such radical antinomian ideas subsequently abandoned their wives and children, and either took up with new, semi-permanent partners, or indulged in a series of casual adulterous relationships. In the case of individuals such as Thomas Webbe, William Francklin and James Nayler, the repudiation of the family appears to have been total and uncompromising. According to the report of a hostile contemporary, Edward Stokes, after deserting his wife and involving himself in a series of relationships with other women, Thomas Webbe 'never went to see his own child born in lawful matrimony, though he rode by the house where it was kept by the mother's friends.'[14] The early Quaker leader, James Nayler, also deserted his wife and children in the early 1650s, and even though he continued for some time after to live near them in the Wakefield area, he refused to have anything to do with them. At the quarter sessions at Appleby in Westmorland in 1652, Nayler told the justices who were examining him that shortly before he left his family he was 'at the Plough meditating on the things of God and suddenly I heard a voice saying unto me "Get thee out from thy kindred and from thy Father's House"'.[15] William Francklin was also accused of claiming that he had received an express command from God to separate from his wife.[16]

The families of these and other similar individuals were certainly casualties of the English Revolution, but it is important to remember that they constituted only a very small proportion of the hundreds of thousands of families which existed in mid-seventeenth-century England.

---

[13] Raine (ed.), *Depositions from York Castle*, pp. 55–6. See also Reay, *The Quakers*, pp. 69–70.
[14] Stokes, *Wiltshire Rant*, p. 82.
[15] DNB, James Nayler (1617?–60); James Nayler, *A Collection of Sundry Books, Epistles and Papers Written by James Nayler* (2 vols, London, 1716), vol. 1, p. 12.
[16] Ellis, *Pseudochristus*, p. 11.

Only a small minority of the families in the country were involved in any major way in the civil-war fighting and, as we have seen, of this minority, certainly less than one family in five, and probably less than one in ten, was 'by the sword divided'.[17] In addition, as was shown in chapter 3, once peace returned in 1646, within many families relatives quickly began to bury the political hatchets of the Civil War, and any divisions which had arisen during the war years were soon put aside. Within a few years of the ending of the war too, the damage that the conflict had done to the network of kinship and cousinage connection was beginning to be repaired by the forging of new marriage links between families which had so recently been sworn enemies. Similarly, the total membership of all the radical sectarian congregations was never more than a small percentage of the population of the country, and only a small section of their number experienced familial conflict as a result of their religious affiliations. While damage was, therefore, done to some families, the serious casualty rate was very low.

Again, even in the midst of revolution, ideology did not always prevail over more prosaic domestic concerns, for many individuals considered the well-being of their families to be at least as great a priority as their political and religious obligations. At the end of the war, many of the Royalists who reluctantly subscribed to Parliament's Solemn League and Covenant and Negative Oath, thereby publicly disowning the king, did so only because they could not otherwise have compounded for their estates and provided for their families' futures. In 1650, the Earl of Leicester grudgingly took the Engagement drawn up by the government of the new republic, primarily so that he could act as official trustee and guardian to his grandchildren, whose father, the Royalist Earl of Sunderland, had been killed during the Civil War.[18] The London merchant, William Walwyn, devoted a great deal of his time and energy during the late 1640s to the Leveller campaign for greater political and religious freedom. But he was also extremely attached to his wife and nearly twenty children, and placed great value upon his private family life. Following his arrest in 1649, he was particularly outraged that the large troop of soldiers sent to his house at Moorfields in the early hours of the morning had caused 'great terror' to his family; in the tract *The Fountain of Slander Discovered*, in which he subsequently defended himself against the accusations of his many critics, he stated that one of the reasons he was determined to refute the slanders made against him was that they

[17] See above, ch. 3.
[18] 'Journal of the Earl of Leicester', in Blencowe (ed.), *Sydney Papers*, pp. 100–1.

wound the Reputation of the Family whereof I am, and may too wound with grief my dear and ancient mother, whom I have the greatest cause to love; my wife and children also are deeply wounded in my reproaches, whom I value ten-fold above my life, and upon whom whensoever I leave the world I would have no blemish.[19]

Nor were the effects of the ideological upheaval of the English Revolution upon the family necessarily wholly malign. At a time when many of the traditional and long-cherished beliefs and institutions of English society were crumbling before their eyes and when serious external dangers were constantly threatening, it is not surprising that many individuals came to see their immediate families as bulwarks against, and refuges from, the uncertainty that surrounded them. Shortly after the start of the Civil War in 1642, the children and grandchildren of Sir John Bramston left their own homes and 'herded together' for protection at Sir John's house at Roxwell in Essex, and more than fifty of them remained under the same roof at Roxwell for much of the war.[20] Edmund Verney also seems to have felt a increased need for family solidarity; writing to his sister-in-law in 1644 to complain that he had not heard from her for over a year, he commented: 'I put it to yourself to judge of whether, think you, these times fit for those whom alliance ties to so strict a unity to live in any distance.'[21]

In addition, as the family and its traditional values appeared to come under mounting attack, conservative writers and ministers began to stress all the more the importance of the institution both in their literary works and pastoral activities. As was seen in chapter 2, throughout the 1640s and 1650s a number of theological writers, such as Jeremy Taylor, Robert Abbot and Thomas Cobbet, laid great stress in their books and sermons upon the importance of a well-regulated and religious family life. Some parish clergymen also made concerted efforts to increase the popularity of family devotions among their parishioners. In the 1650s, the Presbyterian minister Richard Baxter put aside two afternoons each week to catechize the families of his parish of Kidderminster, and in *The Reformed Pastor*, published in 1656, he encouraged other ministers to 'have a special eye upon families to see that they be well ordered and the duties of each relation performed. The life of religion, and the welfare and glory of Church and State dependeth much on family government

---

[19] Walwyn, *The Fountain of Slander Discovered*, pp. 11, 24.
[20] *The Autobiography of Sir John Bramston K.B.*, Camden Soc. Publs, 32 (1845), 109.
[21] *Verney Memoirs*, vol. 1, p. 289.

Conclusion

and duty.'²² Other divines were particularly fastidious in the regulation of their own families; the family of the Presbyterian minister John Angier, for example, was described by one contemporary as a 'well disciplined army, where all knew their proper stations and did carefully attend their post, yea a well instructed Academy, and an organized church.'²³

In the climate of widespread suspicion and confusion which prevailed during and after the war, many individuals also found that their relations with friends and acquaintances were weakened or destroyed, and that only their close kin could be fully relied upon. In 1645, Sir Ralph Verney wrote to a friend:

> I have such unkind (nay I may say unnatural) letters from some so near me, that truly, did I not see it under their own hands . . . I could not have credited that such a total decay of friendship and common honesty could possibly have been amongst those that profess Christianity. These trying times have discovered so much knavery in so many men that heretofore appeared examples of piety, few men can say they have a friend now whose face they knew a week before these troubles.²⁴

During 1650, the exiled Edward Hyde, who was suffering from serious financial difficulties, attempted to recover some of the debts owed him by Royalist friends who had remained in England. Instructing his wife to make contact with them, he told her in March 1650: 'I cannot yet believe that all affections in our friends in England are so dead as utterly to forget us, but that in good time, they who strain their consciences to enjoy plenty there, will administer a share to those who keep themselves entire abroad against that temptation.'²⁵ His confidence, however, in the affection and loyalty of his old friends proved misplaced, for he subsequently discovered that most of them remained deaf to his appeals.

In such a climate, many found that the only people they could entirely trust were their own close relatives. When Lady Brilliana Harley found herself surrounded in Herefordshire during the early months of the war by hostile Royalist neighbours, she wrote frequently to her absent husband, Sir Robert, and son Edward, and in one letter she told Edward

---

²² Baxter, *Gildas Salvianus*, pp. 83–6. See also *Reliquiae Baxterianae*, pp. 83, 85.
²³ E. Axon (ed.), *Oliver Heywood's Life of John Angier of Denton*, Chetham Soc. Publs, NS 97 (1937), 84–6.
²⁴ *Verney Memoirs*, vol. 1, p. 322.
²⁵ HMC *Marquis of Bath MSS*, vol. 2, pp. 89–91.

that she felt she could rely on nobody's advice but Sir Robert's.[26] A year before his outburst about the decay of friendship, Sir Ralph Verney had written to console his uncle, Sir Alexander Denton, after the death of his son, Colonel John Denton; he had assured him that

> ... a day will come (and none knows how soon) not only to put a period to all our miseries here, but to crown us with future glory, and bring us to our old and best friends (for new ones are, like the times, full of inconstancy and falsehood), with whom we shall (without compliment) perpetually remain to one another as I am to you.

When Sir Alexander died the following year, Sir Ralph commented that, during the previous year, his uncle had 'expressed more friendship and affection to me, than in all his life before.'[27] Similarly, at the beginning of 1658, Ralph Josselin recorded in his diary: 'I never had so much care of the family on me, having little help in those about me, indeed our cousin [is] a cosener rather than a help, no trust being in her, which made my wife more dear to me.'[28] Through their experiencing of the fickleness of friends and associates during these years, such individuals came to appreciate all the more the strength and importance of the ties of blood which held the family together.

The institution of the family may also have emerged strengthened from the maelstrom of revolution because many of the individuals who were either temporarily separated from their closest relatives by political exigency, or who faced permanent separation from them by imminent execution, developed as a result a greater awareness of the mutual solace and comfort which could be derived from familial relationships. As was shown in chapter 5, enforced absences between spouses, such as those between Sir Ralph and Mary Verney, Sir Hugh and Elizabeth Cholmley, Sir Richard and Anne Fanshawe, William and Margaret Cavendish, Sir Roger and Isabella Twysden, and Henry and Dorothy Spencer, caused great sorrow and anguish, but at the same time frequently deepened the feelings of fondness and love between husbands and wives.[29] This was certainly true in the case of the parliamentary general, Sir William Waller, whose release from prison in the early 1650s was secured largely through the efforts of his wife and who later recorded his gratitude to

---

[26] Lewis (ed.), *Letters of Lady Brilliana Harley*, p. 181.
[27] *Verney Memoirs*, vol. 1, pp. 320, 322.
[28] Macfarlane (ed.), *Josselin Diary*, p. 416.
[29] See above, ch. 5.

God for 'his comforts and blessings to me, particularly in my enlargement from my long captivity, my return with comfort to my children and family, and that inestimable blessing he hath pleased to bestow upon me in a most dear, good wife.'[30] In the same way, separations could also increase the strength of the emotional bonds between parents and children. As was seen in chapter 6, two individuals as ideologically estranged as Charles I and Henry Marten shared, during their respective periods of imprisonment, the same overriding concern for the safety and well-being of their children.[31]

Among those who came to value family life most highly during these years were some of the political casualties of war and revolution, who were about to be permanently separated from their relatives by their execution. Charles I was just one of a group of civil-war victims who displayed an almost reverential attachment to their families during their last days. The intensity of the emotions felt by these condemned men and their wives and children can be seen in surviving correspondence from the weeks before their deaths, in accounts of their final meetings with their relatives and in the statements they made on the scaffold. When the Parliamentarian Sir Alexander Carew was brought to the scaffold in 1644 for conspiring to surrender St Nicholas Island in Plymouth Sound to the Royalists, he referred in his last speech to the words and writings of his father and grandfather, and chose as a signal for the executioner the last words that his mother had spoken on her death-bed.[32] Despite his earlier refusal to surrender Colchester to the parliamentary forces for the sake of his family, the last meeting between Lord Arthur Capel and his wife and children before his execution in 1649 was an extremely emotional affair. George Morley, a clergyman who witnessed the scene and later attended Capel upon the scaffold, subsequently related how Capel's family had 'assaulted him . . . with passionate looks, gestures and words, bemoaning and bewailing him and themselves – his lady especially – with such sweet and tender expressions of love, sorrow and pity, that the greatest courage in the world must needs have been shaken with it.' Morley further related how, after they had departed, Capel had told him that 'the hardest thing that I had to do here in this world is now past, the parting with this poor woman.'[33] Another Royalist victim of the renewed fighting in 1648, Henry Rich, Earl of Holland, derived great comfort in the days before his execution from his close relationship with

---

[30] Waller, *Recollections*, pp. 132–3.
[31] See above, ch. 6.
[32] *DNB*, Sir Alexander Carew (1609–44).
[33] HMC *Beaufort MSS*, pp. 34–6.

his daughter, Susanna, Countess of Suffolk. According to Samuel Clarke, Susanna visited him frequently during his final days to help him to prepare for his coming ordeal, and at their last meeting, 'being refreshed with these comforts, he cried out "Happy I, that should, from a child of mine own, receive such consolation."' In his speech on the scaffold, Rich also made reference to the importance of the religious upbringing he had received within his family.[34]

Similar sentiments were expressed in the 1650s by several other Royalists who had been condemned for their activities in support of Charles Stuart. In 1651, when Charles invaded England at the head of a Scots army, one of those who joined his cause was James Stanley, Earl of Derby. Taken prisoner after the Battle of Worcester, Derby wrote to his wife from Chester, telling her that 'whatsoever comes my way, I have peace in my own breast, and no discomfort at all but the sense of your grief and that of my poor children and friends.' After he had been tried and sentenced to death, he wrote again to console her, declaring:

> I conjure you, my dearest heart, by all those graces which God hath given you, that you exercise your patience in this great and strange trial. If harm come to you, then I am dead indeed and until then I shall live in you, who is truly the best part of myself; when there is no such thing as I, then look upon yourself and my dear children; there take comfort and God will bless you.

On the scaffold he instructed his son, Lord Strange, to obey and help his mother, and told those around him that 'death had no other bitterness' but that it separated him from his wife and children.[35]

In the spring of 1655, following an abortive Royalist rising in Wiltshire against Cromwell's government, the leader of the rebels, Sir John Penruddock, was captured and sentenced to death. He subsequently wrote from prison to his wife Arundell, telling her not 'to make thyself and my poor children more unhappy by afflicting thyself for me'. Over the ensuing weeks, Arundell devoted all her energies to an unsuccessful campaign to save his life; after she had finally been forced to admit defeat and had visited him for the last time, she wrote to him:

> My sad parting was so far from making me forget you that I have scarce thought upon myself since, but wholly upon you. Those dear

---

[34] Clarke, *Lives of Eminent Persons*, part 2, p. 216; Clarendon, *History of Rebellion*, vol. 4, p. 508.

[35] F. R. Raines (ed.), *The Stanley Papers*, Chetham Soc. Publs, 66–7 (1867), part 3, 1, pp. cc–cci; 2, pp. ccxxvi, ccxliii, ccxliv.

Conclusion

embraces which I yet feel, and shall never lose (being the faithful testimonies of an indulgent husband) have charmed my soul to such a reverence of your remembrances that, were it possible, I would with my own blood cement your dead limbs to life again, and, with reverence, think it no sin to rob heaven a little longer of a martyr.[36]

Another Royalist family which suffered particularly acutely during the Interregnum as a result of its support for the Stuarts was the Fetherstonhaugh family of Kirkoswald in Cumberland. Sir Timothy Fetherstonhaugh, along with two of his sons, fought for Charles Stuart during the summer of 1651; the father was taken prisoner at Wigan Lane in Lancashire and subsequently executed, and both of the sons were killed at the Battle of Worcester. The family's financial losses as a result of their Royalism were estimated to be in the region of £10,000, and in 1661 two of Sir Timothy's younger sons referred to their continuing financial problems when petitioning for positions at the newly restored royal court.[37] A few days before his death in October 1651, in the midst of problems which seemed to be on the point of destroying his family, Sir Timothy sent a letter to his wife asking her to attempt to keep the family together; he wrote to her:

> It is a sad farewell I now must take, and my griefs do superabound for thee and my poor children ... Advise and educate my children in the fear of the lord, and let them never neglect prayers and private duties ... In the presence of God I speak it, thou hast been an unparallelled wife and mother to thy children .... It is time my thoughts and actions were wholly taken up with contemplation of heaven where with comfort I hope we shall meet. And till then God bless thy children and thee, and comfort thee and thy poor, unfortunate dying husband.[38]

That the crisis of the 1640s and 1650s could result in a strengthening of the emotional bonds within those families which had most acutely experienced its tensions and pressures, is perhaps nowhere more clearly seen than in the agonized, but undespairing, sentiments expressed in these letters.

Further confirmation that, even in revolutionary England, familial

---

[36] Ravenhill, 'Records of the Rising in the West, A.D. 1655', vol. 13, p. 133; vol. 15, pp. 1–2.
[37] *DNB*, Sir Timothy Fetherstonhaugh (d. 1651).
[38] HMC *Le Fleming MSS*, p. 20.

considerations continued to obtrude upon newer ideological influences, and that private family matters remained of greater importance to most individuals than the dramatic political and religious changes which were taking place in the country, can be found in the diary of the Essex vicar, Ralph Josselin. Josselin's intense preoccupation with the welfare of his immediate family is evident on virtually every page of this detailed record of his thoughts and actions during the 1640s and 1650s, but its ability to transcend political concerns is particularly vividly illustrated by the juxtaposed comments in the entries for two dates in 1654. On 12 July, the date of the election of MPs for Cromwell's first Protectorate Parliament, Josselin commented in his diary: 'this day set apart for the choice of parliament men through the kingdom, and I set it apart to seek god in behalf of my family'; and six weeks later, on 1st September, he remarked: 'One called and told me that this Friday the Pro[tector] was to be proclaimed Emp[eror]: God good in preserving Ann in a milk bowl, and Jane from swooning, who let her fall in.'[39]

In his autobiography, published in the later seventeenth century, Richard Baxter related a striking parable of the survival of family life in the midst of revolutionary turmoil. He claimed that, following the sack of Bolton by Prince Rupert in 1644, an old woman had found a small baby lying in the street near its dead parents. Taking it home, she put the hungry baby to her own breast, and although she had had no children for over thirty years, 'the Child drew Milk, and so much that the Woman nursed it up with her Breast milk a good while.'[40] Like the apocryphal child of this legend, the family survived the English Revolution, and it did so because the traditional rhythms and sentiments of family life were too strongly rooted to be blown away by the chill winds of material deprivation and ideological ferment which temporarily swept across England during the mid-seventeenth century. Indeed, in some cases these chill winds may actually have enhanced the importance of the family. For those members of the Bramston family who decided to live together during the war years were just one small part of a much larger group of English men and women who, faced with a succession of serious threats to their property, personal safety and most highly valued beliefs and institutions, came to see their families as an important refuge from, and bulwark against the chaos that surrounded them. The general effect of war and revolution upon family relationships, then, seems to have been one of intensification. For where pre-war relations between kin had been cool and distant, the added pressures of revolution could easily lead to conflict and enmity; but where they had been based upon a genuine

[39] Macfarlane (ed.), *Josselin Diary*, pp. 326, 330.
[40] *Reliquiae Baxterianae*, p. 46.

mutual concern and affection, they were often strengthened by the uncertainties of the 1640s and 1650s and came to be held in far greater respect.

Any additional long-term impact that the war and revolution may have had upon the patriarchal nature of family life is extremely difficult to assess. Reviewing the activities of the religious radicals in his article 'Women and the Civil War Sects', Keith Thomas concluded that, as Thomas Edwards had predicted, the call for religious toleration did indeed lead to a 'redefinition of the limits of paternal power'.[41] Lawrence Stone has also argued that the Puritans' acknowledgement of the claims of the individual conscience produced 'a respect for personal autonomy', and has suggested that the assault by the Parliamentarians upon the patriarchal power of the state may have led to a weakening of patriarchy in the family. As evidence of this, he cites the comments of Mary Astell, who argued in her *Reflections on Marriage*, published at the beginning of the eighteenth century, 'If absolute authority be not necessary in a state, how comes it so in a family? Or, if in a family, why not in a state . . . Is it not then partial in men to the last degree to contend for and practise that arbitrary dominion in their families which they abhor and exclaim against in the state?'[42] However, as Mary Astell was herself acknowledging in this complaint against male hypocrisy, patriarchal power remained a strong and widely exercised force for many years after 1660. If, therefore, the absolute authority of husbands and fathers was seriously questioned, perhaps for the first time, during the period 1640–60, these years saw only the tentative opening rounds of a long contest to establish greater rights and freedoms for wives and children. In addition, any discrediting of patriarchy which did occur during these years probably owed as much to the assumption by wives of greater duties and responsibilities, and to the mutual support that many spouses brought to each other in the face of external danger, as it did to conflict and ideological discord.

The English Revolution failed, then, to destroy the family, but the family may have helped to destroy the English Revolution. We have already seen how, after 1646, older familial allegiances soon began to reassert themselves and to dilute the strength of ideological enmities. In addition, as John Morrill has pointed out in a study of the fortunes of the Anglican church during the 1640s, in order to be successful religious revolutions must 'adapt themselves to, as much as they change popular culture'.[43] The problem, however, for the Puritan rulers of Interregnum

[41] Thomas, 'Women and the Civil War Sects', p. 57.
[42] Stone, *Family, Sex and Marriage*, pp. 240, 262.
[43] Morrill, 'The Church in England 1642–9', p. 114.

England was that they found some of the most important aspects of the popular culture of the English people highly objectionable, and were thus unable to harmonize them in any way with their own values. Rather than harnessing the old culture to their revolutionary aspirations, they were responsible for launching a series of ill-judged frontal assaults upon it. Their attempts to introduce major changes in some of the most cherished rituals of family life, in particular the ceremonies associated with baptism and marriage, were, as we have seen, especially resented and widely resisted. Discussing the introduction of civil marriage by Barebone's Parliament in 1653, in his *History of the Commonwealth and Protectorate*, the Victorian historian Samuel Gardiner commented that 'there was nothing in it to give offence to any reasonable person who refused to regard marriage as a purely civil institution.'[44] For once, however, he was wrong; for many people were greatly offended, and the effect of these and other equally unpopular attempts to impose cultural change was to increase the opprobrium in which the revolutionary regimes were held and to contribute substantially to their ultimate downfall.

The return of the Stuart monarchy in 1660 signalled the failure of the English Revolution, and one of the reasons why so many English men and women welcomed Charles II back at the Restoration was that, by the late 1650s, they had come to believe that the well-being of their traditional familial culture would best be provided for by the return to power of the man whom many still regarded as the father of the nation. In June 1660, a few weeks after Charles II's return, the former supporter of Parliament, Ralph Josselin, asked God to make the restored king 'a nursing father to thy people'.[45] A few months earlier, writing to his wife about the prospects for a restoration, the Royalist John, Viscount Mordaunt, had commented: 'After this blessed day which I in no way question that we shall suddenly see, you and I will retire and serve God all our lives and teach our children to serve God and be good subjects.'[46] Of the many enemies which confronted the governments of Interregnum England during the 1650s, none was more powerful or more hostile than the traditional culture of English society, and of this culture, no aspect was more deeply rooted, all-pervasive and resilient than the institution of the family.

---

[44] S. R. Gardiner, *The History of the Commonwealth and Protectorate 1649–1656* (4 vols, New York, 1965 edn), vol. 2, p. 292.
[45] Macfarlane (ed.), *Josselin Diary*, p. 464.
[46] Coate (ed.), *Letter Book of John, Viscount Mordaunt*, p. 164.

Bibliography

1 Primary Sources

Manuscript Collections

D'Ewes family papers, British Library, Harleian MSS 379–83. Feilding family papers, Warwickshire Records Office, CR.2107. Hopkinson MSS, Bradford District Archives, 32D86/17. Neville family papers, Berkshire Records Office, D/EN, F.

Printed Works

Official Records (For primary material incorporated within secondary works see Section 2.)

Atkinson, J. C. (ed.), *Quarter Sessions Records*, North Riding Records Society Publications, vol. 5 (1887).
Bennett, J., and Dewhurst, J. (eds), *Quarter Sessions Records for the County Palatine of Chester*, Lancashire and Cheshire Records Society Publications, vol. 94 (1940).
Calendar of State Papers, Domestic Series, 1640–65.
Commons Journal.
Copnall, H. H. (ed.), *Nottinghamshire County Records* (Nottingham, 1915).
Cunnington, B. (ed.), *Records of the County of Wilts.* (Devizes, 1932).
Fearon, W. A., and Williams, J. F. (eds), *Parish Registers and Parochial Documents in the Archdeaconry of Winchester* (London, 1909).
Firth, C. H., (ed.), *The Clarke Papers*, Volume 1, Camden Society Publications, NS, vol. 49 (1891).
Firth, C. H., and Rait, R. S. (eds), *Acts and Ordinances of the Interregnum 1642–1660* (3 vols, London, 1911).
Green, M. A. E. (ed.), *Calendar of the Committee for Advance of Money* (3 vols, London, 1888).

—— (ed.), *Calendar of the Committee for Compounding* (5 vols, London, 1889–93).
Harbin, E. (ed.), *Quarter Sessions Records for the County of Somerset* Volume 3, Somerset Records Society Publications, vol. 28 (1912).
Hayden, R. (ed.), *Records of a Church of Christ in Bristol 1640 to 1687*, Bristol Records Society Publications, vol. 27 (1974).
James, D. E. Howell (ed.), *Norfolk Quarter Sessions Order Book 1650–7*, Norfolk Records Society Publications, vol. 26 (1955).
Jeaffreson, J. C. (ed.), *Middlesex County Records, OS*, vol. 3 (London, 1954).
Lords Journal
Raine, J. (ed.), *Depositions from the Castle of York Relating to Offences Committed in the Northern Counties in the Seventeenth Century*, Surtees Society Publications, vol. 40 (1861).
Ratcliff, S., and Johnson, H. (eds), *Quarter Sessions Order Book*, Warwick County Records, vol. 3 (1937).
Redwood, B. C. (ed.), *Quarter Sessions Order Book 1642–9*, Sussex Records Society Publications, vol. 54 (1954).
Thurloe, John, *A Collection of the State Papers of John Thurloe* (7 vols, London, 1742).
Underhill, E. B. (ed.), *Records of the Churches of Christ Gathered at Fenstanton Warboys and Hexham 1644–1702*, Hanserd Knollys Society Publications, (London, 1854).
Wake, J. (ed.), *Quarter Sessions Records for the County of Northampton*, Northants. Records Society Publications, vol. 1 (1928).
Wakeman, O., and Kenyon, R. S. (eds), *Shropshire County Records* (Shrewsbury, 1905).

Personal Records – Letters, Diaries and Memoirs (For primary material incorporated within secondary works see Section 2.)

Abbott, W. C. (ed.), *The Writings and Speeches of Oliver Cromwell* (4 vols, Cambridge, Mass., 1937–47).
The Autobiography of Sir John Bramston K.B., Camden Society Publications, vol. 32 (1845).
Axon, E. (ed.), *Oliver Heywood's Life of John Angier of Denton*, Chetham Society Publications, NS 97 (1937).
Bamford, F. (ed.), *A Royalist's Notebook* (London, 1936).
Baxter, Richard, *Reliquiae Baxterianae*, ed. M. Sylvester (London, 1696).
Bray, W. (ed.), *The Diary and Correspondence of John Evelyn* (London, 1906).
de Beer, E. S. (ed.), *The Diary of John Evelyn* (6 vols, Oxford, 1955).
Bennitt, F. W. (ed.), 'The Diary of Isabella, wife of Sir Roger Twysden, bart.', *Archaeologia Cantiana*, vol. 51 (1939).
Blencowe, R. W. (ed.), *The Sydney Papers* (London, 1825).
Cavendish, Margaret, *The Life of William Cavendish, Duke of Newcastle*, ed. C. H. Firth (London, 1886 edn).

Coate, M. (ed.), *The Letter Book of John, Viscount Mordaunt 1658–1660*, Camden Society Publications, 3rd ser., vol. 69 (1945).
Cholmley, H., *Memoirs of Sir Hugh Cholmley Knt. and Bart.* (Malton, 1870).
Collins, A. (ed.), *Letters and Memorials of State . . . Written and Collected by Sir Henry Sydney* (2 vols, London, 1746).
Ellwood, Thomas, 'The Life of Thomas Ellwood', in *Autobiography*, vol. 11 (London, 1827).
Gayton, E. (ed.), *Col. Henry Marten's Familiar Letters to his Lady of Delight* (London, 1662).
Halliwell, J. O. (ed.), *The Autobiography and Correspondence of Sir Simonds D'Ewes, Bart.* (2 vols, London, 1845).
Hart, Kingsley (ed.), *The Letters of Dorothy Osborne to Sir William Temple 1652 to 1654* (London, 1968).
Hervey, S. H. A. (ed.), *The Letter Books of John Hervey, 1st Earl of Bristol* (3 vols, Wells, 1894).
HMC *Appendix to Fourth Report*.
HMC *Appendix to Fifth Report*.
HMC *Appendix to Seventh Report*.
HMC *Appendix to Ninth Report*.
HMC *Beaufort MSS*.
HMC *Buccleuch–Whitehall MSS*, vol. 1.
HMC *Cowper MSS*, vol. 2.
HMC *De Lisle and Dudley MSS*, vol. 6.
HMC *Egmont MSS*, vol. 1.
HMC *Kenyon MSS*.
HMC *Le Fleming MSS*.
HMC *Leybourne–Popham MSS*.
HMC *Marquis of Bath MSS*, vol. 2.
HMC *Portland MSS*, vols 2, 3.
HMC *Various Collections*, vol. 1.
Hodgson, J. C. (ed.), *North Country Diaries*, Surtees Society Publications, vol. 124 (1914).
Hutchinson, L., *Memoirs of the Life of Colonel Hutchinson*, ed. C. H. Firth (London, 1906 edn).
Hyde, Edward, Earl of Clarendon, *The Life of Edward Hyde, Earl of Clarendon* (Oxford, 1827 edn).
Jackson, C. (ed.), *The Autobiography of Mrs Alice Thornton of East Newton co. York*, Surtees Society Publications, vol. 62 (1873).
—— (ed.), *Yorkshire Diaries and Autobiographies in the Seventeenth and Eighteenth Centuries*, Surtees Society Publications, vol. 77 (1886).
'The Journal of Sir Roger Twysden', *Archaeologia Cantiana*, vols 1–4 (1858–61).
'Justice's Notebook of Captain John Pickering, 1656–1660', Thoresby Society Publications, vol. 11 (1900–4).
Kerry, C. (ed.), 'The Autobiography of Leonard Wheatcroft', *Journal of the Derbyshire Archaeological and Natural History Society*, vol. 21 (1899).

Lewis, T. Taylor (ed.), *The Letters of Lady Brilliana Harley*, Camden Society Publications, vol. 58 (1854).
Loftis, J. (ed.), *Memoirs of Anne, Lady Halket and Anne, Lady Fanshawe* (Oxford, 1981).
Ludlow, Edmund, *Memoirs of Edmund Ludlow*, ed. C. H. Firth (2 vols, Oxford, 1894 edn).
Macfarlane, A. (ed.), *The Diary of Ralph Josselin 1616–83* (London, 1976).
Nickalls, J. L. (ed.), *The Journal of George Fox* (Cambridge, 1952).
North, Roger, *Lives of Francis North, Dudley North and John North*, ed. A. Jessop (3 vols, London, 1890).
Parker, K. (ed.), *Dorothy Osborne: Letters to Sir William Temple* (Harmondsworth, 1987).
Raines, F. R. (ed.), *The Stanley Papers*, Chetham Society Publications, vols 66–7 (1867).
Rutt, J. T. (ed.), *The Diary of Thomas Burton 1656–1659* (4 vols, London, 1828).
Schofield, B. (ed.), *The Knyvett Letters 1620–1644*, Norfolk Records Society Publications, vol. 20 (1949).
Slingsby, Sir H., *Original Memoirs of Sir Henry Slingsby* (Edinburgh, 1906).
Tibbutt, H. G. (ed.), *The Life and Letters of Sir Lewis Dives 1599–1669*, Bedfordshire Historical Society Publications, vol. 27 (1946).
—— (ed.), *The Letter Books of Sir Samuel Luke 1644–5*, Bedfordshire Historical Society Publications, vol. 42 (1963).
Waller, William, *Recollections*, in H. Cowley (ed.), *The Poetry of Anna Mathilda* (London, 1788).
Warwick, Sir Philip, *Memoirs of the Reign of Charles I* (London, 1702).

Tracts, Pamphlets and Contemporary Histories

Abbot, Robert, *A Christian Family Builded by God, Directing All Governors of Families How to Act* (London, 1653) (BL E.1233.2).
An Answer to a Book Entitled the Doctrine and Discipline of Divorce (London, 1644) (BL E.17.12).
Baxter, Richard, *Gildas Salvianus. The Reformed Pastor* (London, 1656).
Bloody News from Dover (London, 1647) (BL E.375.20).
Brinsley, John, *A Looking Glass for Good Women* (London, 1645) (BL E.305.23).
Brown, David, *Two Conferences Between Some of Those that are Called Separatists and Independents* (London, 1650) (BL E.601.11).
Burroughs, Jeremiah, *The Glorious Name of God, the Lord of Hosts* (London, 1643).
C.C., *Sad and Serious Thoughts or a Sense and Meaning of the Late Act Concerning Marriages* (London, 1653) (BL E.713.8).
Chidley, Katherine, *The Justification of the Independant Churches of Christ* (London, 1641) (BL E.174.7).

Bibliography

The City-Dames Petition (London, 1647) (BL E.409.12).
Clapham, Jonathan, *A Full Discovery and Confutation of the . . . Quakers* (London, 1656) (BL E.498.7).
Cobbet, Thomas, *A Fruitful Discourse Touching the Honour due from Children to Parents and the Duty of Parents to Children* (London, 1656).
Coppe, Abiezer, *A Second Fiery Flying Roll* (London, 1649) (BL E.587.14).
—— *Some Sweet Sips of Spiritual Wine* (London, 1649)
Coppin, Richard, *Michael Opposing the Dragon* (London, 1659).
A Counter-Buffe (London, 1647) (BL E.399.25).
A Description of the Sect Called the Family of Love (London, 1641) (BL E.168.2).
A Discoverie of Six Women Preachers (London, 1641) (BL E.166.1).
Edwards, Thomas, *Reasons Against the Independent Government of Particular Congregations* (London, 1641) (BL E.167.16).
—— *Gangraena* (London, 1646).
Ellis, Humphrey, *Pseudochristus* (London, 1650) (BL E.602.12).
Farneworth, Richard, *A Woman Forbidden to Speak in Church* (London, 1653) (BL E.726.16).
Featley, Daniel, *The Dippers Dipped* (London, 1645) (BL E.268.11).
Filmer, Sir Robert, *Patriarcha* (London, 1680).
Foord, Edward, *Wine and Women* (London, 1646) (BL E.1189.12).
Fox, George, *The Woman Learning in Silence* (London, 1655) (BL E.870.8).
Fuller, Thomas, *Good Thoughts in Worse Times* (London, 1647) (BL E.1132).
Gauden, John, *Christ at the Wedding* (London, 1655) (BL E.480.3).
Gerbier, Charles, *Elogium Heroinum* (London, 1651) (BL E.1397.1).
Gough, R., *The History of Myddle*, ed. D. Hey (Harmondsworth, 1981).
Hall, John, *Paradoxes*, 1st edn (London, 1650), ed. D. C. Allen (Gainsville, Fl., 1956); 2nd edn (London, 1653).
Hammond, Henry, *A Practical Catechism* (London, 1645) (BL E.305.21).
—— *A Letter of Resolution to Six Queries of Present Use in the Church of England* (London, 1652) (BL E.1326.1).
Harrington, James, *The Commonwealth of Oceana* (London, 1656), in H. Morley (ed.), *Ideal Commonwealths* (New York, 1901).
Herbert, William, *Quadrapartit Devotions* (London, 1648) (BL E.1118.2).
—— *The Child-Bearing Woman* (London, 1648) (BL E.1172.2).
—— *The Careful Father and Pious Child* (London, 1648) (BL E.1117).
Heydon, John, *Advice to a Daughter. In Opposition to the Advice to a Son*, 2nd edn (London, 1659).
Hey-Hoe for a Husband or the Parliamnent of Maids (London, 1647) (BL E.408.19).
Hill, William, *A New Year's Gift for Women* (London, 1659) (BL E.2114.1).
Hobbes, Thomas, *Leviathan* (London, 1651), ed. C. B. Macpherson (Harmondsworth, 1966).
Holland, John, *The Smoke of the Bottomless Pit* (London, 1651) (BL E.662.5).
The Humble Petition of of Many Thousands Wives and Matrons of the City of London and Other Parts of the Kingdom (London, 1643) (BL E.88.13).

Hyde, Edward, Earl of Clarendon, *The History of the Rebellion and Civil Wars in England*, ed. W. Dunn Macray (6 vols, Oxford, 1888 edn).
An Invective Against The Pride of Women (London, 1657) (BL E.669.f.20.56).
Jinnor, Sarah, *The Woman's Almanack* (London, 1659) (BL E.2140.1).
J.S., *A Brief Anatomy of Women* (London, 1653) (BL E.722.2).
A Justification of a Mad Crew (London, 1650) (BL E.609.18).
The Kingdom's Weekly Intelligencer (E.10.7; 714.2).
The Ladies' Champion (London, 1660) (BL E.1053.10).
Little Non-Such or Certain New Questions Moved out of Ancient Truths (London, 1646) (BL E.353.8).
The Maid's Prophecies (London, 1648) (BL E.422.13).
The Man in the Moon (BL E.602.2).
Mercurius Academicus (BL E.324.8).
Mercurius Aulicus (BL E.67.25; 81.19).
Mercurius Democritus (BL E.713.10; 714.5; 714.13).
Mercurius Elencticus (BL E.600.12; 601.2)
Mercurius Politicus, (BL E.494.8; 711.21).
Mercurius Pragmaticus (BL E.421.15; 601.10).
The Midwives' Just Petition (London, 1643) (BL E.86.14).
Milton, John, *The Complete Prose Works of John Milton*, ed. D. Wolfe et al. (8 vols, Yale and London, 1953–82).
—— *An Apology Against a Pamphlet Called a Modest Confutation* (London, 1642).
—— *The Doctrine and Discipline of Divorce* (London, 1643).
—— *The Judgement of Martin Bucer* (London, 1644).
—— *Colasterium,* (London, 1645).
—— *Tetrachordon,* (London, 1645).
—— *Considerations Touching the Likeliest Means to Remove Hirelings out of the Church* (London, 1659).
Mistress Shaw's Tombstone (London, 1658) (BL E.1926.1).
The Moderate Intelligencer (BL E.707.1).
Nayler, James, *A Collection of Sundry Books, Epistles and Papers Written by James Nayler* (2 vols, London, 1716).
Neville, Henry, *The Isle of Pines* (London, 1668).
Ochino, Bernardino, *A Dialogue of Polygamy* (London, 1657 edn).
Osborne, Francis, *Advice to a Son, or Directions for Your Better Conduct* (Oxford, 1656), (BL E.1640.1).
—— *Political Reflections Upon the Government of the Turks* (Oxford, 1656).
Palmer, Herbert, *Scripture and Reason Pleaded for Defensive Arms* (London, 1643).
Pecke, Thomas, *Advice to Balaam's Ass* (London, 1658).
A Perfect Account (BL E.712.2).
A Perfect Diurnal (BL E.217.35).
Peter, Hugh, *Good Work for a Good Magistrate* (London, 1651) (BL E.1364.2).
Philips, Edward, *The Mysteries of Love and Eloquence, of the Arts of Wooing and Complimenting* (London, 1658) (BL E.735.1).

Pordage, John, *Innocence Appearing Through the Dark Mists of Pretended Guilt* (London, 1654) (BL E.1068.7).
A Proclamation Commanding Speedy and Due Execution of the Laws against Drunkenness Adultery and Fornication (London, 1655) (BL E.669.f.20.11).
A Remedy for Uncleanness or Certain Queries Propounded to his Highness the Lord Protector (London, 1658) (BL E.948.3).
A Remonstrance of the She Citizens of London (London, 1647) (BL E.404.2).
The Resolution of the Women of London to Parliament (London, 1642) (BL E.114.14).
The Routing of the Ranters (London, 1650) (BL E.616.9).
Satan Enthroned in his Chair of Pestilence (London, 1656) (BL E.897.2).
The Scourge of Civil Warre, The Blessing of Peace (London, 1645) (BL E.669.f.10.27).
Selden, John, *Uxor Ebraica* (London, 1646).
A Serious Letter Sent by a Private Christian to the Lady Consideration (London, 1655) (BL E.835.2).
Several Proceedings of Parliament (BL E.711.18).
Several Proceedings of State Affairs (E.219.13; 479.24).
Slingsby, Sir Henry, *A Father's Legacy to His Sons* (London, 1658).
The Spiritual Courts Epitomized (London, 1641) (BL E.157.15).
Stokes, Edward, *The Wiltshire Rant* (London, 1652) (BL E.669.5).
A Strange Wonder or a Wonder in a Woman (London, 1642) (BL E.144.5).
Strode, Sir George, *A Discourse of Holy Love* (London, 1652) (BL E.1382.1).
Taylor, Jeremy, *The Whole Works of the Right Rev. Jeremy Taylor*, ed. C. P. Eden (10 vols, London, 1848).
—— *The Rules and Exercises for Holy Living* (London, 1650).
—— *The Marriage Ring or the Mysteriousness and Duties of Marriage* (London, 1653).
A Testimony to the Truth of Jesus Christ (London, 1647) (BL E.423.3).
T.H., *A Looking Glass for Women* (London, 1644) (BL E.2.18).
Thorowgood, G., *Pray Be Not Angry or the Woman's New Law* (London, 1656) (BL E.885.7).
To the Supreme Authority, The Commons. The Petition of Diverse Women of the Cities of London and Westminster (London, 1649) (BL E.669.f.14.27).
A True Copy of the Petition of the Gentlewomen and Tradesmens Wives in and about the City of London (London, 1642) (BL E.134.17).
The Virgins' Complaint for the Loss of their Sweethearts (London, 1643) (BL E.86.38).
Walwyn, William, *The Fountain of Slander Discovered* (London, 1649) (BL E.557.4).
W.B., *The Yellow Book* (London, 1656) (BL E.878.1).
—— *The Trial of the Ladies* (London, 1656) (BL E.878.2).
Whitelocke, Bulstrode, *Memorials of English Affairs* (4 vols, Oxford, 1853 edn).
The Widows' Lamentation (London, 1643) (BL E.88.26).
Winstanley, Gerrard, *The Law of Freedom in a Platform* (London, 1651), in

Christopher Hill (ed.), *The Law of Freedom and Other Writings* (Cambridge, 1983).

2 Secondary Sources

Amussen, S. D., 'Gender, Family and the Social Order, 1560–1725', in A. Fletcher and J. Stevenson (eds), *Order and Disorder in Early Modern England* (Cambridge, 1985).
Aries, Philippe, *Centuries of Childhood* (London, 1973 edn).
Aylmer, G. E., *The State's Servants: the Civil Service of the English Republic 1649–1660* (London, 1973).
Babbage, S. B., *Puritanism and Richard Bancroft* (London, 1962).
Barclay, John, *Select Anecdotes and Instructive Incidents taken from the Publications of Several Members of the Society of Friends* (London, 1822).
Blaauw, W. H., 'Passages of the Civil War in Sussex from 1642 to 1660', *Sussex Archaeological Collections*, vol. 5 (1852).
Blackwood, B. G., *The Lancashire Gentry and the Great Rebellion* (Manchester, 1978).
Blundell, M., *Cavalier: The Letters of William Blundell to his Friends* (London, 1933).
Braithwaite, W. C., *The Beginnings of Quakerism* (Cambridge, 1955 edn).
—— *The Second Period of Quakerism* (London, 1919).
Burghclere, Lady Winifred, *George Villiers, Second Duke of Buckingham 1628–87* (London, 1903).
Capp, B., *Astrology and the Popular Press* (London, 1979).
Cartwright, J., *Sacharissa, Some Account of Dorothy Sidney, Countess of Sunderland* (London, 1893).
Cecilia, Countess of Denbigh, *Royalist Father and Roundhead Son* (London, 1915).
Clarke, Samuel, *The Lives of Sundry Eminent Persons in this Later Age* (London, 1683).
Cliffe, J. T., *The Yorkshire Gentry from the Reformation to the Civil War* (London, 1969).
Cokayne, George Edward, *Complete Baronetage* (6 vols, London, 1900–9).
Cope, E. S., *The Life of a Public Man: Edward 1st Baron Montagu of Boughton* (Philadelphia, 1981).
Corish, Patrick J., 'The Cromwellian Regime 1650 to 1660', in T. W. Moody, F. X. Martin and F. J. Byrne (eds), *A New History of Ireland* (9 vols, Oxford, 1976).
Crawford, Patricia, 'Women's Published Writings 1600–1700', in Mary Prior (ed.), *Women in English Society 1500–1800* (London, 1985).
Davis, J. C., *Fear, Myth and History: The Ranters and the Historians* (Cambridge, 1986).
Davis, W. T. (ed.), *Bradford's History of the Plymouth Plantation* (New York, 1908).

Dictionary of National Biography.
Dixon, H. (ed.), 'An Original Account of the Springett Family', *Gentleman's Magazine*, vol. 36 (1851).
Durston, C. G., 'Berkshire and Its County Gentry 1625–49', Unpub. Ph.D. thesis, Reading University (1977).
—— '"Unhallowed Wedlocks": The Regulation of Marriage during the English Revolution', *Historical Journal*, vol. 31 (1988).
Everitt, Alan, *Change in the Provinces* (Leicester, 1969).
Fletcher, A., *Reform in the Provinces: The Government of Stuart England* (London, 1986).
Fortescue, G. K. (ed.), *A Catalogue of Pamphlets Books . . . Collected by George Thomason 1640–1661* (2 vols, London, 1908).
Fraser, A., *The Weaker Vessel: Woman's Lot in the Seventeenth Century* (London, 1984).
Gardiner, S. R., *The History of the Commonwealth and Protectorate 1649–1656* (4 vols, New York, 1965 edn).
Gentles, Ian, 'London Levellers in the English Revolution: The Chidleys and Their Circle', *Journal of Ecclesiastical History*, vol. 29 (1978).
Glass, R. A., *The Barebones Parliament* (London, 1899).
Greaves, R. L., *Society and Religion in Elizabethan England* (Minneapolis, 1981).
—— and Zaller, R. (eds), *A Biographical Dictionary of British Radicals in the Seventeenth Century* (3 vols, Brighton, 1982).
Gregg, Pauline, *Free-Born John* (London, 1961).
Higgins, Patricia, 'The Reaction of Women, with Special Reference to Women Petitioners', in Brian Manning (ed.), *Politics, Religion and the English Civil War* (London, 1973).
Hill, Christopher, *The World Turned Upside Down: Radical Ideas During the English Revolution* (London, 1972).
—— *Milton and the English Revolution* (London, 1977).
—— (ed.), *The Law of Freedom and Other Writings* (Cambridge, 1983).
Houlbrooke, Ralph A., *The English Family 1450–1700* (London, 1984).
Inderwick, F. A., *The Interregnum* (London, 1891).
Ingram, M. J., 'Ecclesiastical Justice in Wiltshire 1600–1640, with special reference to cases concerning sex and marriage', Unpub. D.Phil. thesis, Oxford University (1976).
Kenyon, J. P., *The Stuart Constitution* (Cambridge, 1966 and 1986 edns).
Laslett, P., *Family Life and Illicit Love in Earlier Generations* (Cambridge, 1977).
—— (ed.), *Patriarcha and Other Political Works* (Oxford, 1949).
—— Osterveen, K., and Smith, R. (eds), *Bastardy and Its Comparative History* (London, 1980).
McArthur, Ellen, 'Women Petitioners and the Long Parliament', *English Historical Review*, vol. 24 (1909).
Mackensie, N. H., 'Sir Thomas Herbert of Tintern: A "Parliamentary" Royalist', *Bulletin of the Institute of Historical Research* vol. 29 (1956).

Mclaren, Dorothy, 'The Marriage Act of 1653: Its Influence on the Parish Registers', *Population Studies*, vol. 28 (1973).
Mather, Jean, 'The Moral Code of the English Civil War and Interregnum', *Historian*, vol. 44 (1982).
Matthews, A. G., *Walker Revised* (Oxford, 1948).
Morley, H. (ed.), *Ideal Commonwealths* (New York, 1901).
Morrah, Patrick, *Prince Rupert of the Rhine* (London, 1976).
—— *A Royal Family: Charles I and His Family* (London, 1982).
Morrill, J. S., *Cheshire 1630–1660: County Government and Society During the English Revolution* (London, 1974).
—— 'The Church in England 1642–9', in John Morrill (ed.), *Reactions to the English Civil War* (London, 1982).
Mount, Ferdinand, *The Subversive Family* (London, 1982).
Muddiman, J. G., *The King's Journalist 1659–89* (London, 1923).
Noble, Mark, *Lives of the English Regicides* (2 vols, London, 1798).
Parker, W. R., *Milton, A Biography* (2 vols, Oxford, 1968).
Proctor, F., and Frere, W. H., *A New History of the Book of Common Prayer* (London, 1951 edn).
Quaife, G. R., *Wanton Wenches and Wayward Wives: Peasants and Illicit Sex in Early Seventeenth Century England* (London, 1978).
Ravenhill, W. W., 'Records of the Rising in the West, A.D.1655', *Wiltshire Archaeological Magazine*, vols 13–15 (1872–5).
Reay, Barry, *The Quakers and the English Revolution* (London, 1985).
Roberts, Stephen, 'Fornication and Bastardy in Mid-Seventeenth Century Devon: How was the Act of 1650 Enforced?', in John Rule (ed.), *Outside the Law; Studies in Crime and Order 1650–1850* (Exeter, 1982).
Rogers, E., *Some Account of the Life and Opinions of a Fifth Monarchy Man* (London, 1867).
Rowe, Violet A., *Sir Henry Vane the Younger* (London, 1970).
Sharpe, J. A., *Crime in Seventeenth Century England* (Cambridge, 1983).
Shaw, Howard, *The Levellers* (London, 1968).
Shaw, William A., *A History of the English Church During the Civil War and Under the Commonwealth* (2 vols, London, 1900).
Slater, Miriam, *Family Life in the Seventeenth Century: The Verneys of Claydon House* (London, 1984).
Smith, Nigel (ed.), *A Collection of Ranter Writings from the Seventeenth Century* (London, 1983).
Stone, Lawrence, *The Family, Sex and Marriage in England 1500–1800* (London, 1977).
Thomas, Keith, 'Women and the Civil War Sects', *Past and Present*, vol. 13 (1958).
—— *Religion and the Decline of Magic* (London, 1971).
—— 'The Puritans and Adultery: The Act of 1650 Reconsidered', in D. H. Pennington and K. V. Thomas (eds), *Puritans and Revolutionaries* (Oxford, 1978).
Townshend, D., *The Life and Letters of Mr Endymion Porter* (London, 1897).

Underdown, David, *Somerset in the Civil War and Interregnum* (Newton Abbot, 1973).
—— *Revel, Riot and Rebellion: Popular Politics and Culture 1603–1660* (Oxford, 1985).
Veall, D., *The Popular Movement for Law Reform* (Oxford, 1970).
Verney, F. P., and Verney, M. M., *Memoirs of the Verney Family During the Seventeenth Century* (2 vols, London, 1904).
Walzer, M., *The Revolution of the Saints: A Study in the Origins of Radical Politics* (Cambridge, Mass., 1965).
Watts, Michael, *The Dissenters*, vol. 1 (Oxford, 1978).
Webster, Charles, *The Great Instauration: Science Medicine and Reform 1626–1660* (London, 1975).
Wedgwood, C. V., *The Trial of Charles I* (Harmondsworth, 1983 edn).
White, B. R., *The English Baptists of the Seventeenth Century* (London, 1983).
Williams, E. M., 'Women Preachers in the Civil War', *Journal of Modern History*, vol. 1 (1929).
Woolrych, A., *Commonwealth to Protectorate* (Oxford, 1982).
Worden, A. B., *The Rump Parliament* (London, 1974).
Wrightson, Keith, 'The Nadir of English Illegitimacy in the Seventeenth Century', in P. Laslett, K. Osterveen and R. Smith (eds), *Bastardy and its Comparative History* (London, 1980).
Wrigley, E. A., and Schofield, R. S. (eds), *The Population History of England 1541–1871* (London, 1981).

Index

Abercromby, Jeremiah 60, 145
Abingdon, Berkshire 26
Abbot, Robert 4, 22, 23, 29, 166
adultery *see* sexual relations, illicit
Adultery Act (1650) 67, 69, 73–5, 98–9, 144, 152–3, 158
Alport, Richard 63, 102
Alport, Susan (née Verney) 63, 102
Anabaptists, *see* baptism; Baptists
Angier, John 167
Anglican Church 3, 121
    Book of Common Prayer of 68, 72, 82, 85, 116, 119, 121, 132
    canon law of 66–7, 74
    courts of 8, 144, 148–9
anticlericalism 84–5
Apsley, Sir Allen 55
aristocracy, divided in civil war allegiance 46
Astell, Mary 173
Attaway, Mrs 19, 97
Aubrey, John 149

Bamfield, Joseph, 67–8
Bankes, Lady Mary 90
baptism 110, 115–21, 174
Baptists 26, 88, 93, 97, 100, 115–16
    congregation of at Fenstanton, Huntingdonshire 65, 72, 86, 96–7, 120, 137
    congregation of at Warboys, Cambridgeshire 65–6, 97, 137
Barebone's Parliament, *see* Parliament
bastards and bastardy 18, 144, 146, 154, 157, 158–9
Baxter, Margaret 102

Baxter, Richard 13, 102, 117, 122, 134, 137, 166, 172
Beauchamp, Lady Anne 35
Belasyse, Henry 36
Belasyse, Thomas, Viscount Fauconberg 36, 50, 72
Berkshire, gentry of and civil war allegiance 45
bigamy, *see* marriages, bigamous
Blount, Anne 77–8
Blount, Mountjoy, Earl of Newport 36, 77
Blount, William 77
Blundell, Anne 92
Blundell, William 92
Blunt family 52
Bodvile, Anne 126
Bodvile, John 126
Book of Common Prayer, *see* Anglican Church
Boyle, Roger, Lord Broghill 84
Bramston, Sir John 166
Bramston family 166, 172
breast-feeding 122–4; *see also* pregnancy and childbirth
Brereton, Sir William 51
Broghill, Lord, *see* Boyle, Roger, Lord Broghill
brothers, divided in civil war allegiance 36–7, 42, 48–9
Brown, David 95
Bucer, Martin 19
Bulstrode, Edward 36
Bulstrode, Sir Richard 36
Bunyan, John 163
Burroughs, Jeremiah 90
Butler, Samuel 88
Byron, Sir Richard 55

Calvert, Elizabeth 93
Capel, Lord Arthur 131, 162, 169
Carew, Sir Alexander 169
Carey, Henry, 1st Earl of Dover 35, 50
Carey, John, Viscount Rochford 35–6
Cavendish, Margaret, Duchess of Newcastle (née Lucas) 64, 94, 103–4, 108, 138, 162, 168
Cavendish, William, 1st Duke of Newcastle 64, 108, 162, 168
Charles I, King of England 3, 4, 5, 24, 28, 34, 38, 39, 40, 47, 48, 52, 89, 113, 129, 135, 139, 149, 169
Charles II, Prince of Wales and King of England 52, 54, 71, 85, 101, 103, 108, 121, 170, 171, 174
Charles Louis, Elector Palatine 38–9, 52
Charleton, Francis 44
Charleton, Mary 44
Charleton, Robert 44
chastity, see sexual relations, abstinence from
Cheshire 82
Chidley, Katherine 13, 93, 95, 162
Chidley, Samuel 95
childbirth, see pregnancy and childbirth
children, see parents
Cholmley, Lady Elizabeth 88, 101, 168
Cholmley, Sir Hugh 88, 101, 168
church courts, see Anglican Church, courts of; High Commission, court of
churching 7, 121–2
Civil Marriage Act (1653) 69–70, 71, 72, 76, 78, 79, 82, 83, 84, 98; see also marriages, civil
Clarkson, Lawrence 20, 132, 151
Claydon, Buckinghamshire 128, 131, 145, 147
Claypole, Elizabeth (née Cromwell) 136
Clement, Gregory 150
Clifton, Sir Gervase 75–6
Cobbet, Thomas 13, 22–3, 130, 134, 160, 166
Cockerill, Edmund 43
Coke, George, Bishop of Hereford 105–6
Coke, Sir John 36, 147
Coke, Thomas 36
Committee for Advance of Money 43, 127, 128
Committee for Compounding 43, 45, 52, 103, 127
composition by Royalists 47, 50–2, 64, 100, 101, 103–4
Convention Parliament, see Parliament
Coppe, Abiezer 12, 15, 20, 151
Coppin, Richard 15

Corbet, John 36
Corbet, Sir John 36
Court of Wards 60–1
courtship, see love and courtship
Crompton, Eyton 44
Cromwell, Elizabeth, see Claypole, Elizabeth
Cromwell, Frances 72
Cromwell, Henry (cousin of Protector) 38, 52
Cromwell, Henry (son of Protector) 53
Cromwell, Lord Thomas of Oakham 52
Cromwell, Mary 36, 72
Cromwell, Oliver, Lord Protector 3, 18, 38, 52, 53, 54, 69, 71, 72, 77, 89, 103, 105, 128, 136–7, 153, 158
Cromwell, Robert 137
Cromwell, Sir Oliver 38
Crowell, Oxfordshire 134–5

Danvers, Henry, 1st Earl of Danby 37, 43
Danvers, Sir John 37, 43, 54
Davies, Richard 137
Denton, Dr William 103
Denton, John 168
Denton, Susan 60, 145
Denton, Sir Alexander 145, 168
Dering, Sir Edward 72
Desborough, John 85
Devereux, Elizabeth, Countess of Essex 89
Devereux, Robert, 3rd Earl of Essex 37, 89, 113
D'Ewes, Richard 46–7
D'Ewes, Simonds 46–7
Diggers, see Winstanley, Gerrard
Directory of Public Worship 68, 72, 118, 119, 122
Dives, Sir Lewis 112
divorce 5, 6, 10, 13, 16, 18–20, 29–30, 98–9; see also marriages, breakdown of
Dormer, Robert, 1st Earl of Carnarvon 37

Earls Colne, Essex 72, 119, 121, 155–6; see also Josselin, Ralph
Edgehill, battle of 35, 40, 48
education 124–6
Edwards, Thomas 4, 5, 13, 29, 72, 93, 97, 116, 133, 160, 173
Elizabeth, Princess (daughter of Charles I) 129, 139
Ellis, Humphrey 152
Ellwood, Thomas 134–5, 163
Ellwood, Walter 134–5, 163
Engagement (1650) 165
Engels, Friedrich 144

Index

Erbury, Dorcas 154
Evelyn, John 119, 122, 126, 133, 136

Fairfax, Lady Anne 89
Fairfax, Mary 54
Fairfax, Sir Thomas 44, 51, 54, 89
Fairfax family 45
families
　broken up by revolution 97–9, 152, 161, 162–3, 164
　brought closer together by revolution 101–9, 137–41, 166–73
　divided in civil war allegiance 6, 33–56 *passim*, 162, 165
　see also family, institution of the
Familists, *see* Family of Love
family, institution of the
　break-up of predicted 5–6, 160
　critics of 10–13, 160
　defenders of 21–32, 166
　history of 1
　literary debate on 10–32 *passim*
　and the state 4–5, 22–3, 24–5, 110, 130–1, 162, 166–7, 173
　suggestions for reform of 13–21, 160–1
　see also families
Family of Love 133, 150
Fanshawe, Lady Anne (née Harrison) 63, 101, 103, 107–8, 112, 124, 168
Fanshawe, Sir Richard 63, 101, 103, 107, 112, 168
Farneworth, Richard 15
fathers, *see* parents
Fielding, Basil, 2nd Earl of Denbigh 35, 39–41, 47–8, 106–7
Feilding, Elizabeth 40
Feilding, Elizabeth, Countess of Denbigh 106–7
Feilding, Harriet 47
Feilding, Susanna, Countess of Denbigh 39–41, 47
Fielding, William, 1st Earl of Denbigh 35, 40–1
Fell, Margaret 93, 100
Fell, Thomas 100–1
Fenstanton, Huntingdonshire, *see* Baptists
fertility 114–15
Fetherstonhaugh, Sir Timothy 171
Fiennes, Nathaniel 85
Fifth Commandment 4, 22, 131
Fifth Monarchists 3, 84
Filmer, Sir Robert 4, 24
Fleetwood, Charles 36, 51
Fleetwood, Sir William 36, 51
Ford, Sir Edward 37, 50, 51
fornication, *see* sexual relations, illicit

Fox, George 15, 93, 96, 100, 143, 155, 157
Franklin, William 98, 152, 164
Frodsham, William 74–5
Fuller, Thomas 127, 149, 156

Gadbury, Mary 98, 152
Gardiner, Cary (née Verney) 35
Gardiner, Thomas 87
Gauden, John 5, 28, 83–4
Gerbier, Charles 14
Gibson, Sir John 140
godparents 7, 116, 118–20
Goffe, Stephen 37
Goffe, William 37, 85
Goodwin, John 95
Goring, Lord George 38, 147
Gough, Richard 146

Halket, Lady Anne (née Murray) 53, 58–9, 67–8, 75, 81–2, 90
Halket, Sir James 75, 81–2
Hall, John 14
Hamilton, James, 1st Duke of Hamilton 40, 47–8
Hamilton, Lady Anne 48
Hammond, Henry 29, 30
Hardwick's Marriage Act (1753) 85
Harlakenden, Margaret 85–6
Harley, Edward 50–1, 91, 138, 167–8
Harley, Lady Brilliana 90, 91–2, 138, 167–8
Harley, Sir Robert 51, 91, 167–8
Harrington, James 16, 125
Henrietta Anne, Princess (daughter of Charles I) 113
Henrietta Maria, Queen (wife of Charles I) 41, 89, 113, 139
Henry, Duke of Gloucester (son of Charles I) 129, 139
Herbert, Philip, 4th Earl of Pembroke 37
Herbert, Sir Thomas 50
Herbert, William 5, 22, 31, 32
Hervey, Sir Thomas 142–3
Heveningham, Arthur 37, 42
Heveningham, William 37, 42, 50
Heydon, John 14, 30
High Commission, court of 149; *see also* Anglican Church, courts of
Hill, William 26, 27
Hillesden House, Buckinghamshire 60, 145
Hobbes, Thomas 24
Holland, Earl of, *see* Rich, Henry, Earl of Holland
Holmes, Jane 95–6, 163–4
homosexuality 31
Hooton, Elizabeth 163

Howard, Thomas 53, 58
Hungerford, Anthony 36
Hungerford, Sir Edward 36
husbands
  authority of over wives challenged 13, 95–6, 163–4, 173
  patriarchal power and responsibilities of 22, 24–5
  see also spouses; wives
Hutchinson, John 42, 54–5, 105, 117
Hutchinson, Lucy 35, 54–5, 105, 111, 117
Hyde, Edward, 1st Earl of Clarendon 39, 48, 105, 108–9, 130, 136, 167

incest 69, 154; see also marriages, incestuous
Independents 93, 95
infanticide 18, 154
Ireton, Henry 37, 50, 51, 131

James, Duke of York (son of Charles I) 90
Jinnor, Sarah 21
Josselin, Ralph 72, 82–3, 85, 86, 106, 114, 117, 118–19, 120, 121, 140, 155–6, 168, 172, 174

Kelsey, Thomas 85
Kenilworth, Warwickshire 83
Kidderminster, Herefordshire 117, 122, 137, 166
Knyvett, Katherine 92, 105
Knyvett, Thomas 62, 63, 92, 105, 140

Lancashire, gentry of and civil war allegiance 45
Langley Burrell, Wiltshire 151
Lenthall, William 51
Levellers 3, 15, 26, 88, 125, 131, 149, 165
Liddell, Sir Thomas 53
Lilburne, Elizabeth 102, 113
Lilburne, Henry 36, 132
Lilburne, John 15, 36, 102, 113, 132
Lilburne, Richard 132
Lisle, John 37, 42
Lisle, William 37, 42
Lister, Sir Matthew 113
Long Parliament, see Parliament
love and courtship 142–3, 145
Ludlow, Edmund 138
Ludlow, Robert 138
Luke, Sir Samuel 150
Lunsford, Katherine 102
Lunsford, Thomas 45, 102
Lunsford family 45

Machin, John 80
Manners, John, 8th Earl of Rutland 39, 121

marriage, institution of
  critics of 10–13
  see also marriages
marriages
  between political opponents 53–4, 165
  bigamous 66–7, 73
  breakdown of 19, 97–9, 148, 152, 154–5; see also divorce
  and choice of spouse 15–16, 53
  civil 7, 16, 28, 58, 66–86 passim, 174; see also Civil Marriage Act
  clandestine 67, 69
  difficulties in contracting 6, 61–4
  dowries and financial settlements in 15–16, 53, 57, 63–4, 93
  forcible 70, 76–7
  incestuous 6, 13, 16–17, 28–9, 69, 73–5
  new opportunities to contract 59–61
  numbers of contracted during revolution 62–3, 75–6
  and parental consent 15, 57–60, 67, 68
  and radical religious sects 16, 65–6, 72, 93, 135, 155
  solemnization of 66–71, 72, 75–6
  see also marriage, institution of
Marten, Henry 52, 139, 149–50, 169
Mauleverer, Richard 37, 42
Mauleverer, Sir Thomas 37, 42
Maurice, Prince 38, 42
May, Isabella 142–3
May Day 4, 153
Mayerne, Sir Theodore 113, 129
Maynard, Sir John 79–80
midwives 111–14, 118, 148; see also pregnancy and childbirth
Milton, John 10, 17, 18–19, 21, 29–30, 36, 52, 84–5, 98, 99–100, 121, 122, 125, 143
Milton, Sir Christopher 36
Milton, Katherine (née Woodcock) 84
Milton, Mary (née Powell) 18, 99–100
Monck, Anne 89
Monck, George 89
Monson, Sir John 37
Monson, Sir William 37
Montagu, Edward, Lord Montagu of Boughton 39
Montagu, Edward, 2nd Earl of Manchester 36, 39
Montagu, Walter 36
moral reform, attempts at 4, 152–4, 158–9
Mordaunt, John Viscount 105, 174
Mordaunt, Lady Elizabeth 105, 174
Morton, Thomas, Bishop of Durham 121
mothers, see parents; pregnancy and childbirth

Moulton, Edward 42
Murray, Anne *see* Halket, Lady Anne
Myddle, Shropshire 145

Nayler, James 154–5, 164
Neville, Henry 36, 52
Neville, Richard 36, 52
Newnham Paddox, Worcestershire 39
Newport, Richard, Baron Newport 161
Newport Pagnell, Buckinghamshire 150
Nichols, Anthony 85

Ochino, Bernardino 17, 18
Oglander, Bridget 58, 59
Oglander, George 47
Oglander, Sir John 34, 47, 58, 104
Osborne, Dorothy 53, 59, 81, 94, 99, 142–3
Osborne, Francis 11, 14, 17, 26, 31
Oxford 11, 63, 124, 135

parents
  authority of challenged 13, 130–1, 133–6, 163–4, 173
  and conflict with children 6, 35–6, 39–41, 110, 130–8, 141, 160
  and deeper relations with children 137–41
  financial problems of 126–8, 161
  responsibilities of towards children 22–5
  separated from children 6, 126–7, 128–9, 138–9, 161, 169
parish registers (registrars) 69–70, 73, 74, 76, 78–80
Parliament
  Barebone's 16, 28, 58, 69, 74, 83, 84, 98, 125, 174
  Convention 71, 99
  First Protectorate 28, 70, 83–4, 172
  Long 2, 19, 36, 68, 121, 125, 149, 152
  Rump 67, 69, 77, 98, 150, 152
  Second Protectorate 71, 84, 85
Pecke, Thomas 11, 18, 26, 27
Penington, Arthur 36
Penington, Isaac the elder 37, 135
Penington, Isaac the younger 36, 135
Penington, Sir John 37
Penington family 135, 163
Penruddock, Lady Arundell 105, 170–1
Penruddock, Sir John 105, 128, 170–1
Percy, Algernon, 10th Earl of Northumberland 38, 46, 51, 119
Peter, Hugh 16, 20
Phayre, Robert 50
Philips, Edward 143
Pickering, John 83

Pierrepont, Francis 35
Pierrepont, Henry 35
Pierrepont, Robert, 1st Earl of Kingston 35
polygamy 5, 6, 13, 16, 17–18, 29, 154, 157
Pordage, John 12, 21, 155
Porter, Endymion 77, 139
Porter, Thomas 77–8, 139
Powell family 52, 100
pregnancy and childbirth 104, 107, 110–14; *see also* breast-feeding
Presbyterian state church 3; *see also* Directory of Public Worship
prostitutes and prostitution 21, 31, 146, 147, 153, 154
Protectorate Parliaments, *see* Parliament
Puckering, Jane 77
Pym, John 136

Quakers 3, 95–6, 97–8, 100, 117, 134–5, 137, 143, 154, 155, 157, 163–4
  and women 15, 26, 93, 96

Ranters 6, 8, 12–13, 20, 21, 25, 31, 96, 98, 132, 144, 145, 151, 157–8, 164
rape 31, 147
regicides 37
Rich, Henry, Earl of Holland 38, 50, 169–70
Rich, Lord Robert 72
Rich, Robert, Baron Rich of Leighs 36, 51
Rich, Robert, 2nd Earl of Warwick 36, 50, 51
Robins, John 98
Rogers, John 102, 113, 132–3
Rogers, Nehemiah 36
Rogers, Timothy 36
Rump Parliament, *see* Parliament
Rupert, Prince 38, 40, 52, 172

Savile, Lady Anne 91, 112
Savile, Sir William 112
Selden, John 19–20
sexual relations 95, 123, 142–59 *passim*
  abstinence from 21, 32, 155
  and civil war soldiers 145–8, 155–6, 159
  illicit 8, 12, 20–1, 30–2, 69, 73, 143, 144, 145–59 *passim*, 164; *see also* Adultery.Act; incest
  literary debate on 20–1, 30–2, 153–4
  and radical religious sects 6, 12, 20–1, 144, 150–2, 154–5, 156, 164
Seymour, William, 10th Earl of Hertford 37
Sheffield family 45
Sidney, Algernon 38, 92, 132
Sidney, Philip, Lord Lisle 38, 119

Index

Sidney, Robert, 2nd Earl of Leicester 38, 51, 132, 165
Sidney family 38
Simmonds, Martha 93, 154
Slingsby, Sir Henry 50, 131
Solemn League and Covenant (1643) 165
Southampton 67
Spencer, Dorothy, Countess of Sunderland (née Sidney) 46, 107, 168
Spencer, Henry, 1st Earl of Sunderland 38, 46, 107, 165, 168
spousals 66, 72
spouses
    absences of 67–8, 105–9, 168
    conflict between 95–7, 109
    mutual appreciation of 101–9
    mutual responsibilities of 22–4
    see also husbands; wives
Springett, Mary 111, 118
Springett, Thomas 111, 118
Stanley, Charles, Lord Strange 128, 170
Stanley, Charlotte, Countess of Derby 89, 90, 170
Stanley, James, 7th Earl of Derby 128, 170
Stapley, Anthony 37
Stokes, Edward 98, 151–2, 164
Stone, Lawrence (historian) 1–2, 46, 66, 94, 173
Strode, Sir George 140
Suffolk, gentry of and civil war allegiance 45
Sydenham family 45

Taylor, Jeremy 22, 24, 28, 31–2, 80, 119, 166
Temple, William, see Osborne, Dorothy
Tomlinson, Matthew 42
Thornton, Alice (née Wandesford) 64–5, 100, 113
Thornton, William 64, 100
Tracy, John Viscount 50–1
Trumbell, William 147
Twysden, Lady Isabella 103–4, 105, 111–12, 118, 168
Twysden, Sir Roger 51, 104, 105, 111–12, 168
Twysden, Sir Thomas 42

Vane, Sir Henry the elder 135–6
Vane, Sir Henry the younger 36, 42, 50, 53, 92, 135–6, 141
Vane, Sir Walter 36
Verney, Cary, see Gardiner, Cary
Verney, Edmund 39, 48–9, 60, 166
Verney, Elizabeth 145
Verney, Henry 60, 64
Verney, John 128
Verney, Lady Mary 87, 97, 103, 104, 108, 112, 114, 120, 124, 128, 131, 145, 166, 168
Verney, Penelope 60, 64
Verney, Sir Edmund 36, 39, 48, 131
Verney, Sir Ralph 36, 39, 48–9, 56, 60, 61, 62, 97, 102, 103, 108, 112, 120, 124, 128, 131, 145, 147, 167, 168
Verney, Susan, see Alport, Susan
Verney, Thomas 147
Villiers, George, 2nd Duke of Buckingham 47, 54

Waller, Lady Anne 102–3, 168–9
Waller, Sir William 102–3, 168–9
Walwyn, William 125, 157, 165–6
Warboys, Cambridge, see Baptists
Ward, Mary 139, 150
Warwick, Sir Philip 149, 156
Webbe, Thomas 20, 151–2, 164
Westminster Assembly of Divines 68, 122; see also Directory of Public Worship
wet-nurses, see breast-feeding
White, Francis 85
Whitelocke, Bulstrode 37
widows 33, 61, 161
Winstanley, Gerrard 16, 25, 30–1, 125
Winter, Samuel 88
wives
    added responsibilities of 91–3, 103–5
    duties to husbands 22–5
    influenced by new ideas 6, 96–7
    see also husbands; spouses; women
women
    as authors 93–4
    political activities of 26, 88–90
    as preachers 26, 95–6, 97, 163–4
    and radical religious sects 93; see also Quakers, and women
    re-evaluation of status of 13–15, 87, 88–9, 90, 94–5
    sexual harassment of by civil war soldiers 146–7, 155–6
    traditional male view of 25–8, 87–8
    see also spouses; wives
Worsley, Charles 82

Yorkshire, gentry of and civil war allegiance 45